D0536641

Transactions
of the
Royal
Historical
Society

SIXTH SERIES

XXIV

CAMBRIDGE
UNIVERSITY PRESS

Published by the Press Syndicate of the University of Cambridge
The Edinburgh Building, Cambridge CB2 8RU, United Kingdom
32 Avenue of the Americas, New York, NY 10013-2473, USA
477 Williamstown Road, Port Melbourne, VIC 3207, Australia
C/Orense, 4, Planta 13, 28020 Madrid, Spain
Lower Ground Floor, Nautica Building, The Water Club,
Beach Road, Granger Bay, 8005 Cape Town, South Africa

First published 2014

A catalogue record for this book is available from the British Library

ISBN 9781107099685 hardback

SUBSCRIPTIONS. The serial publications of the Royal Historical Society, *Royal Historical Society Transactions* (ISSN 0080–4401) and Camden Fifth Series (ISSN 0960–1163) volumes, may be purchased together on annual subscription. The 2014 subscription price, which includes print and electronic access (but not VAT), is £153 (US $255 in the USA, Canada, and Mexico) and includes Camden Fifth Series, volumes 45 and 46 and Transactions Sixth Series, volume 24 (published in December). The electronic-only price available to institutional subscribers is £132 (US $220 in the USA, Canada, and Mexico). Japanese prices are available from Kinokuniya Company Ltd, P.O. Box 55, Chitose, Tokyo 156, Japan. EU subscribers (outside the UK) who are not registered for VAT should add VAT at their country's rate. VAT registered subscribers should provide their VAT registration number. Prices include delivery by air.

Subscription orders, which must be accompanied by payment, may be sent to a bookseller, subscription agent, or direct to the publisher: Cambridge University Press, The Edinburgh Building, Shaftesbury Road, Cambridge CB2 8RU, UK; or in the USA, Canada, and Mexico: Cambridge University Press, Journals Fulfillment Department, 100 Brook Hill Drive, West Nyack, New York, 10994–2133, USA.

SINGLE VOLUMES AND BACK VOLUMES. A list of Royal Historical Society volumes available from Cambridge University Press may be obtained from the Humanities Marketing Department at the address above.

Printed in the UK by Bell & Bain Ltd, Glasgow

CONTENTS

Transactions of the RHS 24 (2014), pp. 1–3 © Royal Historical Society 2014
doi:10.1017/S0080440114000103

INTRODUCTION

This volume of *Transactions* is notable not only – of course – for what it contains, but also for what it does not contain. Readers will find the usual varied fare of papers read at the Society's meetings – the cream of recent scholarship – as well as three of the papers read at the colloquium on 'Croatia and Europe' held at the University of Leicester on 27 March 2013 to mark Croatia's entry into the European Union – an unusual and timely reminder of an important geopolitical story not often included in standard accounts of European history. As for the missing contents – with this volume, *Transactions* will no longer include the Society's annual report and accounts. This change will decouple the publication of report and accounts necessary for the AGM from the publication of *Transactions* and will enable us to include more academic content in the latter. The annual report and accounts will be made more widely available by publication before the AGM in November on the Society's new website (*www.royalhistsoc.org*). I encourage all Fellows and Members to take a look, not only for the full annual report, but also for the wide range of new resources now available on the website: an archive of policy documents (the Society's but also other scholarly and public bodies), on subjects ranging from the school curriculum to freedom of information; podcasts of all of the Society's recent public lectures; information on upcoming events of interest to historians; application forms for proposing new Fellows and Members and applying for the Society's early career research grants and fellowships; a guide for early career historians; and much more relevant not only to the Society's activities but to the rich world of historical research beyond.

We intend in the coming year to extend the usefulness of the website to Fellows and Members: to allow you to pay your dues and buy additional publications online; to encourage you to list your research interests and thus build up an enhanced directory of historical research for public benefit; and to permit online voting for Fellows electing members of Council. This enhancement of the website is part of a renewed effort on our part to improve the services we provide both to our members and to the wider community. For our members, we want to make easier and more regular communication between them and their Society, to encourage more participation in our governance and events, and to migrate our high-quality publications – a tradition we have been maintaining since before our foundation in 1868 (the Camden Series dates from 1838, though we inherited it only in 1897) – to new formats that will keep them vital in the twenty-first century. For the wider community, we want to provide direct access to serious scholarship through our lectures (now all available for free online) and publications (on Open Access to the greatest extent feasible, at moderate subscription rates where not), and to serve as a gateway for news about history and historical events more generally.

In making these changes, we are seeking both to perform the traditional functions of a learned society – support for research and publication, lectures and conferences, recognition of achievement through grants and prizes – and to continue to take on new functions called for in a rapidly changing academic and political landscape. One of the positive features of recent decades has been the growing recognition of historical research in libraries, archives and museums, and we are keen to recruit more Fellows and Members from among researchers in these places, as well as to provide distinctive forms of support for them (such as the Aylmer Seminar for archivists, historians and archivist/historians, that we co-sponsor with the Institute of Historical Research and the National Archives). Less happily, as the network of higher education breaks up into competing institutions with their own interests and bottom-lines firmly in view, we find that we have more and more to perform the functions formerly taken up by government bodies and the network of vice-chancellors, which establish and defend healthy norms for the discipline: access and choice in undergraduate and postgraduate provision for History; the centrality of academic freedom and quality in funding decisions; the importance of ethical peer-review in publication, hiring and promotion decisions; maintaining the conditions for a fulfilling academic career in history and ensuring such a career is open to all comers.

Increasingly, too, we have sought to represent the interests of high-quality historical scholarship in public-policy debates. The two issues that have dominated our agenda this year have been the school curriculum – where, working closely with the Historical Association, representing schoolteachers, we have been intimately involved in the reworking of the curriculum at all levels from Key Stage 1 to A-Level – and Open Access publishing – where we have sought to widen access without sacrificing academic freedom and quality through the wrong kind of regulation. More detailed information on both issues is available in recent newsletters, which are posted on the website. But we have also been engaged in more quiet work on many other issues: defending the freedom of historical research in Brazil and India; playing a role in upcoming commemorations of the centenary of the First World War and the 800th anniversary of Magna Carta; taking a leaf from the scientists' book in raising questions about gender equality in the humanities; drawing attention to the effects of the quasi-privatisation of English Heritage; arguing for the preservation of the decennial census.

None of this would be possible without the hard work and dedication of our small staff – Sue Carr, our Executive Secretary; Mel Ransom, our Administrative Secretary; Jane Gerson, our new Research and Communications Officer – and our voluntary leadership, the officers and members of Council. It is the best part of my job, working with these people, on such a varied diet of enterprises, all of which fly the flag for the best historical scholarship, our goal for nearly 150 years now.

Finally, this is the place to mark the loss on 9 April 2014 of Sir James Holt, President of the Society 1981–5, a great medieval historian and an adornment to the profession.

Peter Mandler
President

Transactions of the RHS 24 (2014), pp. 5–28 © Royal Historical Society 2014
doi:10.1017/S0080440114000012

TRANSACTIONS OF THE
ROYAL HISTORICAL SOCIETY
PRESIDENTIAL ADDRESS

By Peter Mandler

EDUCATING THE NATION I: SCHOOLS*

READ 22 NOVEMBER 2013

ABSTRACT. This paper assays the public discourse on secondary education across the twentieth century – what did voters think they wanted from education and how did politicians seek to cater to those desires? The assumption both in historiography and in popular memory is that educational thinking in the post-war decades was dominated by the ideal of 'meritocracy' – that is, selection for secondary and higher education on the basis of academic 'merit'. This paper argues instead that support for 'meritocracy' in this period was fragile. After 1945, secondary education came to be seen as a universal benefit, a function of the welfare state analogous to health. Most parents of all classes wanted the 'best schools' for their children, and the best schools were widely thought to be the grammar schools; thus support for grammar schools did not imply support for meritocracy, but rather for high-quality universal secondary education. This explains wide popular support for comprehensivisation, so long as it was portrayed as providing 'grammar schools for all'. Since the 1970s, public discourse on education has focused on curricular control, 'standards' and accountability, but still within a context of high-quality universal secondary education, and not the 'death of the comprehensive'.

In these lectures, I will address Britain's transition to a mass education system, at both secondary and tertiary level, over the whole of the last century but especially since the Second World War. I have to report that when I mentioned this to a colleague recently, he said, 'History of education? Really? Well, there goes *your* career.' I thought that an odd comment – not least because my career is much closer to its end than to its beginning – but it does betray a widespread sense in our discipline that the history of education is a dull or marginal or a dead-end subject. I will not now go into *why* that should be, but I will try to demonstrate how misguided it is. Especially for the most modern periods, education is surely one of the most important fields of enquiry, for political, social, cultural,

* I am grateful for many comments from the audience at this lecture, and for subsequent discussions with Laura Carter, Jon Lawrence, Sian Pooley, Gill Sutherland and Selina Todd, which have improved this published version.

even intellectual history. It is one of the principal sites of socialisation – *the* most important site outside the family. It is one of the places where the state enters most regularly and directly into the lives of its citizens. It helps to make us whom we are. It is therefore tightly enmeshed with questions that everyone acknowledges lie at the heart of our contemporary historical agenda – questions of class and gender, of national and other group identities, of social reform and social mobility, of the relationship between state and civil society. For the twentieth and twenty-first centuries, it plays roughly the role that religion played in the preceding centuries.

The specific theme that I will be taking up is the move from an elite to a mass education system, and the consequent emergence of a 'democratic public discourse' about education. I use this term 'democratic public discourse' in two senses. First, I address the question of how Britain changes its educational system in response to the advent of democratic political conditions. Second, I will be focusing more specifically on how public discourse on the provision of education changes – that is, not what are the hidden agendas behind educational change but rather what is or can be said in public about the role of education, by politicians and policymakers (with an eye on the reactions of the democratic electorate), but also, crucially, by the citizens of the democracy themselves, all of whom have direct experience of education as students and most also as parents. Together, these two approaches to the democratic public discourse of education will allow me, I hope, to say what kind of education democracy wants: whom is it meant to serve and for what purpose?

In this first address, I will examine the transition from elite secondary education at the beginning of the century, to universal secondary education in the middle of the century, to mostly comprehensive education from the 1970s to the present day. In the following address, I will chart the rise of mass higher education. Both these addresses will focus on who benefits from the education service. In the third and fourth addresses, I will be considering the purposes of education, taking in turn the thorny question of social mobility and finally the curriculum. Throughout, the focus will remain on the public discourse about who and what education is for; thus questions of funding and administration, though clearly entangled with and placing constraints on what it is possible to say about education in public, will take a back seat.

I start with the advent of universal secondary education over the course of the twentieth century. I should say at the outset that I do not regard Britain as some kind of special case in this regard – still less a 'basket case', as much of the literature holds: to cite the standard work by Andy Green, 'distinctly backward by comparison with other leading western states'.[1] It

---

[1] Andy Green, *Education and State Formation: The Rise of Education Systems in England, France and the USA* (Basingstoke, 1990), vii.

is perfectly true that Britain came relatively late and haltingly to universal primary education – Prussia had 'compulsory attendance laws' from 1763, France had universal provision from 1833, and Britain did not provide free and universal primary education until 1880. But we should beware facile comparisons shaped deliberately to exaggerate British backwardness. The Prussian state was unable to enforce its allegedly compulsory laws and did not provide free and universal primary education until 1868. France did not provide free and universal primary education until 1882. Thus, these three states were roughly in synch by the late nineteenth century.[2]

More importantly, the timing of universal primary education bears little relationship to the timing of universal secondary education because they were largely distinct systems. Universal primary education was driven by nation- and state-building (in Western Europe, mostly in the nineteenth century), as nation-states sought to 'make peasants into Frenchmen' (as the famous instantiation by Eugen Weber put it)[3] by inculcating literacy in the national language and a basic education in civics and patriotism, aimed at small children before they entered the workforce at 11 or 12. Universal secondary education had quite different drivers. In the nineteenth century, a strict divide was erected by most states between primary and secondary education – the first was civic education for all, the second was about elite selection and training, for around 2–3 per cent of the population. There was no need to connect primary and secondary education, as elites did not use state primary education and the masses did not use state secondary education; indeed, elites had an interest in maintaining a barrier between the two, so as to limit the inroads of the masses into the elite to at most a manageable trickle. Almost the sole exception to this rule was the United States, which in the nineteenth century did have an unusual commitment (at least in lip-service) to social mobility.[4]

When in the early twentieth century states began to extend access to secondary education, their motives were driven in large part by novel, democratic considerations. As sociologists of education have argued, the two principal drivers to universal secondary education were humanistic and economic. On the one hand, most Western states (and increasingly non-Western ones) in the twentieth century have viewed education as about the development and socialisation of the individual; this is where education has increasingly assumed the role of religion, in providing for the moral and spiritual needs that are generally assumed to be intrinsic to the human condition. On the other hand, twentieth-century states have

---

[2] *Ibid.*, 3–5, 12–13, and cf. *Mass Education and the Limits of State Building, c. 1870–1930*, ed. Laurence Brockliss and Nicola Sheldon (Basingstoke, 2012), 1–2, 89, 98–101, 118.
[3] Eugen Weber, *Peasants into Frenchmen: The Modernization of Rural France, 1870–1914* (Stanford, CA, 1976).
[4] *Mass Education*, ed. Brockliss and Sheldon, 1–3.

also looked to the economic benefits of education to advance the interests both of individuals and of nations in an increasingly competitive economic environment. Both of these approaches, fortified by (but not requiring) the advent of democracy, have tended to be 'universal, standardised and rationalised'. Over the course of the twentieth century, therefore, secondary education has had a tendency everywhere to be more about individuation than about stratification, and therefore to become less elite-oriented and more democratic.[5]

In this development, Britain did not start out (nor, I will argue, did it become) backward. Though Andy Green scolds backward Britain for excluding working-class children from secondary education before the Second World War, with compulsory schooling ending at 13 or 14, in fact Britain had the latest school-leaving age and the most years of compulsory schooling of any European state in the early twentieth century. In other words, all other countries stopped compulsory schooling at 14 or earlier, and none required the nine years of compulsory primary schooling from 5 to 14 that Britain required before the Second World War. Access to secondary education was limited everywhere, but in the 1930s Britain probably offered as much as France and Germany and by the 1950s and 1960s a good deal more than them.[6] Britain was not the 'slow', 'backward' educator in this period, 'sixty years behind its neighbours', as it has been portrayed in a 'declinist' literature determined to find fault with its social and economic development; it was, rather, where you would expect it to be, comparable to other northern and western European states, and well ahead of the southern European states.[7]

---

[5] John Boli, Francisco O. Ramirez and John W. Meyer, 'Explaining the Origins and Expansion of Mass Education', *Comparative Education Review*, 29 (1985), 145–70, quote at 147–8; Fabrice Murtin and Martina Viarengo, 'The Expansion and Convergence of Compulsory Schooling in Western Europe, 1950–2000', *Economica*, 78 (2011), 501–22. An intermediate position is taken up by *The Rise of the Modern Educational System: Structural Change and Social Reproduction, 1870–1920*, ed. Detlef K. Müller, Fritz Ringer and Brian Simon (Cambridge, 1987), who argue that the early phases of secondary expansion were characterised by both 'systematisation' *and* 'segmentation'.

[6] Michael Sanderson, *Educational Opportunity and Social Change in England* (1987), 119–20. The statistics cited by Sanderson are not strictly comparable – 6 per cent of the 15–18 cohort in England and Wales, 7 per cent of the 11–17 cohort in France, 8.8 per cent of the 11–19 cohort in Germany – but these point to roughly equivalent measures for the 15–18 cohort for Britain and Germany, both somewhat ahead of France.

[7] Brian Jackson and Dennis Marsden, *Education and the Working Class*, 1st edn, 1962 (rev. edn, Harmondsworth, 1966), 236; G. A. N. Lowndes, *The Silent Social Revolution: An Account of the Expansion of Public Education in England and Wales 1895–1965* (Oxford, 1969), 72, 105, and approvingly cited by R. A. Butler in his introduction, iv; I. G. K. Fenwick, *The Comprehensive School 1944–1970: The Politics of Secondary School Reorganization* (1976), 23; Green, *Education and State Formation*, vii, 6, 306–7, 313; Adrian Wooldridge, 'The English State and Educational Theory', in *The Boundaries of the State in Modern Britain*, ed. S. J. D. Green and R. C. Whiting

Like most of its obvious comparators, then, Britain started out the twentieth century with a state secondary system aimed at elite training and ended up with a universal system. How did this happen and why? The conventional view is that Britain moved from an elite-training system in the nineteenth century (based on private schools and quasi-public grammar schools) to an elite-selection system in the mid-twentieth. It was therefore not truly universalistic. The dominant ideology in this period is held to have been the rise of 'meritocracy', the belief that secondary education should add to hereditary social elites a selection from other classes based on 'merit' or intellectual aptitude.[8] I will argue instead that the idea of 'meritocracy' was short-lived and inherently unstable in the public discourse of education. Many competing ideas jostled in the political sphere between the 1900s and the 1950s, and the more universalistic ones were always most likely to triumph.

Both political parties were split in their initial ideas of how to organise access to secondary education. Most attention has focused on Labour, whose limp commitment to universal and equal secondary education is taken to be chiefly responsible for British backwardness.[9] It is true that Labour was divided. On the one hand, its highest hope, voiced by R. H. Tawney (notably in *Secondary Education for All*, the policy document he wrote for the Labour party in 1922), was for 'a single system', 'a progressive course of general education' for all children 11–16.[10] On the other hand, especially on the ground, Labour was dedicated to improving access for working-class children to the existing network of secondary schools – that is, the fee-paying grammar schools, which from 1907 were enabled in return for government subsidy to provide at least 25 per cent of their places free to children who had graduated from state elementary schools and passed a qualifying exam. These 'free-placers' on the whole were higher academic achievers than the fee-payers and so public investment in them was seen to be both meritocratic *and* democratic, a considerable

---

(Cambridge, 1996), 231; Ross McKibbin, *Classes and Cultures: England 1918–1951* (Oxford, 1998), 269.

[8] This view is shared both by champions of 'meritocracy' – e.g. Adrian Wooldridge, *Measuring the Mind: Education and Psychology in England, c. 1860–c. 1990* (Cambridge, 1994), or Sanderson, *Educational Opportunity and Social Change* – and by its critics – e.g. Centre for Contemporary Cultural Studies (CCCS) Education Group, *Unpopular Education: Schooling and Social Democracy in England since 1944* (1981) or Brian Simon, *Education and the Social Order 1940–1990* (1991).

[9] CCCS, *Unpopular Education*, 44, 93–8; Denis Lawton, *Education and Labour Party Ideologies 1900–2001 and Beyond* (Abingdon, 2005), 23–4, 28; Clyde Chitty, *New Labour and Secondary Education, 1994–2010* (Basingstoke, 2013), 33–4; McKibbin, *Classes and Cultures*, 233–5.

[10] *Secondary Education for All: A Policy for Labour*, ed. for the Education Advisory Committee of the Labour party by R. H. Tawney (London: Labour Party, n.d. (1922)), 28–9, 60.

source of local pride.[11] Local authorities were also empowered to provide more free places, either through schools of their own or by buying more places in fee-paying schools; in addition, central government funded its own free places in a group of high-quality grammar schools, the so-called 'direct grant' schools. Labour-controlled local authorities spent much of these cash-strapped decades laboriously building up a supply of 'free' places to meet a growing demand for secondary education amongst their constituents; Middlesbrough, for example, acquired one existing grammar school and opened two more and by 1938 was providing 75 per cent of these places for free to children who had gone to state primary schools, nine-tenths of them from the lower middle and working classes.[12]

Although what Tawney deplored as 'the doctrine of selection or of the educational ladder' extended secondary education only to a small minority (before the war, only 15 per cent entered secondary school), and mostly benefited fee-payers, in places like Middlesbrough the expansion of grammar schools was aimed at poorer children and built up a cohort of labour movement leaders who had reason to be grateful to the grammar schools – figures such as Ellen Wilkinson of Manchester, daughter of a cotton operative, who won scholarships to school and university and ended up as Minister of Education in 1945. As long as the expansion of secondary education meant the expansion of grammar schools, even Tawney celebrated this 'nationalisation' of secondary education and the limited gains made by working-class children within it, as an improvement upon the 'evil' 'doctrine of the two systems. . .of separation'.[13]

Labour, therefore, was ambivalent about the grammar school. But so, too, were the Conservatives. Their leadership continued to think of secondary education as elite training rather than elite selection; for them, elite selection happened elsewhere (to a great extent, in heredity), it did not require an artificial ladder of opportunity such as education was meant to provide. They did not use state secondary education much themselves; in 1938, three-quarters of their MPs were privately educated and over two-thirds still in 1950.[14] They had accepted the ladder of opportunity largely for utilitarian reasons – the need to recruit and train more intellectually skilled labour – and partially to rebuild social solidarity after the General

[11] Olive Banks, *Parity and Prestige in English Secondary Education: A Study in Educational Sociology* (1955), 65–9, 125–8.
[12] J. E. Floud, A. H. Halsey and F. M. Martin, *Social Class and Educational Opportunity* (1956), 9–14, 38; and see Gillian Sutherland, *Ability, Merit and Measurement: Mental Testing and English Education 1880–1940* (Oxford, 1984), 178–80, on central government's restraint of this provision, including the requirement for means-testing 'free' (now 'special') places from 1932.
[13] *Secondary Education for All*, 23–4, 60, 62, 69.
[14] Simon Haxey, *Tory M.P.* (1941), 179–83; H. G. Nicholas, *The British General Election of 1950* (1951), 45.

Strike, but they were anxious that the adhesion of these new recruits not impair the traditional elite-training functions of grammar schools.[15] The purpose of secondary education was to promote the leadership qualities of a minority, and while some saw the expansion of grammar schools as enriching the social elite with new leadership qualities, others were concerned that the grammar schools were diluting rather than enriching. As late as 1951, the Conservative education spokesperson Florence Horsburgh was insisting that in education 'the crucial things are the uncommon things . . . if we are to have good education we must look to these differences in abilities . . . rather than try to get children on to one common ground, as one common child . . . I would infinitely rather have privilege than have children all of one sort'.[16]

Given this ambivalence on both sides, it is not surprising that the advent of secondary education for all in the Butler Act of 1944 amounted to a compromise. As early as the Hadow Report of 1926, a 'bipartite' solution of grammar schools for the minority and a new type of secondary school for the majority, known as the 'modern' school, was mooted. Little came of this under the National government but social and political change in wartime accelerated the policy process considerably and in 1944 the Tory Whips, in the words of a future Tory Education Minister,

> welcomed the prospect of a bill which (unlike Beveridge) entailed no large immediate economic commitment, commanded a wide range of moderate and progressive all-party support, and could be counted on 'to keep the parliamentary troops thoroughly occupied, providing endless opportunity for debate, without any fear of breaking up the government'.[17]

The Butler Act of 1944 was therefore purposefully vague. It required local authorities to provide free secondary education for all, but did not specify what kind, only requiring that provision be suited to different 'ages, abilities and aptitudes'. While local authorities were therefore free to experiment with all kinds of secondary education – 'multilateral' (what we now know as 'all-ability' or comprehensive schools), technical, 'middle' schools and the like – the system almost universally adopted was the bipartite one. This permitted local authorities to retain and expand their carefully nurtured grammar schools (now with 100 per cent free places selected purely on 'merit') and to cater to the remaining 75 per cent of the age cohort with new, cheaper 'secondary modern' schools. This was the model that had been promoted by the Board of Education since Hadow and that was now aggressively promoted by the Coalition government; it was inherited by the Labour government and gingerly defended by Ellen

---

[15] Lowndes, *Silent Social Revolution*, 93–6; Banks, *Parity and Prestige*, 79–80, 119, 122, 124.

[16] *Hansard*, 5th ser., 491 (1950–1), 226.

[17] Edward Boyle, 'The Politics of Secondary School Reorganisation: Some Reflections', *Journal of Educational Administration and History*, 4, 2 (1972), 28.

Wilkinson, the grammar schoolgirl now Minister of Education, for the first few years after the war. In these early post-war years, a delicate political truce was maintained – Labour had got 'secondary education for all', the Tories had preserved elite selection and training – and in Austerity Britain local authorities had little room to breathe. But this truce did not last long; whatever the conventional view, in reality support for meritocracy was actually very fragile and its supposed triumph short-lived.[18]

It is not, perhaps, surprising that Labour – in opposition from 1951 – began to move to the left and retreat from its initial support for the bipartite system. Labour party conference began to pass motions in favour of comprehensivisation as early as 1950. From 1953, it included comprehensivisation in its official programme; its 1955 manifesto promised to promote it and its 1959 manifesto promised to make it law.[19] More surprisingly, the Conservatives were steadily pushed in the same direction. To understand why, we need to consider some underlying social and attitudinal changes that did not necessarily register immediately on the front-benches of the major political parties.

The conventional view is that education was 'a "quiet" area through the cold war', with a consensus behind meritocracy and the bipartite system, either because of a squalid pact between the party leaderships for a 'paternalist' policy that did not ask the public what it wanted, or, possibly, because meritocracy was genuinely popular.[20] I argue that, to the contrary, 'meritocracy' and the bipartite system were from the outset of very uncertain popularity and they became increasingly unpopular, with a rapidly mounting intensity of public opinion (and growing mobilisation at the grass-roots), over the course of the 1950s. There is a clue in the fact that the very word 'meritocracy' was coined by a critic, Michael

[18] Deborah Thom, 'The 1944 Education Act: The "Art of the Possible"?', in *War and Social Change: British Society in the Second World War*, ed. Harold L. Smith (Manchester, 1986), 101–28; Banks, *Parity and Prestige*, 133–44; Simon, *Education and the Social Order*, 58–75, 106, 141–2; Wooldridge, *Measuring the Mind*, 253–9.

[19] Peter Wann, 'The Collapse of Parliamentary Bipartisanship in Education 1945–52', *Journal of Educational Administration and History*, 3, 2 (1971), 24–34; D. E. Butler, *The British General Election of 1955* (1955), 14, 24; D. E. Butler and Richard Rose, *The British General Election of 1959* (1960), 50.

[20] CCCS, *Unpopular Education*, 64; Fenwick, *Comprehensive School*, 103–11, 129; Wooldridge, *Measuring the Mind*, 253–9; Dominic Sandbrook, *White Heat: A History of Britain in the Swinging Sixties* (2006), 314. Bizarrely, Lowndes, writing in 1965, expressed the fear that the historian of the future, 'studying the emotionally charged tirades against the 11+ examination in newspaper articles and editorials of the 1950s and 1960s', would 'exaggerate the width and depth of public feeling on the matter'; he preferred to credit 'the most responsible and best-educated sections of the parents in England and Wales' who were indeed 'vocal in their criticism of the system': *Silent Social Revolution*, 296–8. For an unusual realisation that the 1944 system 'began to crumble even before it was complete, a process that cut across party lines', see Glen O'Hara, *Governing Post-War Britain: The Paradoxes of Progress, 1951–1973* (Basingstoke, 2012), 160.

Young, whose dystopian satire *Rise of the Meritocracy* depicted a populist uprising against educational selection in the year 2034 that was already well underway at the time of publication in 1958.[21] The wellspring of this shift in popular sentiment was the growth of educational aspiration. We have already seen evidence of this in the 1930s, when hard-pressed local authorities like Middlesbrough nevertheless put a lot of money into grammar school expansion in the 1930s. In doing so, they were recognising growing public appetite for free secondary education, as opportunities for better-paid and more secure employment in the clerical and retail sectors expanded, and mothers especially sought education for their children as an alternative to entry into the manual labour market facilitated by fathers' workplace connections. The limited familiarity of working-class families with grammar schools put a cap on this aspiration, but it hardly quenched it, and the advent of universal secondary education from 1944 very much fuelled it. Now education was viewed, like health, as a universal public service, and parents of all classes came to seek the best teachers and schools for their children, just as they came to seek the best doctors and hospitals.[22]

The 'best' schools were widely identified, by all classes, as the grammar schools. This association had already been established before the war, when grammar schools were effectively the *only* secondary schools (thus by definition the best schools and the ones that gave access to non-manual occupations). This association was strengthened after the war by growing familiarity with and aspiration towards non-manual occupations in what was the peak period of social mobility in British history, as non-manual occupations grew from under one third to nearly one half of the labour force. As a result, every social survey into educational aspiration from the early 1950s to the mid-1960s showed that a majority of parents of all classes sought grammar school places for their children, in preference to, as one Bethnal Green housewife put it to social investigators in the early 1950s, 'the ordinary', that is, the secondary modern school. In no poll did preference for secondary modern schools rise much above 10 per cent.[23]

---

[21] Michael Young, *The Rise of the Meritocracy 1870–2033: An Essay on Education and Equality* (1958; Harmondsworth, 1961). Young was not quite the first to use the word in print, but it may still have originated with him: David Kynaston, *Modernity Britain: Opening the Box, 1957–59* (2013), 201.

[22] Selina Todd, *Young Women, Work, and Family in England 1918–1950* (Oxford, 2005), 68–9, 71–2, 101–4, an argument now carried forward into the post-war period in Selina Todd, *The People: The Rise and Fall of the Working Class 1910–2010* (2014), 217, 221–4.

[23] Michael Young and Peter Wilmott, *Family and Kinship in East London*, 1st edn, 1957 (Harmondsworth, 1962), 28–30 ('more than half' chose grammar schools); see also Floud, Halsey and Martin, *Social Class and Educational Opportunity*, 76–9 (56 per cent of S. W. Herts. parents and 54 per cent of Middlesbrough parents); Department of Education and Science (DES), *Children and their Primary Schools: A Report of the Central Advisory Council for Education*

While these preferences for grammar schools were stronger among professional and managerial parents, who had greater familiarity with and much higher rates of success at entrance to grammar school, even amongst the lowest levels of the working-class preferences for grammar school were expressed by around a third of all parents.[24] The most 'frustrated' of all parents were those in the lower middle class and upper working class, where appetite for grammar school was strong and disappointment common: two-thirds of parents in these groups said that their hopes had been frustrated. Thus, support for grammar schools should not be read as support for meritocracy but rather as a desire for the 'best' schools for all children. The corollary of this belief was majority support for the abolition of the 11+ exam and selection.[25] Indeed, the supposedly unaspirational working classes were more likely to support an end to selection, since they were more likely to be 'frustrated' in their aspiration for grammar school and had less opportunity to opt out to private education. The more they knew about a comprehensive alternative, the more they liked the sound of it.[26] But just as there was support for grammar schools across the classes, there was also support for an end to selection across the classes. No

(England) (1967), i.e. the Plowden Report (50 per cent chose grammar schools and 7 per cent comprehensives, 12 per cent chose secondary moderns); D. V. Donnison, 'Education and Opinion', *New Society*, 26 Oct. 1967, a report of a survey of 1,331 adults (46 per cent chose grammar schools, 16 per cent comprehensives, 10 per cent secondary moderns, 12 per cent technical schools). In all of these surveys, 'don't knows' are included, so majorities for grammar schools are even larger amongst those parents with any preferences. Mark Abrams conducted a survey of working-class couples in 1956–7 for Research Services Ltd which asked a wider range of questions and took account of 'don't knows': 34 per cent chose grammar schools, 14 per cent secondary moderns, 9 per cent technical schools, 5 per cent universities, 35 per cent don't know), 'A Pilot Enquiry into Some Aspects of Working-Class Life in London': Mark Abrams Papers, Churchill Archives Centre, Cambridge, 85/1. Kynaston, *Modernity Britain*, 218–22, 242–3, gives more weight to Abrams' rather jaundiced commentary on the gap between working-class aspirations and realities; cf. *ibid.*, 228–34, giving evidence of opinion swinging against selection. But it is clear from Abrams's survey (which was aimed at discovering whether working-class parents would be willing to buy private education) that these parents had high aspirations for their primary-age children, though they were unwilling to blame them personally for 'failure' thereafter, especially as they were satisfied with their labour-market performance regardless of educational experience: compare Tables 5b, 6b, 6d.

[24] Floud, Halsey and Martin, *Social Class and Educational Opportunity*, 82; DES, *Children and their Primary Schools*, 122; Research Services Ltd, 'Pilot Enquiry', Table 5b.

[25] O'Hara, *Governing Post-War Britain*, 162.

[26] A second survey by Abrams for Research Services Ltd, in 1957, asked a nationally representative sample specifically about the bipartite system, broken down by class: 40 per cent of middle-class and 57 per cent of working-class respondents approved of comprehensives when the concept was explained to them, and 42 per cent of middle-class and 59 per cent of working-class respondents when the arguments pro and con were rehearsed for them as well. A separate question – whether it would be better for all children to be educated at the same schools – drew even higher levels of support: 52 per cent of middle-class and 72 per cent of working-class respondents 'agreed completely'. Research

wonder that in the debates over comprehensivisation the Conservatives took the position that they were opposed to the 'destruction of grammar schools'[27] and Labour that they sought 'grammar schools for all' – this latter slogan, taken up by both Gaitskell and Wilson, and much derided in the historiography, expressed very well indeed the preferences of the majority of voters, and particularly 'swing' voters.[28]

This current in public opinion – against selection at 11+ and towards 'grammar schools for all' – has not been widely recognised or, where recognised, not been much admired, either by contemporary pundits or in later historiography. Attention has focused instead on the movement of technical and professional opinion against selection at 11+: sociologists who revealed the class differentials behind 11+ success; psychologists who argued that 'intelligence' was not solely an inherent quality but could be 'acquired', even after age 11; teachers, educational professionals and educational lobby groups who were acutely aware of the mistakes and injustices rendered by selection; and ultimately a series of government enquiries, the Crowther, Newsom and Plowden Reports.[29] But these sections of opinion are emphasised because they tend to be the only ones studied; their actors create articulate and easily accessible texts and organisations. It has been harder to capture or even to locate parental opinion at the grass-roots; yet it was there, highly vocal, 'emotionally charged' as one contemporary pundit admitted, even insurgent. Scorned as well by those who should have been its champions – because working-class opinion did not take the form of organised labour-movement pressure, the New Left preferred to interpret it as somnolence, or at best rank consumerism – what the Catholic archbishop of Liverpool recognised at the time as the 'revolt of the mums' expressed the new common-sense of universal secondary education, what I have called the

Services Ltd, 'Survey of Educational Attitudes', 13–15; Abrams Papers, 3/64; and see further n. 45.

[27] Fenwick, *Comprehensive School*, 94–5, 130–1; Butler, *General Election of 1955*, 21, 36; Butler and Rose, *General Election of 1959*, 56.

[28] Fenwick, *Comprehensive School*, 109; Edward Boyle, Anthony Crosland and Maurice Kogan, *The Politics of Education* (Harmondsworth, 1971), 21–2; Maurice Kogan, *The Politics of Educational Change* (1978), 32; Clyde Chitty, *Towards a New Education System: The Victory of the New Right?* (1989), 40–1; Melanie Phillips, *All Must Have Prizes* (1996), 332–3; but cf. Chitty, *New Labour and Secondary Education*, 38–40, more generous but still seeing a 'contradiction' where none is there. McKibbin, *Classes and Cultures*, 233, points out that the idea of 'grammar schools for all' was already present in Labour circles in the late 1940s.

[29] Sanderson, *Educational Opportunity and Social Change*, 45–54, 86–95; Wooldridge, *Measuring the Mind*, 259–328; Fenwick, *Comprehensive School*, 91–113, and esp. 150, but cf. 163; Kynaston, *Modernity Britain*, 228–34; Alan Kerckhoff, Ken Fogelman, David Crook and David Reeder, *Going Comprehensive in England and Wales: A Study of Uneven Change* (1996), 160–1, 167–9, but cf. 162–4, 169–70.

democratic public discourse of education.[30] And it also told directly on policy.

This pressure registered first where it mattered most, on the local authorities who under the Butler Act had responsibility for the provision and organisation of secondary education in their localities. They had another source of pressure in the 1950s which had to be reconciled with the demand for high-quality schools, that is, a demographic pressure. The advent of the secondary moderns had come at a time when demographic pressure was low. With the baby boom from 1946, that pressure began to grow, and the number of school-age children requiring places swelled from under 5 million at war's end to over 6 million by 1960; at the same time, rising standards and expectations for housing created a housing boom, especially in the public sector.[31] New estates with new schools had to be built. In these circumstances it became increasingly difficult for local authorities, even Conservative ones, to introduce new selective schools. 'I cannot from memory recall a single Conservative, with any interest in the subject, who really favoured building new grammar schools and secondary modern schools, side by side, in an expanding housing estate', commented Edward Boyle, the Conservative Education Minister, about this period.[32] In fact, it was rural authorities, mostly Conservative, who had the most difficulty building new selective schools in thinly populated areas where selective schools would be too small or require too large a catchment. Thus, early experiments in comprehensive schools came not only from big, ideologically committed Labour authorities such as the LCC or Coventry, but also from places like Anglesey, the Isle of Man, Westmorland, Dorset, the West Riding of Yorkshire (then Conservative-controlled) and West Sussex, as well as on new estates built by local authorities of all persuasion – 195 by 1964.[33]

Of course, politicians did sense the power of public opinion on the ground, but because it was easier for national parties to leave this tricky problem to local authorities to solve it was not at first acknowledged in

[30] Lowndes, *Silent Social Revolution*, 265, 296–8. Although there was less bias against working-class children in admission to Catholic grammar schools, there were also fewer places, and rank-and-file Catholic criticism of grammar schools was thus particularly acute: McKibbin, *Classes and Cultures*, 263 n. 173; Todd, *The People*, 225–7.

[31] *Twentieth-Century British Social Trends*, ed. A. H. Halsey with Josephine Webb (Basingstoke, 2000), 186; and see Thom, '1944 Education Act', 120–3.

[32] Boyle, 'Politics of Secondary School Reorganisation', 31; Kerckhoff *et al.*, *Going Comprehensive*, 87–8, 137–42, 162; and see Steven Cowan, Gary McCulloch and Tom Woodin, 'From HORSA Huts to ROSLA Blocks: The School Leaving Age and the School Building Programme in England, 1943–1972', *History of Education*, 41 (2012), 368–9.

[33] Kerckhoff *et al.*, *Going Comprehensive, passim*; Fenwick, *Comprehensive School*, 61–2; Simon, *Education and the Social Order*, 109–10; Sanderson, *Educational Opportunity and Social Change*, 62; O'Hara, *Governing Post-War Britain*, 162; Boyle, Crosland and Kogan, *The Politics of Education*, 121–2.

Whitehall or Westminster. The powers-that-be in those places did their best to dodge or muffle growing unhappiness over selection. Officials at the Ministry of Education expressed the view in 1960 that selection by means of the 11+ 'could not survive the day when [parents'] wishes could gain a hearing'.[34] But parents' wishes were already gaining a hearing. In their electoral addresses, aimed at local rather than national concerns, parliamentary candidates were showing a growing tendency to raise educational issues. Under half of all electoral addresses in 1950 and 1951 mentioned education. This leapt to 72 per cent in 1955 and over 90 per cent by 1959. So much for the 'quiet' period. All prospective MPs, Labour and Conservative, knew education now mattered much more to the electorate, even more than the health service.[35]

Those Conservative MPs most directly concerned with education policy knew this better than most. As Minister for Education for much of the period 1954–62, David Eccles tried at first to placate public opinion (and to cultivate human capital) by pouring money into the education service, to raise the standard of the secondary moderns. Education spending as a proportion of GNP doubled from 2 per cent to 4 per cent. Pupil–teacher ratios fell and secondary moderns were encouraged to offer O-Levels to their students, previously confined to grammar schools. But the dislike of selection was now far too strong to assert the fabled 'parity of esteem' between moderns and grammars. Even as secondary moderns improved, the cap on grammar school places left more frustrated parents – there were no more working-class children in grammar schools in 1961 than there had been in 1950 – and public opinion was at boiling point.

Conservative local authorities were just as concerned as Labour ones. A particularly piquant situation arose in Leicestershire where the Conservative authority had opted for comprehensive 'middle schools' while the Labour-controlled city of Leicester stuck to its grammars. On one occasion, when a routine meeting was called to discuss boundary changes, the boundary commissioners were astonished to find that thousands of people had turned up; as one of the barristers present, later a Labour Lord Chancellor, recalled:

> the vast majority were parents and they were hopping mad because in the city they had secondary and grammar schools whereas the county had comprehensive schools. Some

---

[34] O'Hara, *Governing Post-War Britain*, 161. Most commentators read 'middle-class parents' for 'parents', but the polling evidence, especially on 'frustration', suggests otherwise; and even Kerckhoff *et al.*, the most sensitive commentators, interpret rapid comprehensivisation by Labour authorities as evidence of a lack of a noisy 'grammar-school constituency' (Stoke, Leeds) and/or the presence of 'working-class communities with relatively few education-conscious parents' (parts of Bristol), though they also note extensive public consultation and discussion in such places: *Going Comprehensive*, 87, 98, 112–13.

[35] Nicholas, *General Election of 1950*, 221; D. E. Butler, *The General Election of 1951* (1952), 54; Butler, *General Election of 1955*, 31–3, 36; Butler and Rose, *General Election of 1959*, 131.

of them had sold their homes in Leicester in order to get away from the city education system and the 11-plus and give their children the advantages of a comprehensive school education, and now they were being threatened with being put back into the city again... Of course, I had always known that the 11-plus was not very popular, but I had never known before to what extent it was both hated and feared.[36]

Conservative education ministers, from Eccles on down, knew full well as early as the mid-1950s that selection was doomed. It was most unpopular precisely amongst their target voters – the aspirational lower-middle- and upper-working-class parents who were changing Britain from a pyramidal to a diamond-shaped social structure. Though not explicit in party policy, Conservative government practice shifted from upgrading secondary moderns as such to preparing upgraded secondary moderns for comprehensivisation, following the practice of Conservative-controlled county councils such as the West Riding, Hampshire and West Sussex. Eccles and his successor Edward Boyle encouraged experiments that postponed selection to 14, as in Leicestershire, or 16 (that is, after the school-leaving age), as in Southampton.[37] They began to talk the universalist, individualist language of education that was already the new common-sense: secondary schooling not as elite selection and training but as the normal way in which all individuals would equip themselves for life and work.[38] Thus, although the Conservatives drew on both 'human capital' and more humanistic arguments to motivate their educational policy – the two languages that sociologists tell us are responsible for convergence on universal, standardised secondary education across the developed world – it was the latter argument, for education for individual development, that increasingly won out.[39] It was this Conservative government that commissioned the Crowther, Newsom and Plowden Reports that gave Conservative as well as Labour front-benchers the kind of expert imprimatur that they felt they needed to change public policy. By the time that Boyle succeeded Eccles as Education Minister in 1962, most LEAs had already moved: Boyle was told by his civil servants that 90 out of 163 LEAs had comprehensivisation plans in the works. Only 20 per cent of LEAs were sticking by the 11+.[40] Though Boyle has often

[36] Lord Gardiner, 10 Feb. 1964, in *Hansard*, 5th ser., 263 (1964–5), 245–6. Simon, *Education and the Social Order*, 279, tells this story but unfortunately misattributes it to a Tory minister, Lord Newton.

[37] Wooldridge, *Measuring the Mind*, 332; Boyle, Crosland and Kogan, *Politics of Education*, 121–2, 127; Boyle, 'Politics of Secondary School Reorganisation', 30–3.

[38] Boyle, Crosland and Kogan, *Politics of Education*, 21–2. These were all positions remarkably similar to those enunciated by Tony Crosland, *The Future of Socialism* (1956), 195–207.

[39] Sanderson, *Educational Opportunity and Social Change*, 94–5; Simon, *Education and the Social Order*, 291; CCCS, *Unpopular Education*, 192–3.

[40] Boyle, 'Politics of Secondary School Reorganisation', 32; Lowndes, *Silent Social Revolution*, 304.

been demonised by the New Right as the traitor within the gates who sold out the grammar schools, this again misses the point that the prime movers in educational reform were not in Whitehall or Westminster but in a couple of hundred local authorities, and millions of homes around the country, drawn from all political persuasions.

Thus, comprehensivisation appeared increasingly inevitable from the mid-1950s, though this did not mean it could or should have happened quickly. Implementation took about twenty years, from the first experiments in the mid-1950s to the mid-1970s, by which time most comprehensivisation plans had been approved, leading to the situation today where over 90 per cent of the state sector is represented by these schools. (Throughout this period, the state sector covered 93 or 94 per cent of the entire age-cohort – despite frequent predictions to the contrary, the independent sector has remained resolutely stuck at 6–7 per cent.) But comprehensivisation was no more protracted here than, say, in Sweden.[41] The political problem faced by Labour after 1964 was how to achieve the popular policy of abolishing selection without associating it with the unpopular policy of 'destroying' the best schools. The only way to do this was to persuade parents that comprehensives *were* the best schools – thus the slogan of 'grammar schools for all'.

The evidence is that they were successful in doing so. As early as 1958, when only a bare majority of the electorate had even heard of comprehensives, those who had heard of them favoured them over the bipartite system 3–1; by 1967, nearly three-quarters of those living in areas offering comprehensives, and 85 per cent of those with children actually in comprehensives, favoured them over the bipartite system. As always, the author of this survey commented, 'Respondents were not voting against grammar education; they were voting – massively – against secondary modern education.'[42] In that same year, the Conservative leader Ted Heath publicly asserted that it was 'never a Conservative principle that children should be segregated in different institutions'.[43] In 1970, when the Conservatives returned to power, although they reversed the Labour government's request to local authorities to bring forward comprehensivisation plans, they made a conscious decision not to discourage them, because, as the Education Minister, Margaret Thatcher,

[41] O'Hara, *Governing Post-War Britain*, 166–7, perhaps exaggerating the differences; Kerckhoff *et al.*, *Going Comprehensive*, 1–5. Sweden, Norway and (later) Denmark introduced comprehensive education at lower-secondary level earlier than Britain, but at upper-secondary level at about the same time or later: Susanne Wiborg, 'The Formation of Comprehensive Education: Scandinavian Variations', in *The Death of the Comprehensive High School? Historical, Contemporary, and Comparative Perspectives*, ed. Barry M. Franklin and Gary McCulloch (Basingstoke, 2007), 131–45.
[42] Kynaston, *Modernity Britain*, 234; Donnison, 'Education and Opinion', 585.
[43] CCCS, *Unpopular Education*, 192.

told Heath, 'it was difficult to establish how a child would suffer from the introduction of a comprehensive scheme, particularly as educational opinion, rightly or wrongly, was still strongly in support of comprehensive schools'.[44]

Comprehensivisation was left to local authorities, who were then in the full flood of their plans. At this point, public opinion still seemed – as it had been at least since the mid-1950s – strongly in favour of abolition of the 11+ and of comprehensive schools as the 'best' schools. A few, mostly Conservative, local authorities held local referenda in this period to allow public opinion to settle the question of comprehensivisation, and in each case – Gloucester, Barnet, Cardiganshire, Eton and Slough, Amersham – majorities were returned for comprehensivisation, ranging from 4–1 in Barnet to 2–1 in Eton and Slough and Amersham. None of these results stuck; Barnet LEA's plan was rejected by Thatcher at the DES, the Eton and Slough and Amersham results rejected by the Buckinghamshire LEA.[45] But these were the marginal cases, the ones LEAs found most difficult; in most other places, LEAs saw themselves as in accord with public opinion and comprehensivisation proved, not only uncontroversial, but popular. Thus, it was that Thatcher, through no fault of her own, presided over more transfer from bipartite to comprehensive schools than any other Education Minister.[46] There is a case to be made that this transition to universal secondary education was *more* rather than less popular than in much of the rest of Europe – rather more like America's, in fact, though much later – as a result in Britain of its association with welfare-state universalism as opposed to more technocratic or bargained transitions elsewhere in Europe, where elite-selection in secondary education was taken for granted for longer.[47]

How (if at all) has the democratic public discourse on secondary education changed after the period when comprehensivisation was more or less complete, that is, since the 1970s? Political debate about education in this period has revolved around a set of issues – curriculum reform, 'standards', accountability, parental choice – that to some extent

[44]'Discussion at Chequers on Education', 13 Jan. 1972: The National Archives, PREM 15/863.

[45]Caroline Benn, 'Referenda – do they help or hinder decision-making?', *Education*, 21 Apr. 1972, 374–5; Caroline Benn, 'Polling the People', *Where: The Education Magazine for Parents*, Nov. 1975, 304–5. The Gloucester result was complicated by a tortuous set of questions, which made it possible for majorities to be counted for both comprehensives and grammar schools.

[46]Simon, *Education and the Social Order*, 408, 420.

[47]Cf. *The State of Welfare: The Economics of Social Spending*, ed. John Hills and Howard Glennerster (Oxford, 1998), 67: 'It took a generation finally to free ordinary people from the belief that they had no right to higher education or to take school-leaving qualifications.' The evidence is that many 'ordinary people' did have these beliefs, though it took a generation to realise them.

represents a continuity with the rising expectations of the post-1944 period, but which also incorporates new themes of scepticism about the alleged 'permissiveness' of 1960s culture and about the performance of public services, associated with the New Right. These latter associations have led historians of education (mostly themselves writing from the Left) to characterise this period in nearly apocalyptic terms: the return of selection, the 'dismantling' of the comprehensive system, the 'steady abandonment of the comprehensive ideal', even 'the death of secondary education for all'.[48] Here, I will emphasise the elements of continuity as well as change. The New Right itself represented some currents of continuity: its very diverse cast of characters included frank advocates of a return to selection, but also advocates of comprehensive education who were traumatised by the permissiveness of the 1960s, yet sought to reverse it by means of standards *rather* than selection, and an entirely new element of market ideologists who were not so concerned about 'permissiveness' (in some ways, they were for it) and for whom selection and comprehension were not the main issues.[49] New Labour drew on a similar mix, though with fewer advocates of selection.

Because comprehensivisation had proceeded 'from the bottom up', with working-class districts going first, there were still some LEAs with strong middle-class 'grammar school constituencies' holding out for selection by the time the Conservatives returned to power in 1979. Thatcher had by then undoubtedly registered (and capitalised upon) the growing scepticism about both the 'permissiveness' of the 1960s and, even more so, the performance of public services. She withdrew pressure on the holdout LEAs to convert; many of them retain the bipartite system today, representing about 7 per cent of the age-cohort. But while public opinion in these holdout districts remained generally supportive of their existing system, so did public opinion in comprehensivised LEAs. Attempts in the 1980s by Conservative LEAs to roll back comprehensivisation in Solihull, Redbridge, Wiltshire and Berkshire were all stymied by united parent

[48]E.g. Chitty, *Towards a New Education System*, 175–6, 178; Chitty, *New Labour and Secondary Education*, ch. 5; Richard Pring, *The Life and Death of Secondary Education for All* (2013). In the 1980s, both Left and Right were predicting the return of selection; though this did not happen, subsequent analyses from the Left have tried to demonstrate that it did (see below, pp. 23, 26). Even the more temperate Kerckhoff *et al.* were convinced they were witnessing the return of selection in the early 1990s: see the section on 'Comprehensive Education: A Bleak Future' in *Going Comprehensive*, 42–4.

[49]For some helpful typologies of New Right thinking on education, see Roger Dale, 'Thatcherism and Education', in *Contemporary Education Policy*, ed. John Ahier and Michael Flude (1983), 233–55; Brian Salter and E.R. Tapper, 'The Politics of Reversing the Ratchet in Secondary Education, 1969–1986', *Journal of Educational Administration and History*, 20 (1988), 57–70; and Christopher Knight, *The Making of Tory Education Policy in Post-War Britain 1950–1986* (Lewes, 1990), though the latter undoes some of his more subtle distinctions by too often lumping them together as 'Conservative educationalists' or 'preservationists'.

and teacher pressure. Apparently, while parent pressure was no longer mobilised against existing bipartite schools, it was still impossible to get parents to accept new ones – perhaps another sign of scepticism, not so much about public services, as about politically motivated changes of any kind. In sharp contrast to the period of comprehensivisation, as well, demographic and fiscal pressures were running against new schools and LEAs had little appetite for more upheaval that would require money they did not have. The mainstream of public debate, in both parties, therefore, focused on persuading parents that their children were being offered the 'best' schools without requiring selection, which has generally remained throughout this period the untouchable 'third rail' of educational politics.[50]

Probably the most important policy decisions of the Thatcher governments themselves were those involving curriculum, which certainly represent continuity more than change, and indeed can be seen as putting the *coup de grace* to the bipartite system and consolidating comprehensivisation. First was the decision in 1984 to merge the two examination systems left over from the bipartite system, CSE and GCE O Level, into a single GCSE exam at 16, which even right-wing critics have described as 'the triumph of the comprehensive principle in the curriculum'.[51] Next came the move to draft a national curriculum. This had a more ambiguous pedigree. Curriculum had traditionally been left very much to local control – to the local authority, even to the individual school or teacher – on the principle that central government in a liberal society should not be dictating on matters of individual conscience and belief. This decentralising principle was one of the healthy sources of vagueness in the Butler Act of 1944, which left so much in the hands of local authorities.

Teachers had, of course, come to consider curricular freedom a prerogative of their own, particularly in the 1960s – the golden age of teacher autonomy. Successive waves of educational reformers, on both Right and Left, had emphasised the need for more central control of curriculum in order to level up standards and improve the student experience, especially in a highly mobile society, starting with David Eccles who in 1960 had regretted the failure of politicians of any stripe to make inroads into what he termed resonantly 'the secret garden of the

[50] Kerckhoff et al., *Going Comprehensive*, 41–2, 208, 226; *The State of Welfare*, ed. Hills and Glennerster, 29–41. Cf. Dominic Sandbrook, *Seasons in the Sun: The Battle for Britain, 1974–1979* (2012), 196–216, which argues more anecdotally for a much sharper turn on the part of all classes back towards grammar schools.
[51] Wooldridge, *Measuring the Mind*, 400–1; Phillips, *All Must Have Prizes*, 137–8; for more grudging accounts of GCSE from the Left, see Simon, *Education and the Social Order*, 508–10, Chitty, *Towards a New Education System*, 161–3, but cf. Andrew Adonis, *Education, Education, Education: Reforming England's Schools* (2012), 25.

curriculum'. The subsequent rise of progressive educational methods in the 1960s kept the garden not so much secret as roped off from political control; one of the sources of opposition to the CSE–GCE merger even from advocates of comprehensive education was teachers' feeling that they had more curricular control over CSE, even if it deprived their students of access to A-Levels and higher education.[52]

On the other hand, it was an article of 'declinist' faith on the Left as well as the Right that the lack of a national curriculum on the French model was one of the factors keeping British education in the amateurish dark ages.[53] Furthermore, the same forces that had been driving comprehensivisation – pressure for a unitary system from parents seeking equality and also from both employers and unions making 'human capital' arguments – encouraged both parties to undertake central reform of the curriculum. No doubt local authorities and teachers' unions were right to deplore this as a power grab by the Education Department, but it was a power grab facilitated by demands for a modern, unitary school system from a wide array of interests. A 1979 survey showed that local authorities were not exercising any effective oversight on curriculum. The Education Department stepped into this vacuum, seeking to organise 'a national consensus on a desirable framework for the curriculum'.[54] As the debate over the draft history curriculum amply demonstrated, there were risks entailed in opening the 'secret garden', but it was also still possible in the 1980s to have a robust public discussion amongst parents, teachers, academics, civil servants and politicians, and to produce a curriculum that commanded a substantial degree of consensus around a 'desirable framework'.[55] Like the creation of GCSE in 1984, the drafting of the national curriculum between 1988 and 1995 in the end is much more plausibly seen as the culmination of the process of comprehensivisation than as the beginning of its end.

Something similar can be said about 'standards'. The language of 'standards', employed with increasing insistence from the 1970s, is another element of recent educational reform jargon closely associated with the New Right. It is seen as representing a 'preservationist' or 'restorationist' position with regard to the grammar schools, and part of a concerted campaign to discredit comprehensive education. 'Excellence'

---

[52] Simon, *Education and the Social Order*, 311–16; Chitty, *Towards a New Education System*, 129.

[53] Green, *Education and State Formation*, vii–viii, 314–15; Peter Scott, *Knowledge & Nation* (Edinburgh, 1990), 155–7; Chitty, *Towards a New Education System*, 139.

[54] Boyle, Crosland and Kogan, *Politics of Education*, 25–8, 170–3; Chitty, *Towards a New Education System*, 61–3, 106–26, 142–4, 153–4. Chitty seems to be in favour of a common exam at 16 and a national curriculum, in principle but not in practice.

[55] Robert Phillips, *History Teaching, Nationhood and the State: A Study in Educational Politics* (1998). I will have more to say on the subject of the history curriculum in my fourth address.

is taken to be a code word meaning grammar schools.[56] But again it is just as plausible to see the language of standards as bolstering rather than undermining public support for comprehensive schools. Since the 1950s, parents had learned to seek the 'best' schools for their children: initially, this meant grammar schools; later, it meant comprehensive schools. The language of 'standards' was therefore bound to be used by advocates of *both* grammar schools *and* comprehensives. The authors of the Black Papers, the notorious founding documents of the New Right in education, who were reacting against 'permissiveness' in education and not always against comprehensive schooling *per se*, in fact used the language of 'standards' in both ways. Some felt in the traditional way that the grammar schools were the only reliable bastions of excellence; others, acknowledging that 'a majority [of the electorate] probably favour some kind of comprehensive school', focused their energies on promoting excellence in comprehensives.[57] Whereas the New Right was understandably ambivalent about excellence in comprehensives, New Labour was not. Tony Blair's leading education advisor, Andrew Adonis, did identify 'excellence' with the teaching practices of independent and grammar schools but devoted all his energies to transplanting them into comprehensives: the old Labour policy of 'grammar schools for all'. His Blairite counterpart, Alastair Campbell, who put the phrase 'bog-standard comprehensive' into circulation, was even more of a comprehensive stalwart: for him 'excellence' was not something associated with one kind of school or another, but rather something at which all schools ought to aim. Both used the language of 'failing comprehensives', but this was hardly an attempt to delegitimate comprehensiveness; rather it was an attempt to meet rising expectations amongst parents. Adonis himself defined failure in the 1990s as leaving school with fewer than 2 or 3 GCSEs of any kind, but defines failure today as leaving school with fewer than 5 GCSEs above a C grade.[58] As Alison Wolf has argued, the language of standards in Britain differs from similar language elsewhere in Europe, focused on 'certification' for all

---

[56] Notably in Knight, *Making of Tory Education Policy*, 86, 95–6, 99, 110, 151–3.

[57] C. B. Cox and A. E. Dyson, *The Black Papers on Education* (1971), 9, 26–9. In the pro-selection camp were Angus Maude, two psychologists who believed in the heritability of intelligence (Cyril Burt and Richard Lynn) and Tibor Szamuely; in the anti-selection camp, at least at first, were Rhodes Boyson and the prime movers of the Black Papers, Cox and Dyson. See further Brian Cox, *The Great Betrayal* (1992), 145–7, 150, 156–7, 177–9, 213, 222.

[58] Adonis, *Education*, xii, 11–19, 37, 113; Peter Hyman, *1 out of 10: From Downing Street Vision to Classroom Reality* (2005), 308–12. Blair himself was a secret admirer of selection, but he knew better than to say so in public. *The Alastair Campbell Diaries*, I: *Prelude to Power, 1994–1997*, ed. Alastair Campbell with Bill Hagerty (2010), 531, 732.

rather than elite-selection – further evidence of the persistent importance of welfare-state universalism in public attitudes to education here.[59]

'Accountability' is another catchphrase of the post-1970s period that is taken to be a New Right synonym for selection. For New Right champions of 'standards', the only way to measure educational quality was testing, and the publication of test results for individual schools (or even individual teachers) would promote competition between schools and thus drive standards up further. 'Accountability' was thus primarily about exposing schools to market tests. But accountability also derives, as standards do, from rising parental expectations. As we have seen, the Education Department had done its best to shield bipartite schools from parental pressure in the 1950s. Comprehensive schools were not at first much more exposed to parental pressure either. It was not only the curriculum that was secret, so were inspection reports – not available for individual schools – and internal management – no parent representatives were required on governing bodies under the 1944 Act, and many local authorities monopolised control of those governing bodies through the 1960s. In the 1960s and 1970s, there was mounting pressure from parents for both informal and formal participation in the running of schools; this was a different, more vocal form of parental opinion than we found in the 1950s, but in many ways a logical extension of it. It was, of course, part of a wider ethic of 'community participation' building in the 1960s and 1970s, and it became effective from the bottom up, only retrospectively sealed by legislation. A study in the mid-to-late 1960s found almost no parental representation on governing bodies. By 1975, the practice had become pretty general; it became statutory in 1979.[60] Other forms of accountability – such as the publication of inspection reports, required from 1983, and examination results, required in the 1988 Education Reform Act – cannot be detached from this demand for parental involvement in schools. Like the language of 'standards', accountability reflected both an assertion of parental involvement in schools and a distinctive New Right demand for market tests. Indeed, the New Right's populist successes here as elsewhere owed much to this dovetailing with well-established and non-partisan demands for popular participation which were only fitfully connected to market ideology.

A final demand of the New Right, for 'parental choice', was in many ways the most controversial. In its extreme form – the 'voucher' scheme,

[59] Alison Wolf, 'A Comparative Perspective on Educational Standards', in *Educational Standards*, ed. Harvey Goldstein and Anthony Heath (Oxford, 2000), 28. I am grateful to Gill Sutherland for this reference.

[60] DES and Welsh Office, *A New Partnership for Our Schools* (1977), i.e. the Taylor Report, esp. 5–10. The teachers' unions and LEAs both opposed parent participation in governing bodies. CCCS, *Unpopular Education*, 224–5.

whereby parents were credited with the cost of a state education and could spend it anywhere they liked, including independent and other selective schools – 'parental choice' *was* a means of restoring selection through the back door, though it was also (primarily, for the New Right) just another way of introducing market mechanisms into the education system to drive up standards. But like 'standards' and 'accountability', 'parental choice' could be many things to different people. In the hands of New Labour, it could be about embracing multiculturalism – offering parents the choice of schools oriented to particular faiths or other identities. In the hands of both parties, it could be about 'specialism' – offering parents the choice of schools oriented to particular subjects or pursuits: technology or the humanities or art and music or sport. 'Specialism' itself was ambiguous with regard to selection; in theory, it could be used to restore the bipartite system by introducing academic and vocational specialist schools. Keith Joseph talked about specialism in terms of 'differentiation', a heavy hint at a return to the bipartite hierarchy.[61] Other Tories liked to tease Labour with this ambiguity. John Patten, Education Secretary in 1992, wrote an article in the *New Statesman* entitled, 'Who's afraid of the "S" word?', where the S-word turned out to be specialism and not selection.[62] In the event, the Conservatives could not do more than tease. They never seriously considered voucher schemes. For Patten as well as for Joseph, 'specialism' always remained a matter of parental choice between types of school, not academic selection by the back door. This was even more the case for New Labour, which saw specialism as a way to create a 'new type of all-ability state school', not a way of introducing selection at all.[63]

But the biggest problem with 'parental choice' is that it was not very popular. Parents wanted the 'best' schools for their children, but they also wanted their neighbourhood school to be the best school – not some other school miles away. They much preferred 'parental voice' to 'parental choice'.[64] The Conservatives knew even better than Labour that

---

[61] Chitty, *Towards a New Education System*, 158–61. Both Right and Left – e.g. Wooldridge, 'English State and Educational Theory', 248–54, Knight, *Making of Tory Education Policy*, 152, 157, 180, Stewart Ranson, 'Towards a Tertiary Tripartism: New Codes of Social Control and the 17+', in *Selection, Certification and Control: Social Issues in Educational Assessment*, ed. Patricia Broadfoot (1984), 221–44 – treat differentiation and selection as nearly synonymous.

[62] Chitty, *New Labour and Secondary Education*, 58–9. Patten made clear that specialism was *not* selection in the old sense: 'The selection that does take place is always parent-driven. The principle of open access remains.'

[63] Adonis, *Education*, xii, 44–7.

[64] This was particularly true in Scotland, where parents seemed to welcome the introduction of self-management through governing bodies (that had already been available in England) but not the greater degree of choice than was available in England inserted into Scottish educational legislation by the Thatcher governments. See Margaret A. Arnott, '"The More Things Change. . .?": The Thatcher Years and Educational Reform in Scotland', *Journal of Educational Administration and History*, 43 (2011), 181–202.

'choice did not resonate at all with target voters'. In both the 1997 and 2005 general elections, they soft-pedalled their ideological commitment to 'choice' in favour of a more voter-friendly emphasis on 'standards', which no one could be against.[65] 'Specialism' has so far turned out to be something of a damp squib – a device whereby heads obtain extra funding for their schools rather than a significant criterion by which parents actually choose schools for their children.[66]

To sum up the period since the comprehensivisation process was virtually completed in the 1970s: the democratic public discourse about schools has been dominated by a diverse set of issues – curricular reform, 'standards', accountability, 'parental choice'. The leaderships of all three governing parties have ensured that selection is no longer on the table; it is notable, for example, that one of the Liberal Democrats' few recent policy successes came when Michael Gove attempted to restore a two-tier exam at 16, a proposal which so little excited the Conservative party that it capitulated to Nick Clegg's expostulations almost without debate. Emphasis has been placed instead on driving up quality in all state schools. On the whole, though not entirely, the Right has done better in setting the terms of this public discourse than the Left. New Right ideas about market competition have inspired new testing regimes, league tables, better information for parents about school performance, independent management of schools and parental choice. The Left has criticised most of these measures, for aggravating social segregation and introducing selection by the back door, but it has had few alternatives to propose to capture the public imagination and improve the quality of state education. While correctly holding that privileged families do better in market competition, the Left offers as alternatives to market mechanisms only alleged instruments of collective control – local authorities, teachers' unions, class consciousness – that have lost salience and public support. In doing so it often finds itself doubting the ability of ordinary citizens to make decisions for themselves. When Shirley Williams proposed in 1977 to introduce measures for parental choice into the Labour government's electoral programme, Tony Benn wrote to her, 'To raise parental expectations in this way might lead to a greater dissatisfaction and parental anxiety, and would certainly lead to a

[65] David Butler and Dennis Kavanagh, *The British General Election of 1997* (Basingstoke, 1997), 22; Dennis Kavanagh and David Butler, *The British General Election of 2005* (Basingstoke, 2005), 41. Education was less of an issue in the 2001 and 2010 elections.

[66] By 2003, government had come to see school specialism as a matter more of driving standards than of improving parental choice. Michael Shaw, 'More Specialist Schools Will Not Mean More Choice', *Times Education Supplement*, 17 Jan. 2003; Mike Baker, 'What Is the Point of a Specialist Future?', *Times Education Supplement*, 28 May 2004. Cf. *The State of Welfare*, ed. Hills and Glennerster, 66, sceptical about specialism as a factor in either choice or standards.

terrific pressure on the local education authorities, on the ministers and, of course, MPs as well.' Despite twenty years or more of rising parental expectations precisely among Labour's core constituency, the man in Whitehall still, in 1977, knew best.[67]

The Left's best cards have been curricular. Though legislated by Conservative governments, both the unitary GCSE exam at 16 and the national curriculum had been old Labour proposals aimed at improving prospects for the disadvantaged and delivering quality education for all. These curricular reforms combined quality and equality in a compelling way. Other proposals from the Left have tended to emphasise equality without meeting public demand for quality – such as the largely unsuccessful attempt to introduce 'banded' admissions to ensure truly comprehensive intakes, or renewed campaigns against the remaining grammar schools. In truth, however, neither the Right nor the Left have established a 'big idea' for education to rival the crusade for the 'best' schools for all that did capture the popular imagination between the 1950s and the 1970s. While politicians acknowledge that good schools and hospitals remain highly popular doorstep issues, neither market nor corporatist nostrums to secure these things carry much conviction nowadays.[68] It may be that privatisation, if explicitly embraced by the Conservatives after 2015, will be the spark that relights a real education debate. In the meantime, however, the consensus established in the immediate post-war decades behind a universal service, without selection but promising constantly improving provision for all, at least to 16, has weathered the ideological storms of the last forty years remarkably well; and Britain remains, like most developed countries, committed to a 'universal, standardised and rationalised' education system that strives (at least in public discourse) to give equal opportunities for personal development and socialisation to all. More up for public debate in the last forty years has been how far these agreed goals for secondary education should be extended to further and higher education – and it is to that debate that I will turn in my second address, next year.

---

[67] Chitty, *Towards a New Education System*, 157–8; Lawton, *Education and Labour Party Ideologies*, 91, 101–3; CCCS, *Unpopular Education*, 224–5; and see *ibid.*, 251–65, for some awareness of the need for (and lack of) a counter-hegemonic discourse.

[68] David Butler and Dennis Kavanagh, *The British General Election of 1992* (Basingstoke, 1992), 126; Butler and Kavanagh, *British General Election of 1997*, 110–11; Kavanagh and Butler, *British General Election of 2005*, 176.

Transactions of the RHS 24 (2014), pp. 29–55 © Royal Historical Society 2014
doi:10.1017/S0080440114000024

THE 'FEUDAL REVOLUTION' AND THE ORIGINS OF ITALIAN CITY COMMUNES*

The Prothero Lecture

By Chris Wickham

READ 10 JULY 2013

ABSTRACT. This article takes two major moments of social change in central medieval Europe, the 'feudal revolution' in France and the origins of Italian city communes, in order to see what they have in common. They are superficially very different, one rural one urban, and also one whose analysts focus on the breakdown of political power and the other on its construction or reconstruction; but there are close parallels between the changes which took place in France around 1000 or 1050 and those which took place in Italy around 1100. The contrast in dates does not matter; what matters is that in each case larger-scale political breakdown (whether at the level of the kingdom or the county) was matched by local recomposition, the intensification or crystallisation of local power structures which had been much more *ad hoc* before, and which would be the basic template for local power henceforth. In Italy, the main focus of the article, the different experiences of Pisa and Genoa are compared, and the development of urban assemblies first, consular collectives second, communal institutions third, are all analysed from this perspective, as guides to how the city communes of the peninsula developed, however haltingly and insecurely. The article finishes with a brief comment on the sociology of Pierre Bourdieu.

I want here to take two major moments of social change in central medieval Europe, the 'feudal revolution' in France and the origins of Italian city communes, and see what they have in common. They are superficially very different, one rural one urban, and also one whose analysts focus on the breakdown of political power and the other on its construction or reconstruction; but some of that differentiation is because each has a considerable protective colouring which derives from their separate importance for two different national grand narratives, of France and Italy. In fact, they have more similarities than you might think. The first has often been denied to have occurred, the second never; but I would argue, and will argue here, that the second strengthens some of the arguments for the first – as well as making it less specific, less focused on a French problematic and, indeed, on a problematic which has often

* I am grateful to Simone Collavini, Maria Elena Cortese, Alessio Fiore and Charles West for critiquing this text.

seemed to make sense only in France. I will, however, talk more here about Italy than about France, for it is my expertise, and anyway the French experience is better known in the English-speaking world.

The debate about the 'feudal revolution' in France and its neighbours around the year 1000 and, more widely, in the eleventh century has been going on for over twenty years now.[1] It could be posed as an important and fecund one, as it has gone on so long; but it could also be thought of as tired, with most of its positions reiterated a dozen times. A case for the latter position can easily be made, in fact; it is not chance that many of its major protagonists, such as Thomas Bisson and Dominique Barthélemy, have more recently focused their attention elsewhere.[2] But a case can also be made for coming back to the debate as well, because it genuinely did place in centre stage some basic problems about how to understand medieval social structures and medieval social change which are very far from being resolved; recent and innovative work by some people who were not involved in the debate at its high-point, the 1990s, also allows us to reframe some of its parameters in fruitful ways.[3]

Briefly, what the debate has been about is the real underpinnings of the breakdown of political power which was so much a feature of the history of France in the tenth and eleventh centuries. Georges Duby claimed in the 1950s, in an argument which was reformulated in 1980 in an influential book by Éric Bournazel and Jean-Pierre Poly, that the major change was not the collapse of royal power in the early tenth century in 'West Francia' – the western third of Charlemagne's empire, and the ancestor of modern France – because the rights of kings were simply devolved to the twenty-odd dukes and counts whose local territories made up the kingdom; rather, it was the break-up of the territories of (most of) these counts into a myriad of castle territories, a century later, which marked the real socio-political shift.[4] The rulers of these castle territories, 'castellans' or simply 'lords', ruled their territories using the 'banal' powers which they had usurped from kings and counts – rights of justice, rights to take

---

[1] Useful historiographical guides (none of them, of course, neutral) include C. Lauranson-Rosaz, 'Le débat sur la mutation féodale', in *Europe around the Year 1000*, ed. P. Urbanczyk (Warsaw, 2001), 11–40; S. MacLean, 'Apocalypse and Revolution: Europe around the Year 1000', *Early Medieval Europe*, 15 (2007), 86–106; D. Barthélemy, *The Serf, the Knight and the Historian*, trans. G. R. Edwards (Ithaca, NY, 2009), 1–11, 302–13; C. West, *Reframing the Feudal Revolution* (Cambridge, 2013), 1–9.

[2] T. N. Bisson, *The Crisis of the Twelfth Century* (Princeton, 2009), is not really about the 'feudal revolution' but about its aftermath in the late eleventh and twelfth centuries; Barthélemy has become more interested in the Peace of God and knighthood (see, among others, *Chevaliers et miracles* (Paris, 2004)).

[3] West, *Reframing the Feudal Revolution*; Mark Whittow is also preparing a book on this subject.

[4] G. Duby, *La société aux XIe et XIIe siècles dans la région mâconnaise*, 2nd edn (Paris, 1971), esp. 137–90; J.-P. Poly and É. Bournazel, *La mutation féodale, Xe–XIIe siècles* (Paris, 1980).

dues of all kinds from the territories subject to them, whether they owned those particular lands or not – but, once power had been privatised in this way into the *seigneurie banale*, 'banal lordship', it changed form. The old public world dissolved. Justice, for example, became less of a formalised (again, 'public') process, with the assignment of victory and defeat to litigants, as it had been up to 1000 or so, and in seigneurial courts was often replaced by arbitration, reaching peace by compromise rather than the rule of law. Personal bonds everywhere replaced official roles. A new stratum took effective power, a very small-scale aristocracy of *milites*, whose ancestors might have often been noble cadets, but also often no more than fighters in counts' clientèles, and in some cases men of rich peasant origin. They would have been unrecognisable to the 'imperial aristocracy' of Charlemagne's time, who had dozens of estates each and neither needed nor wanted to control the peasantry with the oppressive detail which a castellan both could and had to use to keep control of his much smaller-scale lands, around his castle. The appearance of this stratum as major political players was what constituted the 'revolution' of the period, if anything did (and you may well think that it was therefore not a very happy word; indeed, opinion has always veered between using 'revolution' and preferring 'mutation' or 'transformation' – although some people think a mutation is a greater change than a revolution, and some think the opposite). But the way that power was refigured with respect to both the level of the kingdom/county and the level of lord–peasant relations marked an enormous structural change, only reversed by patient processes of reconstruction on the part of kings and major regional leaders from the late twelfth century onwards.

Everything about this formulation has been contested. Did this 'revolution' only take place in parts of France (including Catalonia and Flanders, then part of West Francia), or did it have analogues and parallels elsewhere? Was the early eleventh century really a more serious break than the early tenth? How sharp a change was it, over a couple of decades (i.e. fast and violent), or over a century (i.e. slow and sometimes imperceptible)? Did it bring with it a larger degree of local violence, as the new lords established themselves at the expense of both counts above and the peasantry below, as well as against their peers and rivals, or did it not, either because the Carolingian period before it was just as violent and domineering, or else because eleventh-century violence was more targeted and strategic than contemporary complaints, normally rhetorical and self-seeking, would suggest? Indeed, how far does the linguistic turn enable us to recognise the degree to which many of the 'changes' of the period were simply the results of different narrative strategies? How did these changes relate to the history of serfdom, or to the Peace of God? Did justice really change in its form after 1000, with new castellan courts, or did they replicate previous practices? Is the distinction between 'public' and 'private' of any analytical value in this period? Were banal dues really more oppressive than their equivalents had been under the Carolingians, or is it just that people talked about them more? Were the practical exercise of lordship, and lordly values such as honour, so regular between the ninth century (at the latest) and the twelfth that the whole period could best be seen in a frame of near-total continuity? Was there in general any real difference, apart from scale, between a single castellany in the eleventh century and a kingdom 200 years earlier? And all this without even starting on the troubled word 'feudal' and all its various meanings; but these questions will do to give a sense of the issues involved.[5]

I got involved in these debates myself, partially because I was annoyed at the Francocentricity of many of the participants, and also at the tendency of many of them to generalise on the basis of the single region they knew well and to forget the issue of local difference even inside France; partly because I was very interested in how land disputes worked, and I could indeed see differences there between a 'before' and an 'after'; partly because the debate, however skewed it sometimes became, did seem to me to be about important structural issues.[6] And it still does. The opponents of 'mutationism' have recently several times announced that they won, but for my part I still see Carolingian royal and aristocratic power as genuinely distinct from that exercised by castellans, focused as the latter came to be on castles, points of bounded power in the landscape, rather than on the wider and less structured domination which greater lords can often get away with – even if the new lords were not all as violent as has been claimed, and even if their sense of honour and their political stage-management (Gerd Althoff's *Inszenierung*) had not changed so very much.[7] I found this in lordships (*signorie*) in Italy – where the echoes of this

---

[5] See esp., beyond the citations in n. 2, D. Barthélemy, *La mutation de l'an mil a-t-elle eu lieu?* (Paris, 1997), 13–28, and R. E. Barton, *Lordship in the County of Maine c. 890–1160* (Woodbridge, 2004) (both against); the debate between T. N. Bisson and several commentators in *Past and Present*, 142 (1994), 6–42, 152 (1996), 196–223, 155 (1997), 177–225; J.-P. Poly and É. Bournazel, *Les féodalités* (Paris, 1998) – only a small number of the contributions, but perhaps the main ones which stand now to represent it.

[6] My own contributions included 'Debate: The "Feudal Revolution"', *Past and Present*, 155 (1997), 196–208; and 'Property Ownership and Signorial Power in Twelfth-Century Tuscany', in *Property and Power in the Early Middle Ages*, ed. W. Davies and P. Fouracre (Cambridge, 1995), 221–44 (partially reprising 'La mutación feudal en Italia', in *Los orígenes del feudalismo en el mundo mediterráneo* (Granada, 1994), 31–55), as the most focused examples, but reading through my 1990s articles I find echoes of the debate in many other pieces too.

[7] G. Althoff, *Spielregeln der Politik im Mittelalter* (Darmstadt, 1997), discusses the tenth and eleventh centuries; *idem, Die Macht der Rituale* (Darmstadt, 2003), 38–67, discusses the ninth, and 68–135 the tenth–eleventh again, in less detail. The analyses are developed in, among others, C. Pössel, 'Symbolic Communication and the Negotiation of Power at Carolingian

debate have not, in fact, been strong at all – quite as much as in France.[8] I argued then, and would still argue, that what marked this change was that local practices of domination, which had always existed informally in the countryside but had been regarded as illegal by legislators (including the Carolingians, but not only them), henceforth, after 1000 (or 1050, or 1100, depending where one was), *constituted* legality. A long-standing dialectic inside power relations on the ground between the legal and the technically illegal therefore became much weaker. I also argued, and would still argue, that what I will call the formalisation of power on the ground, the greater boundedness of all its elements, what Robert Fossier called *encellulement*, became much greater after 1000/1050/1100, precisely to make up for the break-up of formal power at the level of the kingdom.[9] Charles West in an important recent book has developed this latter point very effectively, in a study of the French–German borderlands, Champagne and Lorraine, between the Marne and the Moselle: he shows how the new *seigneuries banales* were indeed distinguished from the past by a formalisation of justice and other political rights, of local power itself, in such a way that they became in themselves forms of property, which could be (and occasionally were) alienated as a whole or in bits to other lords; he proposes furthermore, more radically, that this was not only an intensification of the local oppressiveness of Carolingian practical power relations but also, particularly in the sharpening of concepts of property and jurisdiction, a completion of the highly theology-influenced Carolingian royal political programme itself.[10] I do not want to pursue

Regnal Assemblies, 814–840' (Ph.D. thesis, University of Cambridge, 2003), and West, *Reframing the Feudal Revolution*, 87–95.

[8] Italian historiography, even the strong contribution made to it by French scholarship, has in general been much less interested in the debate: François Menant, for example, who is of course fully aware of it, as his *thèse* shows (*Campagnes lombardes au moyen âge* (Rome, 1993), e.g. 563), does not even mention it in his important synthesis 'La féodalité italienne entre XIe et XIIe siècles', *Settimane di studio*, 47 (2000), 347–87. A. Barbero, 'La polemica sulla mutazione feudale', *Storica*, 3 (1995), 73–86 (a sharp-eyed review of Barthélemy's own *thèse*), and S. Carocci, 'Signoria rurale e mutazione feudale', *Storica*, 8 (1997), 49–91 (one of the best analytical surveys of seigneurial power) treated it as an essentially French, not an Italian, debate. A. Fiore, 'Dal diploma al patto', in press, is certainly what the French would call 'mutationiste' but does not refer to the French problematic (I am very grateful to the author for a copy of the text). The historiography of the *signoria* is in fact at least as developed as that on the *seigneurie*, but its focus has been different, as a glance at *Strutture e trasformazioni della signoria rurale nei secoli X–XIII*, ed. G. Dilcher and C. Violante (Bologna, 1996) (notwithstanding Barthélemy's contribution to it), or the two volumes of *La signoria rurale nel medioevo italiano*, ed. A. Spicciani and C. Violante (Pisa, 1997–8), shows. My own views are summarised in 'La signoria rurale in Toscana', in *Strutture e trasformazioni*, ed. Dilcher and Vi, 343–409.

[9] R. Fossier, *Enfance de l'Europe* (Paris, 1982), 288.

[10] West, *Reframing the Feudal Revolution*.

this latter point, which takes me well away from my theme, but West's views about local formalised power I shall come back to later in this paper.

As to the origins of city communes in Italy, the other side of my equation: I will be talking about this in rather more detail later, but for now, the basic parameters can be set out briefly. Signorial, lordly, power developed very slowly in the countryside in Italy, more slowly and with less of an obvious crisis than in much of France, although by 1100 there were quite as many castles in Italy as in France and often more.[11] This is partly because of the force of Italy's cities, which were unusually large and politically influential by Western European standards, not least because most major landowners lived in them, including castle-holding lords. The traditional Carolingian-style counties, which the Kingdom of (north-central) Italy had as much as did France, were mostly run from cities as well, and Carolingian-style collective, 'public', justice continued well into the eleventh century, as hundreds of documents for *placita*, assembly-based judicial hearings, tell us.[12] This fitted with the survival of royal power: this was experienced intermittently in Italy, for after 962 its holders were based in northern Germany, but it held the Kingdom together as a single unit until the wars between Henry IV and Gregory VII after 1080. Those wars were also civil wars, and they brought with them a delegitimisation of traditional power structures, as emperor and pope deposed each other and rival bishops appeared in many cities. Royal power rapidly weakened in the last decades of the eleventh century and was not revived again, apart from the grand attempt to do so by the German emperor Frederick Barbarossa in 1158–77, which failed. Urban leaders reacted by taking over the running of cities themselves, and, increasingly, they did so as organised collectivities, which by the second quarter of the twelfth century were coming to be called by a new term, *commune*: city communes. When these managed to establish themselves as structured bodies, and when they took over their own rural territories as well (often, even if not always, fairly similar to the older Carolingian counties), we find ourselves in a world of

[11] A good regional-based model for northern Italy is Menant, *Campagnes lombardes*; the other key monographic works are H. Keller, *Signori e vassalli nell'Italia delle città (secoli IX–XII)* (Ital. trans., Turin, 1995); A. A. Settia, *Castelli e villaggi nell'Italia padana* (Naples, 1984); and the collective *La vassalità maggiore del Regno Italico*, ed. A. Castagnetti (Rome, 2001). For the frequency of castles, see for Tuscany *Castelli*, I, ed. R. Francovich and M. Ginatempo (Florence, 2000). Tuscany, however, faced a sharper rural crisis because political breakdown all happened very late in the eleventh century, as we shall see later; a good local study of that is M. E. Cortese, *Signori, castelli, città* (Florence, 2007).

[12] See C. Manaresi, *I placiti del 'Regnum Italiae'* (3 vols., Rome, 1955–60), for almost all the texts; F. Bougard, *La justice dans le royaume d'Italie de la fin du VIIIe siècle au début du XIe siècle* (Rome, 1995) for the basic analysis.

city states with collective leaderships, a radically different one from the Carolingian world.[13]

Historians have chased the beginning of such communes by looking for the first references in each city to the word which came to be used for a member of the annually changing communal ruling group, *consul*. This is a hopeless task, for these are in every case purely chance references, and the word 'consul' anyway did not mean an official urban ruler for some time, sometimes decades, after its first appearance in a document for the Kingdom of Italy, for Pisa in 1080–1. Rather, I would prefer to look for the slow development of the different elements of an ideal type of the early city commune, which I would characterise as consisting of: conscious urban collectivities, which included either all (male) city-dwellers or a substantial part of them, usually held together by oaths; a regularly rotating set of ruling magistracies, chosen or at least validated by that collectivity (not often in any 'democratic' way, but at any rate not chosen by superior powers such as kings or bishops); and a *de facto* autonomy of action for the city and its magistrates, including in warfare and justice, and eventually taxation and legislation – the basic elements of early and central medieval government. These appeared in different orders in different cities, although all of them characterised nearly every city of the by-now evanescent Kingdom of Italy in 1150 or so, and indeed outside it, in Venice and Rome. The crystallisation of communal government came most visibly with the development of regular communal tribunals for justice, which in most of the precocious cities was in the 1130s, although in Pisa and Genoa the date was as early as around 1110; these tribunals certainly mark a consciousness of political autonomy which was then built on more systematically later. When we reach these tribunals, the other elements of the communal ideal type can usually be found as well.[14]

Posed in these terms, the debate over the origins of Italian city communes might well seem to be an entirely different type of problematic from that concerning the development of castellan power in France, except for the obvious fact that the geographical scale of political practice had become more localised. Let us look at the experiences of some actual

[13] Good introductions (out of several in the last decade or so) include F. Menant, *L'Italie des communes (1100–1350)* (Paris, 2005); G. Milani, *I comuni italiani* (Bari, 2005).

[14] I discuss this in greater detail in *Sleepwalking into a New World* (Princeton, in press); see ch. 1 for the historiography (but a good recent survey is already P. Grillo, 'La frattura inesistente', *Archivio storico italiano*, 167 (2009), 673–700) and the ideal type. H. Keller, 'Gli inizi del comune in Lombardia', in *L'evoluzione delle città italiane nell'XI secolo*, ed. R. Bordone and J. Jarnut (Bologna, 1988), 45–70, is basic for the invisibility of communal origins. The document for Pisa in 1080–1, actually issued by a Sardinian ruler and in the Sard language, is most recently edited in *I brevi dei consoli del comune di Pisa degli anni 1162 e 1164*, ed. O. Banti (Rome, 1997), 107–8; for its dating to 1080–1 (rather than to the wider limits of 1080–5) and a good analysis, see M. Ronzani, *Chiesa e 'Civitas' di Pisa nella seconda metà del secolo XI* (Pisa, 1996), 190–9.

cities, however, to see what problems they pose, and what insights they give us as to how social development worked; these, I shall argue, have more analogies with France than might be obvious at first sight. That will give us something more concrete to handle when we come back to comparisons at the end. I will discuss two cities here as case-studies, Pisa and Genoa, the two earliest-developing city communes of all as I have just said: for the kinds of problem I wish to set out are already visible in their evidence. They were not typical cities; they were both ports, the most active commercial ports of the Kingdom of Italy in fact, and, although they were fairly similar to each other, many of their experiences were not shared by their inland neighbours, even major internal commercial entrepôts like Milan and Cremona. But as far as the problems I want to set out here are concerned, they are certainly typical enough to be going on with.

Pisa first, then. Pisa's ruling structures remained stable into the 1070s; it was part of the March of Tuscany, which was among the last of the territories of Carolingian Europe to remain governed according to more or less the same principles as had been used in the time of Charlemagne. Up to 1080, the *placitum* assembly met regularly in the city, normally in the presence of the marquis or marquise, to make judicial decisions, and the landed elite of Pisa turned out to it on a regular basis too, as witness-lists show – influential Pisans came to the assembly at Pisa, that is to say, just as influential Lucchesi turned out to similar assemblies at nearby Lucca, and so on, city by city, elsewhere too. The solid political aggregation of the Kingdom of Italy was clear here; every city had its own public political community (for, whatever problems the word 'public' may cause historians, the term *publicus* was used in our period with much the same range of meanings as it has today),[15] which could be called to the assembly by recognised hierarchical superiors: here, the marquis, elsewhere imperial *missi* (themselves generally local elite figures) and bishops. Pisa was an unusually protagonistic city, with over half a century's worth of naval military expeditions at its back, raids of rich Muslim cities in the southern Mediterranean for the most part, but at home it was happy to be part of a political structure with very old roots. This changed after 1080, for the civil wars in Italy began, and already

---

[15] See, as one example out of many, *Monumenta Germaniae Historica* (henceforth *MGH*), *Die Urkunden und Briefe der Markgrävin Mathilde von Tuszien*, ed. E. and W. Goez (Hanover, 1998), nn. 52, 52, 56, 61, for Tuscany in 1099–1100. Cf. for northern Europe L. Genicot, 'Sur la survivance de la notion d'état dans l'Europe du Nord au haut moyen âge', in *Institutionen, Kultur und Gesellschaft*, ed. L. Fenske *et al.* (Sigmaringen, 1984), 147–64; Y. Sassier, 'L'utilisation d'un concept romain aux temps carolingiens', *Médiévales*, 15 (1988), 17–29; and, for the continuing force of 'public' justice well after 1000 in France, even if in a county (Anjou) with a fuller survival of public power than many, B. Lemesle, *Conflits et justice au moyen âge* (Paris, 2008), 41–6.

in 1081 Henry IV was in Pisa giving concessions to the city collectivity, the 'faithful citizens', having deposed Matilda, the ruling marquise of Tuscany and a close ally of Gregory VII. The Pisans switched back to Matilda a few years later, once Henry had left Tuscany for the last time in 1084, but Matilda did not return from her lands in northern Italy to her March for fifteen years, and, when she did, did not base herself in Pisa again; her palace would end up under the control of the commune.[16] There was a power vacuum in the city in the 1080s as a result; indeed, for four years there was no bishop in the city either. In 1090, however, a new bishop, the pro-Gregorian Daiberto, was asked by the city's *commune colloquium* to arbitrate on the height of tower-houses in the city. In the text of his arbitration, made with the help of 'strong and wise men', who are named, and are from the city's traditional elite, he determined the maximum height towers should in future be in the city (21 metres), and named the two towers which could remain higher than that (the towers of other elite figures), although men could not in future go up to their tops. This arbitration hints at civil discord, presumably in the context of Italy's civil war, but also at its resolution, and indeed Pisa is not known to have been politically divided again for over half a century. The policing of towers was left to the city's *commune colloquium* to ensure, and the whole agreement was confirmed by a collective and renewable oath of all Pisa's adult males.[17]

The *commune colloquium* is the key player in this text. It was the city's assembly, of the *populus* or the *cives*; it shows the continuing importance of assembly politics for the city, an issue I shall come back to; but it was not the same as the judicial assembly of the *placitum*. For a start, it was not making judgements here, which was the *placitum*'s core role – the Pisans had had to call in the bishop to do that, as in effect an external arbiter, for the bishop of Pisa had no traditional role as an urban leader, and Daiberto was not himself a Pisan – but also, crucially, it was not called by anyone in a hierarchy stretching upwards, be it king or marquis; it was defined by the Pisans themselves, and from now on, if not already, by their collective oath. Daiberto's arbitration was sworn to by all incoming

---

[16] For the palace, see G. Garzella, *Pisa com'era* (Naples, 1990), 86–8, 109–11. For the political history see esp. Ronzani, *Chiesa e 'Civitas' di Pisa*, and *idem*, 'L'affermazione dei Comuni cittadini fra impero e papato', in *Poteri centrali e autonomie nella Toscana medievale e moderna*, ed. G. Pinto and L. Tanzini (Florence, 2012), 1–57; for the wars, most recently E. Salvatori, 'Lo spazio economico di Pisa nel Mediterraneo: dall'XI alla metà del XII secolo', *Bullettino dell'Istituto storico italiano per il medioevo*, 115 (2013), 119–52 (I am very grateful to the author for a copy of the text before publication).

[17] G. Rossetti, 'Il lodo del vescovo Daiberto sull'altezza delle torri', in *Pisa e la Toscana occidentale nel Medioevo*, II (Pisa, 1991), 25–47; cf. M. Matzke, *Daibert von Pisa* (Sigmaringen, 1998), 61–5.

consuls of the commune of Pisa by the mid-twelfth century, indeed.[18] But conversely, and for all that, the arbitration cannot usefully be seen as a communal document either. The city has no stable leaders here. The Pisans already called members of their elite 'consuls' on occasion as we have seen, but there are no consuls here either. The city assembly seems pretty well defined by 1090; this was almost certainly in response to the power vacuum of the 1080s. The assembly, that is to say, took formal shape as a defensive reaction to the civil war and the sudden absence of traditional powers, a point I shall come back to. But its leadership remained informal. There is absolutely no sense in Pisa of the city's leadership leaping into the breach offered by the absence of traditional powers – nor of the bishop doing that either. Daiberto was influential (he even managed to turn his office into an archbishopric), but he does not appear again as the city's arbiter, and anyway left in 1098 with the Pisan contingent to the First Crusade and stayed in Jerusalem as its first Latin patriarch; Pisa did not have an archbishop again until 1106.

Consuls in Pisa appear as political actors in texts from 1109, and fast take centre stage in our main document collections. They were city representatives in 1109; in 1110, in the same role, they are referred to as representing the *commune* of Pisa, almost the earliest citation in Italy of the noun; in 1111, they were the representatives of the city assembly too, and also made a trade treaty with the Byzantine emperor Alexios Komnenos; in 1112, they ran the first documented consular court case, together with the city's *populus*, held, symbolically, outside the old palace of the marquis, which is also, even more symbolically, the only documented consular-run case from anywhere in Italy which uses the *placitum* format; in 1113–15, they were the city's political and military leaders in the largest naval expedition of all, the Balearic campaign, which ended with the sack of Palma de Mallorca and generated not only vast booty but also a huge sub-Virgilian praise-poem about the city and its leaders, the *Liber Maiorichinus*.[19] The Pisans were on a roll, and they stayed proud and happy, violent and protagonistic, under the continuous leadership of their consuls, from then onwards, with regular communal judges appearing in the 1130s and the first communal legislation in the 1140s, culminating in their commissioning of the city's ambitious Roman-law legal code, the

[18] *I brevi dei consoli*, ed. Banti, 60, 88.

[19] *Carte dell'Archivio arcivescovile di Pisa*, II, ed. S. P. P. Scalfati (Pisa, 2006), nn. 10–12 (a. 1109), 14 (a. 1110), 19 (a. 1111), 20 (a. 1112); *Documenti sulle relazioni delle città toscane coll'Oriente cristiano e coi Turchi*, ed. G. Müller (Florence, 1879), 43–5, 52–4 (the 1111 trade treaty); *Liber Maiolichinus de gestis Pisanorum illustribus*, ed. C. Calisse (Rome, 1904). For 1109, see M. Ronzani, 'Le prime testimonianze dell'attività dei consoli pisani in quattro documenti del 1109', in *Quel mar che la terra inghirlanda*, ed. F. Cardini and M. L. Ceccarelli Lemut (Pisa 2007), 679–705.

double *Constitutum* of 1161.[20] The consuls, once we see them and know their names, were overwhelmingly from the elite already documented in the eleventh century. Then, they had been happy to be the dependants of the marquis; in the intervening period, they were the informal leaders of the city assembly; but from here on they would be the city's consuls – annually changing, but essentially showing us a continual turnover of members of the same fifteen or so families which ruled Pisa without much of a break, or even all that much renewal, from the early eleventh century to the early thirteenth.[21] Running the city was sufficiently attractive that a text of 1091–2 even shows a group of the leading families of Pisa giving up the signorial rights they had recently constructed over villages some 10 kilometres north of the city in favour of urban jurisdiction, and Pisa from then onwards gained a control over most of its diocese unusually rapidly, a diocese which also – another very unusual feature – contained few signorial territories apart from those of the bishop (by now archbishop).[22]

The establishment of the commune in Pisa was, as I have said, early. It was also not that difficult; it had little opposition as far as we can see. But this does not mean that it was a straightforward substitution of one governmental system for another. Our best evidence for this, as usual in this period, is the documentation for disputes. The Pisan consuls were prepared to imitate the *placitum* in a judgement of 1112, which shows that they could indeed see themselves as in some sense the heirs of the Kingdom and the March (Matilda did not die until 1115, but her hegemony was already weaker, and the March effectively collapsed after her death). But that was the first surviving Pisan dispute document which was not an arbitration for over thirty years, and the last (except for a late and by now outlying imperial-run case in 1116) for another twenty.[23] Dispute documents are so regular in Italian archives,

---

[20] The code is edited in *I Costituti della legge e dell'uso di Pisa (sec. XII)*, ed. P. Vignoli (Rome, 2003), 64–5, 105 for 1140s laws, and cf. C. Storti Storchi, *Intorno ai Costituti pisani della legge e dell'uso (secolo XII)* (Naples, 1998), 72–4. For communal development, see in general Ronzani, 'L'affermazione dei Comuni cittadini'.

[21] See the lists in M. L. Ceccarelli Lemut, 'I consoli e i magistrati del comune di Pisa dalla comparsa del consolato (1080/1085) al 1189', *Bollettino storico pisano*, in preparation (I am very grateful to the author for a copy of the text); for the elite continuities in Pisa, see Wickham, *Sleepwalking*, ch. 3.

[22] The 1091–2 text is edited in *I brevi dei consoli*, ed. Banti, 108–10; a good study (among several) remains G. Rossetti, 'Società e istituzioni nei secoli IX e X', in *Atti del 50 congresso internazionale di studi sull'alto medioevo* (Spoleto, 1973), 209–337, at 320–9. For the general history of the Pisan expansion into its contado, see G. Volpe, *Studi sulle istituzioni comunali a Pisa*, 2nd edn (Florence, 1970), 1–123; for the restricted role of signorial territories, M. L. Ceccarelli Lemut, 'Terre pubbliche e giurisdizione signorile nel *comitatus* di Pisa (secoli XI–XIII)', in *La signoria rurale*, ed. Spicciani and Violante, II, 87–137.

[23] *Carte dell'Archivio arcivescovile di Pisa*, II, ed. Scalfati, n. 48 (a. 1116). *Ibid.*, n. 67 (a. 1125) is also a canon-law case, decided by the archbishop.

from the late eighth century onwards, that gaps in their survival are always potentially significant; and this fifty-year low-point for Pisan formal justice is certainly significant. The fact that it is also typical of every other well-documented city in the Kingdom of Italy in the same period reinforces the point: the old legitimate judicial fora were failing or had already failed.

When consular judicial documents restart in Pisa, in 1135, they do not imitate the *placitum* any more. Instead, they are matter-of-fact texts, generated by the communal judges, who are 'chosen by the archbishop, the consuls and the whole *populus* to end cases both private and public', and who judge with the agreement of the parties. The involvement of the archbishop dropped out of the formula by 1138, but otherwise this pattern persisted from then on. The first such case has a large witness-list, indicating that the case was probably connected with the city assembly, but after that fewer people sign, often only consuls. These judgements tend to stress the agreement of the parties, which may make them seem like arbitrations, and I am sure that early consular justice was indeed, everywhere, in part based on practices of arbitration, which had always existed and which are also more prominent in our documents after 1080. This does not mean that the communal judges did not have full judicial powers, however; already by 1142, they judge in contumacy, i.e. in the absence of one of the parties, which shows that they could make judgements even without consent. But as important, in my view, is that even then communal justice is not at all frequent in Pisan documents; it only takes off in the 1150s, and arbitrations are more common in our documentation until then.[24] Although Pisa's commune started so early, and with a self-confidence already very clear in the early 1110s, it took another generation and more for this to be turned into lasting political structures. The early Pisan consuls and consular judges operated with a degree of informality, and indeed an often very *ad hoc* set of powers, which it would be wrong to underestimate. It could indeed be argued – I argue it elsewhere – that they were barely aware that they were creating a totally new political structure at all.[25]

Genoa, Pisa's maritime rival and by the 1120s its firm enemy, had a similar trajectory, but with some interesting differences. We cannot track its leaders back into the eleventh century, for Genoese documents hardly begin before 1100, but its consular elite after that, although often seriously divided, was almost as long-lasting as Pisa's. The first difference is that its commune had an early chronicler, Caffaro of Caschifellone (*c.*1080–1166), who was active in it for thirty years as a consul and ambassador,

---

[24] *Ibid.*, II, nn. 105, 124; A. D'Amia, *Diritto e sentenze di Pisa* (Milan, 1962), n. 2, for the three cited cases. See in general C. Wickham, *Courts and Conflict in Twelfth-Century Tuscany* (Oxford, 2003), 108–14.

[25] See Wickham, *Sleepwalking*.

and who strongly stressed the organisational structure of the commune (here called a *compagna*) in his *Annals* from the start, in 1099, where he links the formation of the *compagna* to the Genoese participation in the First Crusade; from then onwards he gives the names of the consuls for every three- or four-year term, or, after 1122, for every year, names which seem, on the basis of the documents which survive, to be pretty accurate. Indeed, the first known consul of Genoa appears already in a text of 1098, in an apparently official role, i.e. even before Caffaro's formal date for the first *compagna*, which fits the fact that Caffaro in another work says casually that Genoa had already had a *consulatus* in the late 1090s. All the same, the neatness of the 1099 start of the commune in the *Annals* is undermined here; and, since Caffaro probably started writing the *Annals* only in the late 1140s, and since he shows us such a strong ideological commitment to the relationship between the commune and civic concord, which was often hard to achieve in Genoa (much harder than in Pisa), we should be cautious of his wider claims for how the very early structuring of the *compagna* actually occurred.[26] The Genoese certainly used the word 'consul' for ordinary military leaders as well, for example, as Caffaro's account of the First Crusade also shows; and the first document with a set of consuls making an agreement, an oath to the king of Jerusalem in 1104, probably reflects that. Other similar texts for the city from the decade of the 1100s only mention the Genoese *cives* or *populus*, not any formal leadership.[27] For the early part of that decade, in fact, I doubt that the Genoese commune had much of a structure at all.

Already by 1104–5, however, communal formalisation inside the city was rather more developed, for from then begin Genoa's consular court cases, which were (unlike in Pisa) presided over and judged by the consuls themselves. These are never in *placitum* format; in fact, Genoa quickly developed a format for recording such cases which is unlike that of any

---

[26]Two recent unpublished theses, L. Filangieri, 'Famiglie e gruppi dirigenti a Genova (secoli XII–metà XIII)' (dottorato di ricerca, Università degli studi di Firenze, 2010), and A. Inguscio, 'Reassessing Civil Conflicts in Genoa, 1160–1220' (D.Phil. thesis, University of Oxford, 2012), are the best discussions of the Genoese elite. Citations of Caffaro: *Annali genovesi di Caffaro e de' suoi continuatori*, I, ed. L. T. Belgrano (Rome, 1890), 5, 17, 111. For him as chronicler, see G. Petti Balbi, *Caffaro e la cronachistica genovese* (Genoa, 1982); *eadem*, 'Caffaro', *Dizionario biografico degli italiani*, XVI (1973), 256–60. For his uniqueness among communal chroniclers (including Bernardo Maragone in Pisa), see C. Wickham, *Land and power* (1994), 295–303. For the 1098 text, see *Codice diplomatico del monastero di Santo Stefano di Genova*, I, ed. M. Calleri (Genoa, 2009), n. 96. The best overall study of the early commune of Genoa is R. Bordone, 'Le origini del comune di Genova', in *Comuni e memoria storica* (Genoa, 2002), 237–59.
[27]*Codice diplomatico della repubblica di Genova*, I, ed. C. Imperiale di Sant'Angelo (Rome, 1936) (henceforth *CDGE*), nn. 16 (a. 1104, cf. *Annali genovesi di Caffaro*, ed. Belgrano, I, 11), 20, 24, plus 22 (a. 1108), with a consul as one member of a wider *populus*. Cf. also Filangieri, 'Famiglie e gruppi dirigenti a Genova', 73–80.

other Italian city, but it is even shorter and brisker than those elsewhere. Early cases here, as in Pisa, were decided in the presence of the city's assembly, again usually called a *compagna* or else *parlamentum*, although by the 1130s this practice was falling out of use and consuls henceforth more often judged on their own. These were more numerous than in Pisa. There, as we have seen, they are not common until the 1150s; but in Genoa they are visible in different church archives already in the 1110s and 1120s, and are common by the 1130s.[28] In Genoa, consuls were by 1130 also legislating, changing some of their traditional city customs – which are documented in the eleventh century – on their own authority (in Pisa the first dated law is 1140); and we have a large set of customs and legislative acts documented in the first consular *breve*, the list of duties that the consuls swore to at the start of their official term, which is from 1143 (in Pisa the first surviving *breve* and consular oath is from 1162).[29] If this was a race, then, from a common starting point around 1110, the Genoese were usually ahead in the period up to 1150, although the Pisans caught up and surged ahead with their monumental law code of 1161, which the Genoese did not match for a long time.

Conversely, the *compagna* was not as much a synonym for the city and its political community as this account might make seem. The word *compagna* is in fact otherwise (including in Genoa itself) used to mean a commercial consortium, and it did not include all Genoese; the 1143 *breve* refers, for example, to people who 'who were not called, or whom we [consuls] decided that were not suitable, to enter into our *compagna*',

---

[28] For the first court-case, which is unpublished, see *Liber instrumentorum Monasterii Sancti Fructuosi de Capite Montis, Codice 'A'*, Archivio Doria Pamphilj (in Rome), bancone 79, busta 12, fo. 8rv, concerning rights to the falcons of Capodimonte. Subsequent court cases to 1140, not in order: *CDGE*, nn. 45, 49, 50, 77, 93; L. T. Belgrano, 'Il registro della curia arcivescovile di Genova', *Atti della società ligure di storia patria*, 2.2 (1862), 27–8, 56–60; *Le carte di Santa Maria delle Vigne di Genova (1103–1392)*, ed. G. Airaldi (Genoa, 1969), nn. 3, 6; *Le carte del monastero di San Siro di Genova (952–1224)*, I, ed. M. Calleri (Genoa, 1997), n. 73; *Le carte del monastero di Sant'Andrea della Porta di Genova (1109–1370)*, ed. C. Soave (Genoa, 2002), n. 2; *Codice diplomatico del monastero di Santo Stefano*, I, ed. Calleri, nn. 104, 110, 115; *I libri iurium della Repubblica di Genova*, 8 vols., ed. D. Puncuh *et al.* (Genoa, 1992–2002), I/3, n. 524 (this partially supersedes *CDGE* as an edition, but *CDGE* is easier to use, and I cite it by preference where there is overlap). Surprisingly, there is no study of these texts as a whole. M. Vallerani, 'La riscrittura dei diritti nel secolo XII', in *Zwischen Pragmatik und Performanz*, ed. C. Dartmann *et al.* (Turnhout, 2011), 133–64, at 153–60, is the best brief discussion.

[29] *CDGE*, nn. 53, 67–8, 96–7, 102, 128 (the *breve*); some of the cases listed in n. 28 are halfway to legislation too. Eleventh century: *CDGE*, n. 3, and in general A. Fiore, 'Giurare la consuetudine', *Reti medievali rivista*, 13.2 (2012), 47–80, at 50–2, for Liguria. The Pisans had local customs, at least for seafaring, too (*MGH, Heinrici IV. Diplomata*, ed. D. von Gladiss (Berlin, Weimar and Hanover, 1941–78), n. 336 – the diploma is interpolated, but almost certainly not in this clause); so may many other cities have had. We do not know how they were put into practice, although a Savona text of 1058 refers to local *non-placitum* justice (Fiore, 'Giurare la consuetudine', 51, for references and discussion).

which could certainly include people from the city, for another section of the *breve* discusses what to do with a Genoese who is indeed so invited but refuses to join – if so, he cannot be a communal official, and no one in the *compagna* can 'carry his money overseas'. (Pisa, by contrast, was more inclusive from the start; its leaders were uncontested, but its oath-swearing, which was at the base of the whole developing communal structure, explicitly included every Pisan male over fifteen in the 1090 tower arbitration.) By now, the Genoese used the word *commune* too – in effect in the 1143 *breve* as a synonym for *compagna*; but a document of 1135, an agreement with Marquis Aleramo, a powerful rural lord, shows some differences, for the text involves Aleramo swearing the oath of the '*compagna* of the commune of Genoa . . . as do other Genoese citizens who swear to this *compagna* which is now of the commune of Genoa or will swear to other *compagnae* of the commune of Genoa'.[30] The commune might thus be seen as the community of the city, and the *compagna* its apparently in theory temporary political expression, although this by no means shows that the commune extended to more people than did the *compagna*. Genoa was a coherent commune pretty early, but this image of temporaneity and exclusivity may explain why it was that even around 1150 agreements with the commune sometimes included clauses which covered what would happen if it ceased to exist.[31]

Gioacchino Volpe, the most interesting medieval historian of his generation in Italy, argued in 1904 for the 'privatistic' origins of the commune, based on voluntary associations held together by oaths, which were thus a world away from the 'public' institutions of the old Kingdom of Italy.[32] Partly, he did so because he, like most historians at the time (and a few legal historians still today), believed that communes did not have any standing in public law until Frederick Barbarossa conceded legal rights to them in the 1160s to 1180s – this does not stand up as an argument, for judicial assignments in contumacy, and the first documents exiling citizens, which both begin in Italy in the 1140s, clearly assume full public rights of that sort.[33] Partly, he argued this because he, like many people around 1904, saw the urban vitality of the communes as one of the main steps forward in Italian medieval history, and he wanted to stress the voluntarism of that vital spirit, a state of mind which would lead him to his later role as an ideologist for the Fascist party. Historians from the 1960s onwards were keen to stress instead that city leaders in Italy had a public role from the start, representing the whole of their cities and

---

[30] *CDGE*, n. 128, at pp. 155–6, for the *breve*; n. 73 (a. 1135).
[31] E.g. *CDGE*, n. 205 (a. 1150); see also n. 97 (a. 1139), an internal Genoese oath which envisages that there might be a time without consuls (*si autem consules Ianue tunc non fuerint*).
[32] G. Volpe, *Medio evo italiano* (Florence, 1961), 87–118, esp. 100–4.
[33] G. Milani, *L'esclusione dal comune* (Rome, 2003), 27–34.

claiming rights to rule, judge, take to war and, a generation on, tax as well.[34] In legal terms, they were right; but early communes were more uncertain than that, as Volpe also knew, with, not least, leaderships who were by no means sure that leading their neighbours and inferiors was more honorific than the traditional hierarchies of dependence stretching up to kings, where these still existed. I have argued before for a rather more informal, quasi-Volpean, position for early communes, using the example of Lucca, whose commune, first documented in 1119–20, was much more uncertain than that of its neighbour Pisa until its own consular court cases start in the 1130s, or indeed later.[35] But it is important to stress here that even Genoa, with its early judicial texts and legislation, shows the city as being ruled by something which remarkably resembles the private association which Volpe sketched out – although it did indeed also claim the right to judge everyone in the city, members of the *compagna* or no, as with the rule over India by the East India Company up to 1858. Conversely, even Pisa, although it had a less restricted community of the oath and no signs of the temporaneity of some Genoese texts, did not systematically make good the public role for its consular leadership which it undoubtedly claimed, until communal dispute settlement became more important for the city's inhabitants, in the 1150s.

Pisa and Genoa were the earliest Italian communes, as I have stressed, and also, in their different ways, the earliest Italian communes to develop a clear and solid institutional structure. Even Pisa and Genoa, however, show lasting signs of a relative informality for at least some of their communal practices; others, as with Lucca, did so much more. Take Cremona, for example: this city had been long active as an urban community, with a history of urban opposition to and uprisings against its ruling bishop which went back to before 1000, and with the first reference to a *comunum* anywhere in Italy, in 1097; Cremona subjected some of the major centres in its territory in agreements of the 1100s–20s, and its city assembly is fronted in some of these, as in 1118 and 1120. Nonetheless, its communal judicial documents do not start until the 1130s, like Lucca and Milan and to an extent even Pisa; and its ruling consuls, although first referred to in the 1110s, are otherwise nearly invisible: they are named

[34] See G. Cassandro, 'Un bilancio storiografico' (1959), in *Forme di potere e struttura sociale in Italia nel Medioevo*, ed. G. Rossetti (Bologna, 1977), 153–73, often cited but even sketchier than Volpe; O. Banti, '"Civitas" e "Commune" nelle fonti italiane dei secoli XI e XII' (1972), in *ibid.*, 217–32; G. Tabacco, *The Struggle for Power in Medieval Italy* (1973), trans. R. Brown Jensen (Cambridge, 1989), 182–90, 321–44; Tabacco is by far the most influential voice here for modern historiography. Tax: basic is P. Mainoni, 'A proposito della "rivoluzione fiscale" nell'Italia settentrionale del XII secolo', *Studi storici*, 44 (2003), 5–42.

[35] Wickham, *Courts and Conflict*, 19–40. So does Banti, '"Civitas" e "Commune"', 222: 'an emergency solution'. But the social changes involved in the crystallisation of the commune were often greater than Banti and his generation took into consideration.

only once before the 1150s. This commune was active and independent, but remained informal, and very tied to the collectivity of its assembly.[36] Many communes were a good deal less active than that, such as Vercelli, now the type example of what Giuliano Milani calls a 'latent' commune, where consuls appear acting autonomously in the 1140s, but they were mostly also vassals of the local bishop. This was true of many communes, for city leaders often had episcopal associations for a long time, but such vassalage did not necessarily circumscribe their activities. In Vercelli, however, the commune drops out of our documentation altogether in the period 1150–65, and episcopal government is all we can find in our sources – here, that is to say, the bishop could return the city to more traditional hierarchies without recorded difficulty, and we must wonder how much the commune's leadership in the 1140s, however city-based (for urban leaders here had few rural connections), ever thought that communal rule was more legitimate and honorific than episcopal dependence. In Florence, too, another late commune (first reference to consuls in 1138, first surviving court case in 1172), consular activity, although here partially based on newer elites than in Pisa and Genoa and also not visibly associated with the bishop, was 'one power among others' even in the final decades of the century.[37] If even in Pisa and Genoa the commune began informally and uncertainly, it would not be surprising that in less precocious and more uneasy communes like Vercelli and Florence such a lack of certainty was still clearer. Even in Milan, however, we find signs of that. In this large and powerful city, with an urban elite which was very boisterous in the eleventh century, the close feudal ties of the major elite families to the equally powerful archbishop meant that the latter exercised a great influence over the city assembly of the 1090s and onwards, and over the first documented consuls in 1117 and 1130, who were very much part of the archbishop's entourage, to the extent that the contemporary chronicler Landolfo of S. Paolo could refer to them as 'his', the archbishop's, consuls. Here, only the 1140s, when a new stratum of influential consuls with judicial expertise and little land is attested in the fast-increasing sequence of consular court cases, did the commune really begin to separate itself from episcopal power; that separation was complete by the 1150s, when Milan became Barbarossa's major opponent, but it was not two decades old by then.[38]

[36] F. Menant, 'La prima età comunale', in *Storia di Cremona*, II, ed. G. Andenna (Cremona, 2004), 198–281. The most convenient edition of the documents of 1097, 1118 and 1120 is *Le carte cremonesi dei secoli VIII–XII*, II, ed. E. Falconi (Cremona, 1984), nn. 242, 273, 279.

[37] See P. Grillo and A. Barbero in *Vercelli nel secolo XII* (Vercelli, 2005), 163–75, 293–7; E. Faini, *Firenze nell'età romanica (1000–1211)* (Florence, 2010), 262–320, 361–3, and 263 for the quote. For 'latente', Milani, *I comuni italiani*, 24–6.

[38] See Wickham, *Sleepwalking*, ch. 2; *Gli atti del comune di Milano fino all'anno MCCXVI*, ed. C. Manaresi (Milan, 1919), nn. 1, 3 (aa. 1117–30); Landolfo Juniore, *Historia Mediolanensis*, ed. C.

I could continue with sketches like these, of the different experiences each Italian city had with the halting development of its commune; but, although fascinating (at least to me), they would not add to the points I want to make on a more general level. Rather, I want to explore what they tell us about the problem of the formalisation of local power in Italy. Here, it is useful to begin with the urban assembly. This body is not always very prominent in our twelfth-century evidence (it is not in Lucca or Florence, for example), but it is certainly so in Pisa and Genoa, as also Cremona and Milan, and many other places as well, as two important recent studies, by Edward Coleman and Paolo Grillo, have stressed.[39] What did it consist of, and in what way was it new?

We have seen that in the Carolingian period assembly politics was a central part of political practice; indeed, a whole political habitus presupposed it, in Francia and Italy alike (as, also, further afield, in England, and indeed elsewhere as well).[40] Legitimation of rulership by large social groups, including, in theory at least, the whole free male population, had old roots, therefore, and the great *placitum* assemblies, surviving in Italian cities into the second half of the eleventh century, were simply part of that. Twelfth-century Italian urban assemblies might have simply seemed, and have been felt, to carry this tradition of mass legitimisation on, very occasionally even extending their participation to women, as was also a feature of a minority of earlier assemblies, most often visible in England.[41] Conversely, if membership of communal assemblies often seems by the mid-twelfth century to have become the right only of more restricted groups (explicitly so with the Genoese *compagna*, but more and more elsewhere too, either because fewer people participated in the main assembly or because more exclusive executive assemblies, the

Castiglioni (Bologna, 1934), cc. 44, 48 bis. Here, the classic point of reference is Hagen Keller: see his 'Die Stadtkommunen als politische Organismen in den Herrschaftsordnungen des 11.-13. Jahrhunderts', in *Pensiero e sperimentazioni istituzionali nella 'Societas Christiana' (1046–1250)*, ed. G. Andenna (Milan, 2007), 673–703, which is perhaps his fullest statement of his argument about the 1120s–40s institutionalisation of the Milanese commune, and which refers to his previous work.

[39] E. Coleman, 'Representative Assemblies in Communal Italy', in *Political Assemblies in the Earlier Middle Ages*, ed. P. S. Barnwell and M. Mostert (Turnhout, 2003), 193–210 (which includes previous bibliography); Grillo, 'Una frattura inesistente', 692–6; and cf. also R. Celli, 'Il ruolo del parlamento nel periodo formativo dei Comuni', in *Poteri assemblee autonomie (il lungo camino verso la sovranità popolare)* (Udine, 1989), 17–40, for a more legalistic argument along similar lines.

[40] C. Wickham, 'Consensus and Assemblies in the Romano-Germanic Kingdoms', *Vorträge und Forschungen*, in press, provides a survey; S. Reynolds, 'Assembly Government and Assembly Law', in *Gender and Historiography*, ed. J. L. Nelson *et al.* (2012), 191–9, makes some important analytical points.

[41] Classic for Italy, but atypical: Landolfo Juniore, *Historia Mediolanensis*, c. 44 for Milan in 1117. For England, *Anglo-Saxon Charters*, ed. A. J. Robertson (Cambridge, 1939), nn. 66, 78; *Charters of St Albans*, ed. J. Crick (Oxford, 2007), n. 7.

credenza in Lombard cities, the senate in Pisa, gained importance),[42] then that had long been a *de facto* feature of the Carolingian world too.

But there were important novelties as well. The practice of the Carolingian period was that such assemblies were called by rulers or their representatives; the major exceptions were in Scandinavia, where kingship was very weak. They made formal decisions, but according to scripts; and in Italy, their functions were above all to hear royal commands, to decide on disputes, and, in general, to underwrite, by making public, a wide variety of legal transactions.[43] The assemblies of the early twelfth century were different. There is no evidence that most of them were dependent on a superior power to be called – they were generally called by consuls by the 1150s, but that was after consular authority was fully established, and earlier on we cannot assume it. In Milan, for example, it is true that the powerful Archbishop Giordano could call a large penitential assembly in front of the cathedral after the great earthquake of 1117, but when a year later he 'inflamed the crowd of the assembly to do vengeance' to get it to declare war on Como in 1118, the event shows not only that he could not declare war on his own, but also that he had gone to a preexisting assembly to do so.[44] They were indeed deliberative about a wide range of issues, as we shall see in a moment. They were a reinvention of a concept of assembly politics which had only recently ceased to exist, and, not surprisingly, they made some of the same assumptions about group decision-making and legitimacy, but they were not the same, any more than a large Union-called general meeting in a modern UK University is the same as the University's Senate or Congregation. And they were never called *placita*, and only very rarely indeed (once in Pisa, as we have seen) used *placitum* notarial traditions in the recording of their decisions. They were in fact both less and more than *placita*. They evidently could not claim the *placitum* tradition as legitimately theirs, and, although justice was often done in front of them initially, their main function was not as a law court; indeed, non-criminal justice rapidly passed to much smaller

[42] *Gli atti del comune di Milano*, lxxiv–vi; *I brevi dei consoli*, ed. Banti, 48, 76. For the complexities involved, especially in decision-making, see G. De Angelis, '"Omnes simul aut quot plures habere potero"', *Reti medievali rivista*, 12 (2011), 151–94.

[43] Bougard, *La justice*, esp. 307–46; C. Wickham, 'Justice in the Kingdom of Italy in the Eleventh Century', *Settimane di studio*, 44 (1997), 179–255. The criticisms of this focus on the end of judicial assemblies made by Stephen White in his 'Tenth-Century Courts at Mâcon and the Perils of Structuralist History', in *Conflict in Medieval Europe*, ed. W. C. Brown and P. Górecki (Aldershot, 2003), 37–68, are fair as regards the Mâconnais, where judicial assemblies had a different history, but do not seem to me to reflect the Italian situation. For France, the best monographic analysis of the continuity of judicial assemblies into the eleventh and twelfth centuries is now Lemesle, *Conflits et justice*, 33–81, for Anjou.

[44] Landolfo Juniore, *Historia Mediolanensis*, cc. 44, 47.

groups of experts, and for the most part lost its assembly element entirely.[45] Conversely, they also did many things that *placitum* assemblies less often did: choose consuls and other urban officials (however restricted that right really was), very occasionally chase consuls out (maybe only in Brescia in 1135, but the example is still significant),[46] decide to go to war and make peace and alliances, approve legislation and other major political decisions. They had a wide variety of names: *concio, arengum, colloquium, parlamentum, consilium, consulatus,* varying from city to city but also inside the practice of the same city. This in itself indicates that they were local developments, in parallel across the old Kingdom of Italy, to meet similar needs, although also, doubtless, with considerable copying of practice from one city to the next.

In this form, the *concio* or *colloquium* had roots in the past as well. There had been occasional earlier non-*placitum* assemblies in Italian cities, too, in the ninth century and later, and in the urban uprisings of the mid-eleventh these assemblies had had an identifiable role, as did the oaths which they swore to each other. Some of them – one example is probably Liguria, in Genoa and Savona – seem to have been associated with the generation and ratification of local customs already in the eleventh century. These were evidently much more direct ancestors of the *concio* than the *placitum* assembly was, and are indeed cited in every account of the origins of the communes in these terms.[47] In the middle third of the eleventh century in troubled cities like Cremona and Milan, they were *ad hoc* oppositional bodies, too. But what marked the novelty of the period from the 1090s onwards is that these assemblies were increasingly regular, increasingly visible, increasingly well defined; they increasingly *were* the city, in its decision-making role. You might say that in (say) 1050 in a city like Milan there was a dialectic between a formal *placitum* assembly and

---

[45] Wickham, *Courts and Conflict,* 19–40, and *idem,* 'Public Court Practice', in *Rechtsverständnis und Konfliktbewältigung,* ed. S. Esders (Cologne, 2007), 17–30. I would now make some modifications: in Milan, large witness groups for civil judgements continue on and off until the second half of the twelfth century (*Gli atti del comune di Milano, passim*); in Rome, where memories of the *placitum* were particularly strong, collective judgements continue until c.1190 (cf. C. Wickham, 'Getting justice in twelfth-century Rome', in *Zwischen Pragmatik und Performanz,* ed. Dartmann *et al.,* 103–31, at 118).

[46] *Annales Brixienses,* ed. L. Bethmann, *MGH, Scriptores,* XVIII (Hanover, 1863), 811–20, at 812, cited in Grillo, 'La frattura inesistente', 694.

[47] For a good brief account, see Milani, *I comuni italiani,* 16–23. For earlier analyses, see among many W. Goetz, *Le origini dei comuni italiani,* trans. I. and R. Zapperi (Milan, 1965), 34–6, 81–4, 94–5 – influential in its time, but now very dated; H. Keller, 'Mailand im 11. Jahrhundert', in *Die Frühgeschichte der europäischen Stadt im 11. Jahrhundert,* ed. J. Jarnut and P. Johanek (Cologne, 1998), 81–104, at 93–8 (one of several parallel analyses by the author); and Tabacco, *The Struggle for Power,* 185. They indeed argue that the oath-based collectivities of mid-century Milan were definitely proto-communal, 'the premise for the future commune' (Tabacco). This seems to me too teleological. See Fiore, 'Giurare la consuetudine', 50–2, for Liguria.

the informal and as yet occasional oath-based *colloquium* of concerned citizens, which when there was conflict could easily be, and was, defined by traditional powers as illegal (as the Cremona uprising was by Henry III, and the Pataria in Milan was by its opponents);[48] and that, when the formal assembly failed, what was abandoned was this dialectic. Instead, the informal assembly formalised itself, regularised itself, turned itself into a *de facto* legal entity: the Cremonese *comunum* which took over the neighbouring town of Crema in benefice from Matilda in 1097, the Pisan *colloquium* which could call in Bishop Daiberto to make a ruling about Pisan tower-houses and engage itself to police the decision afterwards, the Pisan *populus* which could decide to send an expedition to the Balearic islands in 1113,[49] the Milanese *concio* which could start the long-lasting and bloody Como war in 1118, the *plenum parlamentum* in which the Genoese consuls set up some of the rules for the city's new mint in 1140.[50] What had been illegal now defined legality; as a defensive measure in front of political breakdown, but through a set of increasingly formal practices which would last.

This is where the parallels with France lie, then, in Italian cities a century later: in the formalisation of informal practices which had previously existed on the ground, the legalisation of the illegal, the end of the previous dialectic between formal and informal. I will come back to that shortly, but in the Italian context I want first both to nuance and generalise it.

As to nuancing: I have been characterising the early commune as informal until much later than the newly defined assemblies of the 1090s. This is because I am using an ideal-type characterisation of the commune which is more elaborate than, simply, the appearance of a clearly characterised city assembly. That assembly had formalised itself in many cities by 1100, but communal government remained uncertain for a long time, with city leaders who may well have – must have – dominated assembly deliberations, but who had not developed official status yet; that process of formalisation, institutionalisation, as we have seen, did not occur until around 1110 in Pisa and Genoa and the 1130s in other early cities, and in others rather later than that. I would guess that this was associated with a lessening of the defensiveness of the previous generation, when cities had had to deal as best they could with the breakdown of the hegemony and political structures of the Kingdom of Italy, and also with the steady regularisation of practice which must have slowly taken place

---

[48] *MGH, Heinrici III. Diplomata*, ed. H. Bresslau and P. Kehr (Berlin, 1931), n. 319; Landolfo Seniore, *Mediolanensis historiae libri IV*, ed. A. Cutolo (Bologna, 1942), III, 15, 18.

[49] *Liber Maiolichinus*, ed. Calisse, lines 1, 40, 82, etc.

[50] *CDGE*, n. 102, cf. 96–7 – though note that previous consular legislation in the 1130s, nn. 53, 67–8, does not mention the city assembly.

everywhere. City leaders were, however, as uneasy about the legitimacy of self-made communal government as were traditional powers like kings and bishops; many of them stayed out of the crystallising commune for a long time; and few of them realised quite what a break with the past it was until some time later too. The process of formalisation of local power-structures was therefore a slow one, which took in some cases two generations to complete.

As to generalising: we have been looking here at cities, but the Italian countryside faced exactly the same situation, of the breakdown of the hegemony of the Kingdom, and reacted in similar ways. The development of the Italian equivalent of the *seigneurie banale*, generally called the *signoria territoriale*, that is to say lordship and the ability to exercise rights over all inhabitants of a single territory, be they tenants of the lord, tenants of other lords or independent landowners, was a long process in Italy. Already in the ninth century, large landownership sometimes brought some judicial rights, *iustitia domnica* as it was often called; in the tenth century, royal cessions of land (and sometimes of castles or castle-building rights, but often not) increasingly often included *districtiones*, rights of justice, plus rights to take tolls of different types, attached to the land. These did not develop further until the eleventh century in the Po plain. The decades after 1030 see many more references to *districtus* or *placitum et districtum* as a normal part of rural rights, especially if a castle is attached to the territory; but it is not until the 1070s or so that we start to find references to signorial rights held over people who were not tenants of the lord, and this is not generalised in neat legal terms as *dominatus loci*, something which can itself be an object of transactions, until after 1100. Such a *dominatus* could derive from legal means – transactions between the holders of different types of legally delegated power – but it could also be, and probably usually was, the result of creative and coercive improvisation on the part of lords, generalising out from other sorts of rights which they already had, as in France. This latter was initially illegal, and sometimes called (again as in France) *malae consuetudines*, but it too was later accepted as a legal *dominatus*: as with, for example, the local *signorie* enjoyed by the *capitanei*, episcopal vassals, who held tithes in fief from the archbishop of Milan, but frequently managed to extend this quite precise and restricted local right into a much more wide-ranging domination.[51]

The point about this is twofold. First, that the move towards the ability to coerce people in the countryside, whether by running their

---

[51] For all this, classic texts are C. Violante, 'Pievi e parrocchie nell'Italia centrosettentrionale durante i secoli XI e XII', in *Le istituzioni ecclesiastiche della 'societas christiana' dei secoli XI–XII* (Milan, 1977), 633–799 (who stresses, at 666–8, 717–21, that tithe fiefs did not bring signorial rights at the start); Keller, *Signori e vassalli*, esp. 118–36; Menant, *Campagnes lombardes*, 395–477, 728–35, 757–65.

legal disputes, or by extracting tolls and wood-rights from them, or by forcing them to build and guard castles (or by other means: the list is long), had begun, slowly, well before the Kingdom of Italy broke up in the civil wars after 1080. The full public rights of the Kingdom persisted most of all, precisely, inside the walls of cities and in the urban-focused *placitum* assemblies which were so much an Italian particularity by now;[52] and not every city had complete control over its countryside. But, second, and not less important, there is no doubt that signorial rights extended rapidly after 1080 or so. All our best evidence is from after that date in northern Italy. And in Tuscany, where, as we have seen, the March preserved Carolingian political practices unusually fully, signorial rights are hardly visible at all before 1080. There were a few, attached to comital families and the like, who were the first in the region to privatise their local powers; as early as 1075 we have a signorial court case for the powerful Guidi counts in one of their power-bases, in the hills east of Florence. But it was only after 1080 that that 'all power lost its strength, and justice died and perished in our land', as the peasants of Casciavola in the territory of Pisa said in their plea to the city against the coercion of local lords, in a famous text of *c.* 1100. From then on, once again, references to signorial rights, including over whole territories, become much more numerous, and also normalised; what had been illegal turned into legality, and could also, from now on, be seen as a basket of discrete quasi-proprietorial rights which could be sold or otherwise alienated. In the territory of Florence, it is also this period which sees medium-level lords detach themselves from a city focus and concentrate on more local rural territories, which they could now rule in greater depth, using developing signorial powers, and indeed they had to, given the competition of others. In general, indeed, a specialisation by certain families in signorial lordship in the countryside sometimes caused a political separation between city and country which would take a long time to reverse.[53]

If the Kingdom of Italy had lasted, many territorial *signorie* would certainly have developed anyway, and would not necessarily have been considered by kings, counts and bishops as a diminution of their power at all – indeed, the latter two groups contained some of the keenest examples

[52] Cf. esp. Tabacco, *The Struggle for Power*, 331–42.

[53] *I più antichi documenti del monastero di S. Maria di Rosano (secoli XI–XIII)*, ed. C. Strà (Rome, 1982), n. 9 (cf. S. Collavini, 'Le basi materiali della signoria dei Guidi tra prelievo signorile e obblighi militari (1075 c.–1230 c.)', *Società e Storia*, 24 (2007), 1–32); *I brevi dei consoli*, ed. Banti, 105–7 (*c.* 1100); C. Wickham, *The Mountains and the City* (Oxford, 1988), 313–14 (the basket of rights); *idem*, 'La signoria rurale in Toscana'; Cortese, *Signori, castelli*, esp. 231–48 (Florence); *eadem*, 'Aristocrazia signorile e città nell'Italia centro-settentrionale (XI–XII sec.)', in *I comuni di Jean-Claude Maire Vigueur*, ed. M. T. Caciorgna *et al.* (Rome, 2014), 69–94 (where she shows that many signorially orientated families had, after all, the necessary nuances, relatively little to do with early communes in north central Italy).

of aggressive local lords. Many city communes, later, particularly in northern Italy (less so Tuscany), once they reestablished structured power over the countryside (which they were already beginning to do by 1150), were equally unworried by such rural lordships, as long as they were loyal to the city. But what happened after the civil wars was that formal lordly power in the countryside extended over more people, and what was as yet informal became formalised; the countryside divided itself up between different blocs of *dominatus loci* in an increasingly homogeneous way. It began to be possible, indeed, to see all, or nearly all, the countryside of the former Kingdom as being divided up between signorial territories, whether weak or strong, as a matter of course. And, it must be added – I have discussed the point elsewhere, so I can be brief – that the same is true of other forms of rural territorialisation, that of the parish, crystallising around nearly every one of the numerous rural churches which had until 1100 had few autonomous religious and fiscal rights; and also that of the village itself, for village boundaries in Italy had very often been unusually vague by European standards until then. Rural communal structures would develop next, following these territories, which indeed were often superimposed, one on the other: first in large and relatively city-like rural centres (they would be called towns in northern Europe) and in villages with unusual legal autonomy from lords, but soon in villages of every size and level of dependence. All these were developments which were potential but incomplete before 1080, and became rapidly more complete from then on, in a process which was not always fast, here either, but which firmly took shape in the twelfth century above all.[54]

I do not want this to seem an eirenic process. Italian rural lords, like urban elites indeed, were domineering, unpleasant and badly behaved in all respects. This was not new either, but the late eleventh century and the early twelfth gave them many more opportunities to show it, just as the early eleventh century had done in France. How violent and unjust the countryside was or became is not, however, the point here. Rather, the points I wish to stress are that powers, and the very boundaries of powers and rights, in the countryside became much more clearly delineated in and after the 1080s; that this was a real and significant change; and that this process of delineation and formalisation exactly matches that of, first, the urban assembly, and soon the structures of the city commune. Personal relationships, whether vertical (the feudo–vassalic bond, lord–community agreements) or horizontal (private agreements of aid and friendship between lords) gained a rather greater formality in

---

[54] C. Wickham, *Community and Clientele in Twelfth-Century Tuscany* (Oxford, 1998); P. Guglielmotti, *Ricerche sull'organizzazione del territorio nella Liguria medievale* (Florence, 2005), 28–35; for autonomous villages, see e.g. Fiore, 'Dal diploma al patto'.

the same period too.[55] In these respects, the signoria and the commune in Italy are both examples of the same general process, the process by which informal (and illegal) power-structures become formal (and legal) ones.[56] The signoria was very hierarchical, the commune was much more associative, and indeed maintained the city assembly, the principal form of an imagery of mostly phony egalitarianism, in some form for a long time. But the contrast between lordship and collectivity was the main way in which they were opposed. Neither (contrary to a traditional Italian historiography) was older, more legal, or more 'public' than the other. The two models for local organisation would have a long history together, indeed, as rural communes began to run signorial lordships and, later, urban *signorie* came to take over cities, in future centuries.

To conclude: the homology between the commune and the signoria in Italy of course makes even clearer the point I have already started to make, that there are close parallels between the changes which took place in France around 1000 or 1050 and those which took place in Italy around 1100. The contrast in dates does not matter; what matters is that in each case larger-scale political breakdown (whether at the level of the kingdom, the march or the county) was matched by local recomposition, the intensification or crystallisation of local power structures which had been much more *ad hoc* before, and which would be the basic template for local power henceforth. Here, I do see something of a difference between cities and the countryside, however, for the causal process was not so clear-cut in the latter. In the latter, the formalisation model set out by West for the old Frankish heartland fits Italy pretty well, not least in the emergence of the assumption that the basket of banal rights – and the power derived from them – were by now sufficiently clearly defined that they could henceforth be treated as forms of property, which I find in Italy just as he does in the north.[57] Where Italy may differ from Francia is in that these changes in the Po plain and Tuscany can indeed, in my view, best be seen as a partially defensive response to the weakening of those larger structures, even though it had independent origins as a process. In general, West sees the formalisation of local power as being the completion of Carolingian categorisations of political and property rights, and not a consequence of Carolingian failure. I am happy to accept that in large part, again particularly for Francia; but it is also arguable that in a world dominated by a politics based on land transactions, a lack of systematic

[55] Menant, 'La féodalité italienne'; S. Reynolds, *Fiefs and vassals* (Oxford, 1994), 215–35; Fiore, 'Dal diploma al patto'.

[56] For the homology between signoria and commune, see also P. Racine, *Plaisance du Xème à la fin du XIIIème siècle* (Paris, 1979), 372, but he said so for different reasons (city government as being *just like* the 'feudal' social relations in the countryside) and I do not follow him there – see further Cortese, 'Aristocrazia signorile e città'.

[57] West, *Reframing the Feudal Revolution*, 184–90, 196–8, 255–63.

attention to local power relations in the countryside, such as we see in the actions of both emperors and major lay aristocrats (although less so monasteries) in the ninth century, was indeed potentially dangerous for them, and that these local power relations, once they became formalised enough for whatever reason to manipulate politically, which in a land-based political system was always on the cards, might indeed slip out of the hands of greater powers.[58] That is a rural argument, however. Inside Italian urban politics by contrast – an arena virtually absent in Francia, of course – I do not see anything except a defensive reaction to political crisis in the decades after 1080 or so. Power carried on being exercised in Italian cities in Carolingian ways without all that much difficulty until then, and, until that traditional structure failed, the inchoate forms of local political practice which also existed, urban assemblies in particular, were not going to replace it anywhere. Indeed, the generation-long uneasiness about the new communal political structures which developed in its absence is itself a clear demonstration of the lasting hegemony inside city walls of the hierarchical presuppositions of the past.

These two, city and country, are nonetheless linked tightly by the fact that newly formalised structures replaced informal local ones, in the context of the failure (as it can be said to be in Italy) of the previous overarching structures of formal political power. The dialectic between informal and formal was here lost – at least until new informal practices developed again, which in Italian cities they would soon enough, urban factions, the *popolo*, and onwards from there. In Italy as in France, it was that which was the major change of the period, and it can be analysed in very similar ways. But I would like to end with a more sociological point, which I think follows from what has been argued in the foregoing. Informality of practice, it seems to me, is *always* in dialectic with formal social and political structures, and cannot exist without them. And I think this means that Pierre Bourdieu was not entirely right about one aspect of his theory of habitus, which has been so influential for me, and not only for me. He proposed that everything was habitus, and that formal structures were only secondary: a *post facto* power-play imposed on top of the durable informality of practice.[59] I would say, however, that that practice, the gamesmanship of which Bourdieu was the greatest theorist, presupposes not just a formal structure which the games-playing subverts – creative and successful cheating on the football field cannot

---

[58] As with Marc Bloch's 'fragmentation of authority' (*Feudal society*, trans. L. A. Manyon (1962), 446 – the French original says *pouvoirs* for 'authority', however).

[59] P. Bourdieu, most lucidly in *In Other Words*, trans. M. Adamson (Cambridge, 1990), 76–86; the most theoretically elaborated characterisation of habitus, leaving more implicit its relation with formalisation however, is in his *The Logic of Practice*, trans. R. Nice (Cambridge, 1990), 52–65.

exist without the rules of the Football Association (Bourdieu of course knew this) – but also that, if the subversion becomes more total, so that the formal structure fails, then part or all of the habitus has to turn itself into a newly formal structure to replace it: because at least some element of formal structure in the practice of everyday political and social life is essential, in societies with any degree of elaboration at all.[60] From that standpoint, in France, the formalisation of local power, which remains for me the most essential element of the 'feudal revolution', could not have failed to occur. What happened in Italy in the decades around 1100 seems to me to bear out the point as well. What Italians did with it, however, as they proceeded uneasily into the future, while looking backwards into the past, is another matter.

[60] And perhaps in any society. Charles West suggests to me that the 'big-men' societies discussed by Marshall Sahlins and others (e.g. M. D. Sahlins, 'Poor Man, Rich Man, Big-Man, Chief', *Comparative Studies in Society and History*, 5 (1962–3), 285–303) might sometimes be different, structurally more informal. I am not sure here; that is certainly the way Sahlins presents it; but the closest medieval Europe visibly came to that, in Iceland before 1262, the structures of *goðord* and *thingar*, judicial rights over free men held by the equivalents of 'big men' and the assemblies in which those rights were expressed, seem to me, whatever their weakness and their practical subversions, to have had clear formal elements – see for a survey J. Byock, *Viking-Age Iceland* (2001), 118–38.

Transactions of the RHS 24 (2014), pp. 57–77 © Royal Historical Society 2014
doi:10.1017/S0080440114000036

PREACHERS AND HEARERS IN REVOLUTIONARY LONDON: CONTEXTUALISING PARLIAMENTARY FAST SERMONS

By Ann Hughes

READ 27 SEPTEMBER 2013

ABSTRACT. Studies of preaching in England during the 1640s and 1650 have focused on the high-profile sermons, preached before the parliament on fast days and other special days of thanksgiving, relying in particular on analysis of preachers' texts as published in print. This paper explores ways of placing the fast sermons in broader contexts, drawing on the lively scholarship on early modern sermons that presents them as events as well as texts, dynamic encounters between preachers and hearers. This paper thus explores the responses of conscientious hearers to sermons in London in the 1640s and 1650s, through a variety of notes kept by pious Puritans, broadly sympathetic to the parliament's cause, including the artisan Nehemiah Wallington, John and Katherine Gell from the provincial gentry and John Harper, a city fishmonger. For these hearers, sermon note-taking had enduring purposes, for reflection, meditation and discussion, sometimes across generations; recording the immediate political context or the polemical arguments of the fast sermons was not necessarily their priority. Hearers' notebooks place the fast sermons within a broader context of attendance at more 'routine' pastoral and didactic preaching in London parishes, revealing also that a preacher like Stephen Marshall, best known for his dynamic sermons before the parliament, spent most of his time on less controversial series of sermons on central issues of Protestant faith. Note-taking practices suggest that too sharp a contrast between polemical and routine preaching would be misleading; the fast sermons could be apprehended in a variety of ways by conscientious Puritan hearers, while sermons with a more pastoral focus nonetheless exhibited clear signs of the tensions and dilemmas provoked by the religious conflicts of the period.

In 1661, a contemptuous broadside rejoiced in the downfall of the godly Presbyterian clergy of London:

> Say are the Presbyterian Champions fled?
> Is sturdy Vines, and thundering Marshall dead?
> . . . Time was my Masters, you could draw a sword,
> Beat Drums, sound Trumpets, and then fall abord
> The Enemy, mount the next Pulpit thence,
> Curse Meroz for his sloth and negligence,
> Stand stifly to the Cause, never give o'er,
> Witnesse your Brother Ash at Marsenmore.

Time was when you could fight with lips & hands,
Could turn your classes into Trained Bands.[1]

Some twenty years after its first delivery, *Meroz Cursed*, Stephen Marshall's
sermon on Judges V, verse 23, remained the characteristic political sermon
of the 1640s.[2] Preaching before the House of Commons in February 1642,
in the shadow of the Irish rebellion and the king's flight from London,
following his failure to arrest prominent leaders of the parliament,
Marshall urged his hearers to avoid the curse on the people of Meroz who
had acted as 'neuters, who stand aloofe off' and 'came not to the help of
the Lord against the mighty'. Marshall urged his congregation that 'many
great things are yet to be done, much rubbish to be removed . . . Ireland to
be relieved, Religion to be established'; and he clearly raised the prospect
of military action. Prayer would do much but it might be that men would
be 'called, as souldiers, to spend your blood in the Churches cause'.[3]

For sympathetic contemporaries, also, *Meroz Cursed* was a memorable
civil war sermon, as the poet Anne Bradstreet, writing from distant New
England had it:[4]

Blest be thy Commons, who for Common good,
And thy infringed Lawes have boldly stood.
Blest be thy Counties which do aid thee still
With hearts and states, to testifie their will.
Blest be thy Preachers who do chear thee on,
O cry: the sword of God, and *Gideon*:
And shall I not on those wish *Mero*'s curse,
That help thee not with prayers, arms and purse.

The hostile broadside, however, took its title – *The Downfall of the Ark
or the Morning Exercise at an End* – from what might be appear to be a
different mode of 1640s preaching. The Morning Exercise was a regular
series of short sermons preached over a month in a single London
parish and presented by its orthodox godly or Presbyterian backers as
an uncontroversial pastorally focused enterprise. The royalist broadside,
however, did not distinguish between the exercise and the more directly
'political' preaching of the parliamentary fasts, smearing all Presbyterian
preaching as support with 'lips and hands' for rebellion. This paper seeks

---

[1] *The Downfall of the Ark, or the Morning-Exercise at an End* (1661).
[2] The text is: 'Curse ye Meroz, said the angel of the Lord, curse ye bitterly the inhabitants
thereof because they came not to the help of the Lord against the mighty.' Jordan S. Downs,
'The Curse of Meroz and the English Civil War', *Historical Journal*, 57 (2014), 343–68.
[3] Stephen Marshall, *Meroz Cursed or, A Sermon Preached to the Honourable House of Commons*
(1642), 3–4, 48, 53.
[4] Anne Bradstreet, 'A Dialogue between Old England and New, concerning their Present
Troubles. Anno 1642', in *Kissing the Rod*, ed. Germaine Greer *et al.* (1988), 132.

to place the high-profile parliamentarian preaching within a broader context, by relating the fast sermons to the more routine preaching available in London in the 1640s and 1650s, and by stressing reception as much as delivery. It will return to the preaching at the Morning Exercise by way of conclusion.

I

Within modern scholarship, discussions of the parliamentary fast sermons, amongst which *Meroz Cursed* looms large, have dominated studies of preaching in the 1640s and 1650s. Between February 1642 and February 1649, the parliamentarian regime kept the last Wednesday in the month as a solemn fast throughout the kingdom with two high-profile sermons preached before the Commons and, from October 1644, two in the Lords. There were also *ad hoc* or special days of humiliation and thanksgiving that marked conflict, setbacks and defeat on the one hand, or victory and reconciliation on the other.[5] After 1649, the regular fast days were abandoned for a variety of reasons: fear of giving preaching opportunities to London Presbyterians and other opponents of the new regime; radical Puritan anxieties that the fasts had become merely 'formal observance' and perhaps sheer exhaustion. A newsletter reported in April 1649 that the fast days had 'almost wearied all the Preachers and Hearers of England'.[6] Nonetheless, days of fasting, humiliation and thanksgiving continued throughout the 1650s, and in all there were more than 130 of these days of special worship in the 1640s and 1650s.[7] Some provincial sermons were printed, and more of those delivered in prestigious London churches, while as many as three-quarters of all sermons preached before the Commons reached the press. Not to be printed was in itself worth notice, the London bookseller and collector George Thomason writing on his copy of the sermon given by Stephen Marshall at the thanksgiving for the miraculous victory at Naseby, 'Mr Vines not printed'.[8] The majority

---

[5] Christopher Durston, '"For the Better Humiliation of the People": Public Days of Fasting and Thanksgiving during the English Revolution', *Seventeenth Century*, 7, 2 (1992), 129–49, provides an essential analysis, now extended by the fundamental research of the Durham project, 'British State Prayers, Fasts and Thanksgivings, 1540s to 1940'. See *National Prayers. Special Worship since the Reformation*, I: *Special Prayers, Fasts and Thanksgivings in the British Isles 1533–1688*, ed. Natalie Mears, Alasdair Raffe, Stephen Taylor and Philip Williamson (with Lucy Bates), *Church of England Record Society*, 20 (2013), for the texts of ordinances and orders for fasts and thanksgivings. I regret that I have not yet been able to take account of the research of Dr Lucy Bates, 'Nationwide Fast and Thanksgiving Days in England, 1640–1660' (Ph.D. dissertation, Durham University, 2012).

[6] *Moderate Intelligencer*, 19–26 Apr. 1649, quoted in Durston, '"For the Better Humiliation of the People"', 142.

[7] Durston, '"For the Better Humiliation of the People"'.

[8] Stephen Marshall, *A Sacred Record to be Made of God's Mercies to Zion* (1645), British Library (BL) E. 288 (36).

of the preachers before the parliament were members of the Westminster Assembly, mainstream Puritans or Presbyterians, although Independents or 'Congregationalists' were also represented in the early 1640s, and increasingly prominent from the later 1640s. Of the men denounced in *The Downfall of the Ark*, the Essex minister Stephen Marshall preached most often before the Long Parliament, acting on twenty-two occasions before 1649 with sixteen of these sermons printed; Richard Vines was almost as prominent, preaching eleven sermons, of which seven were printed, while Simeon Ashe had four out of his six parliamentary sermons printed, and, as chaplain to parliament's general, the earl of Manchester had brought news to London of the victory at Marston Moor in 1644.[9]

The texts of these printed fast sermons – the words on the page in about 250 small tracts – have proved attractive sources for political scientists, historians, theologians and literary scholars. A lively and still influential article by Hugh Trevor Roper elucidated the ways in which the preachers engaged with specific and immediate polemical contexts, 'tuning the pulpits' to justify particular parliamentarian initiatives. Stephen Marshall is defined as parliament's 'clerical tribune', and 'if Marshall holloa'ed the parliamentary pack onwards into war in 1642, [Hugh] Peter in 1647 would holloa the army onwards into revolution'.[10] If this judgement is commonly now regarded as overly conspiratorial, scholars continue to explain how theological exegesis and scriptural narratives, accounts of God's purposes for his chosen people, had an undisguised relevance to the pressing political and religious dilemmas of the 1640s and 1650s, rallying listeners to the parliamentary cause in the early 1640s, or intervening in intra-parliamentarian divisions.[11] The printed texts have been used, for example, to debate the relative importance of religious and political frameworks for parliamentarian justifications of resistance.[12]

[9] John Wilson, *Pulpit in Parliament: Puritanism during the English Civil Wars 1640–1648* (Princeton, 1969), 109–14; Tom Webster, 'Marshall, Stephen (1594/5? – d. 1655)', *Oxford Dictionary of National Biography* (*ODNB*).

[10] H. R. Trevor-Roper, 'The Fast Sermons of the Long Parliament', in his *Religion, the Reformation and Social Change* (1967), 294–344, at 298 and 324. The metaphor is from hunting, and *Meroz Cursed* is discussed at 307–8.

[11] Amongst many examples: Michael Walzer, *The Revolution of the Saints* (Cambridge, MA, 1965; New York, 1974, pbk), 293–9; Wilson, *Pulpit in Parliament*; Paul Christianson, *Reformers and Babylon: English Apocalyptic Visions from the Reformation to the Eve of the Civil War* (Toronto, Buffalo and London, 1978); Stephen Baskerville, *Not Peace but a Sword: The Political Theology of the English Revolution* (1993); Christopher Hill, 'Fast Sermons and Politics', in his *The English Bible and the Seventeenth-Century Revolution* (1993; 1994 pbk), 79–108. A very recent essay, Rachel Foxley, 'Oliver Cromwell on Religion and Resistance', in *England's Wars of Religion Revisited*, ed. Charles W. A. Prior and Glenn Burgess (Farnham, 2011), 209–30, discusses *Meroz Cursed* specifically at 210–11.

[12] Glenn Burgess, 'Was the English Civil War a War of Religion?', *Huntington Library Quarterly* (*HLQ*), 61 (1998), 173–201; Edward Vallance, 'Preaching to the Converted: Religious Justifications for the English Civil War', *HLQ*, 65 (2002), 395–419.

Most recently, the literary historian Achsah Guibbory has shown how 'a deepened sense of the historicity of the narratives of Biblical Israel', an empathetic identification with the Israelites combating the idolatrous Canaanites, or struggling to rebuild the Temple after the Babylonian exile, enabled the preachers to offer complex constructions of the English nation as a chosen people.[13]

This is a rich and still relevant body of work, but the seductive power of these easily available printed texts obscures broader understandings of preaching in the 1640s and 1650s. There has been relatively little discussion of the fast sermons themselves as events or experiences; rather the texts are used unreflectively as sources to elucidate more general issues.[14] How did ministers, whether confident and well connected like Marshall, or initially inexperienced provincials like Charles Herle, prepare to address their eminent auditors? Herle desired readers of his first fast sermon 'to pardon the want of Quotations, for that (being a Stranger) he had neither Bookes or Notes by him at the penning of what followes'.[15] Herle's sermon was preached on 30 November 1642 and available in printed form by Thomason on 22 December; we need to know more about the printers and publishers who made this rapid production possible, and about how hasty and almost automatic printing affected the relationship between the sermon as oral and as printed communication. The histories of print culture and the book that interrogate how the words came to be on the printed page in particular ways have had relatively little influence here. We do not know enough about how fast sermons were apprehended by readers of the printed sermons or by hearers at their delivery, beyond very general assumptions of enthusiasm or indifference. Fast sermons were clearly not routine occasions, but there is no systematic work on how, for preachers and hearers alike, they took their place amongst more everyday preaching in parish churches. This is a demanding agenda for long-term research, and some preliminary and particular findings are presented here. My focus is on London preaching, particularly as recorded by broadly Puritan hearers sympathetic to the parliament; I explore how conscientious sermon goers located the parliamentary fast sermons within their own contexts of preaching attendance and personal piety. The general impact of the fast sermons and comparisons with

[13] Achsah Guibbory, *Christian Identity, Jews and Israel in Seventeenth-Century England* (Oxford, 2010), 10, 111 and 89–120.

[14] The most comprehensive study of the fast sermons, by John Wilson, has 'Puritanism during the Civil Wars' as its sub-title and uses the printed texts as a way of discussing the changing career structures and religious outlooks of the preachers, as emblematic of broader religious change.

[15] Charles Herle, *A Payre of Compasses for Church and State* (1642), BL E. 130 (3).

royalist fast sermons during the civil war are both vital topics, but they await further research.[16]

II

In London, the parliamentary fasts inaugurated distinct experiences of time and space, an intermixture of mobility and contemporaneity. Popular preachers moved from pulpit to pulpit through one exhausting day; although lay people were supposed to observe the day in their own parish, many chose more exciting or more congenial preachers. For the London radical and future Leveller, William Walwyn, fast days were occasions for sociability and intellectual recreation. 'It fell upon a Fast day in the morning' that Walwyn and two friends 'hastned abroad', discussing religion as they went. They first heard the Presbyterian James Cranford at Christ Church, but finding him not to their taste, they 'went at last to Basing-shaw Church, it being where my Lord Mayor was to be, as expecting to hear some excellent man there; being there some time, we found the matter so lamentable, as we were all three weary of it . . . so we all three at once together went away, but so as we could give no offence to the congregation, being not in the body of the Church'. Walwyn denied that he and his friends had 'been from Church to Church' but he implied that many others in the city did.[17] The Presbyterian wood-turner Nehemiah Wallington, in contrast, confined himself to preaching at his parish church and experienced fast days as a mixed blessing, occasions for morbid reflection and exhaustion as much as inspiration. In May 1643, following some benefit from his parish minister, Henry Roborough:

> when the next man had gone on a while I began to grow weary and wished he had done for faine I would be at home and there was no more expected to perform any more. But Mr Ash being come (weary in) not makeing acount to have don any thing yet with much parswasion did goe up which did grive & was ierksome to my carnall & unregenerat part.

[16] Durston concluded that the authorities failed to 'enforce conformity to their godly ideals' with the 'great mass' of the English people repudiating this culture of preaching and fasting: '"For the Better Humiliation of the People"', 145–6. A more qualified judgement on the successes and failures of godly reform and Puritan preaching is Bernard Capp, *England's Culture Wars: Puritan Reformation and its Enemies in the Interregnum* (Oxford, 2012).

[17] William Walwyn, *Walwyn's Just Defence* (1649), 8–9, recounting events from the mid-1640s. Walwyn claimed it was more characteristic of his critics amongst John Goodwin's congregation to move from preacher to preacher: 'passing to and fro from place to place on the Lords, and Fasts dayes, 4 and 6 of a company spying, watching,and censuring of doctrines'.

In the event, the 'unexpressable love of my God to me his pevish & unworthy Childe' melted Wallington's heart and Ashe's sermon was 'sweet & profitable unto mee so that the time did seeme short'.[18]

The bustle and variety of preaching on a London fast day was less characteristic of provincial England, but the high profile given to fast days through print and parliamentary proclamations meant that provincial supporters of the parliamentary cause felt a sense of identity with their more prominent comrades. In December 1646, for example, a Coventry preacher planning his theme for a day of humiliation praying for God's forgiveness following a 'great judgement of rain and water', imagined his fellow-ministers doing likewise: 'my thoughts led me, That others of my Brethren, as their lot fell, would rouse up their Auditors, Whether the Princes, or the People of the Land, some to take better notice, some to reform, and some to repent of these disregarded Sins'. Bryan's response was a rousing defence of the parliamentarian regime, defending high taxes as necessary to the defence of 'Lives, Liberties, Priviledges, Estates and Religion', and cautioning against a precipitous peace with the king.[19] On the other hand, the city Presbyterian Francis Roberts, in the only sermon of the four preached before the parliament to be printed, offered the Lords a bitter denunciation of the delays in establishing a reformed national church: we 'languish, faint and dye under those cursed diseases of error, heresie, blasphemy, licentiousness, divisions, disorder and confusion, horrid Atheisme, and all manner of prophaneness? . . . Whither are we falling?'[20] The degree to which the programme of national fasts achieved a shift, albeit partial and temporary, in what David Cressy has termed 'Calendrical consciousness' and in spatial awareness would repay further examination.[21]

The importance of fast days, as repeated experiences, and of the sermons as a *series*, is evident in their printed character. Some bookseller-publishers deliberately presented fast sermons to readers as a series, appending chronological lists or 'catalogues' of all those preached to date at the end of an individual sermon, noting those not printed. These lists were often in sermons preached late in December so that

---

[18] BL Add. MS 40,883, fo. 102v. This was a common experience for Wallington who had hoped at the April fast that Ashe would not turn up, but ultimately benefited from his sermon: *ibid.*, fo. 92v; *The Notebooks of Nehemiah Wallington, 1618–1654. A Selection*, ed. David Booy (Aldershot, 2007), 189–90.

[19] John Bryan, *A Discovery of the Probable Sin* (1646), Preface, 3, 13.

[20] Francis Roberts, *A Broken Spirit, God's Sacrifices. Or the Gratefulnesse of a Broken Spirit unto God* (1646), 34. We should not automatically assume that provincial preaching was less committed than that delivered in London.

[21] David Cressy, *Bonfires and Bells. National Memory and the Protestant Calendar in Elizabethan and Stuart England* (Berkeley and Los Angeles, 1989), 13. There is brief discussion of the fast sermons at 45–8.

the previous year's preaching could be summed up, and lists were sometimes highlighted on title pages.[22] Individual printed sermons were relatively cheap, and perhaps ephemeral publications but although fast sermons were usually printed, and often acquired singly, they were avidly collected and preserved by readers.[23] The later seventeenth-century book auction catalogues of ministers prominent in the 1640s and 1650s reveal them as indefatigable collectors of each others' sermons which they organised as a special category. Thomas Jacombe's library included a 'Compleat Collection of Sermons preached before the Houses of Lords and Commons in the time of the late civil wars bound in eleven volumes', while Thomas Manton had organised his alphabetically by author: volume 36 of 'pamphlets bound together in quarto' included '17 sermons preached by Mr Stephen Marshall before the two Houses of Parliament upon several occasions' while volume 42 covered preachers whose names began with 'S' with sermons by Obadiah Sedgwick, William Strong, Henry Scudder, Lazarus Seaman, William Spurstow and John Strickland between 1644 and 1647.[24] Amongst laymen, George Thomason and the iconoclast William Dowsing had near-complete collections of printed fast sermons. Thomason added the occasional endorsement – 'this sermon I heard preached' on Herle's November 1642 text, or the note that John Ley's *The Fury of Warre, and Folly of Sinne*, preached in April 1643 was

---

[22] John Strickland, *Gods Work of Mercy in Sions Misery* (1644), listed sermons preached from 17 Nov. 1640 to 27 Dec. 1643, advertising the 'Catalogue' on the title page; Thomas Case, *God's Rising, His Enemies Scattered* (1644), like Strickland printed for Luke Fawne, extended the list to Apr. 1644. John Whincop, *God's Call to Weeping and Mourning* (1645), was preached before the Commons on 29 Jan. 1644/5 and published shortly afterwards; a second edition (1646), printed for Nathaniel Webb and William Grantham, included 'A Continuation of the Catalogue' of sermons before the Commons and the Lords from 29 Jan. 1644/4 to 31 Dec. 1645. The Commons' Catalogue is described as 'the fourth volume' and the continuations are placed before 'A Catalogue of All the Sermons Preached upon the Dayes of Publike Thanksgiving before Both or Either Houses of Parliament', 7 Sept. 1640 to 12 Mar. 1645/6. There is no catalogue in the first edition. Thomas Horton, *Sinne's Discovery and Revenge* (1646), preached before the Lords on 30 Dec. 1646 and printed for Samuel Gellibrand, included a brief list of 'The Names of the Preachers before the Parliament: Anno 1646' with the texts of their sermons but no dates (p. 40), while William Goode, *Jacob Raised or the Means of Making a Nation Happy* (1646), also preached before the Lords on 30 Dec., and printed for Nathaniel Webb and William Grantham, had 'A Continuation of the Catalogue of Sermons Preached upon the Dayes of Publique Humiliation' before the Lords and the Commons, Jan. 1645/6 to Dec. 1646, with a note 'Reader Be pleased to take notice, Those whose Texts are not quoted are not yet printed'; followed by 'A Continuation of the Sermons preached upon the Dayes of Publique Thanksgiving' before both or either of the Houses of Parliament, Apr.–Nov. 1646 (after p. 29). Cf. Wilson, *Pulpit in Parliament*, 237–8.
[23] An exception is Cornelius Burges, *Two Sermons Preached to the Honourable House of Commons* (1645) which included a sermon preached 30 Mar. 1642 but not preached until paired with one on a similar theme from 30 Mar. 1645.
[24] *Bibliotheca Jacombiana* (1687), 90; *Catalogus Variorum & Insignium Librorum . . . Thomas Manton* (1678), 49–50.

the gift of the author.[25] For Dowsing, we have suggestive evidence of repeated, thoughtful engagement with the printed texts. He purchased some 158 printed sermons preached to the Long Parliament, almost all of those preached before the Commons at the regular fast days from 1642 to 1646, along with twenty-eight sermons on special occasions and a smaller number of sermons before the Lords. Dowsing accumulated his collection through 'piecemeal' purchases usually paying 5d a sermon, sometimes buying shortly after publication but often much later. He noted dates of purchase, and of first reading, applied any errata and added biblical references, marginal emphases and occasional comments. The sermons were bound into six systematically arranged volumes in October 1646, and Dowsing then reread them all again.[26]

Dowsing's active response to the fast sermons indicates how much the study of preaching in the 1640s and 1650s has to gain from the enormously productive scholarship on Tudor and early Stuart preaching associated with Ian Green, Mary Morissey, Peter McCullough, and especially Arnold Hunt. This work insists that sermons were events as much as they were texts, and that the responses of hearers are as important as the aims and methods of preachers. Analysing printed sermons alone and in isolation limits attempts to understand 'the two-way relationship between the preacher and his audience', in Arnold Hunt's words. Sermons, in this framework, were at once speech acts, performances and public events; moving oral encounters between preachers and hearers.[27] A fuller understanding of such encounters in years of political upheaval, civil wars and religious fragmentation is particularly pressing, yet has been rarely attempted.[28]

---

[25] BL, E. 130 (3), E. 103 (1).

[26] John Morrill, 'William Dowsing and the Administration of Iconoclasm', 6–10, and John Blatchly, 'Dowsing's Collection of Parliamentary Sermons', 327–33, both in *The Journal of William Dowsing*, ed. T. Cooper (Woodbridge, 2001).

[27] Ian M. Green, *Continuity and Change in Protestant Change in Protestant Preaching in Early Modern England* (Friends of Dr Williams's Library, 60th lecture, 2009); Mary Morissey, 'Interdisciplinarity and the Study of Early Modern Sermons', *Historical Journal*, 42, 4 (1999), 1111–23, at 1112, for 'events and texts'; *idem, Politics and the Paul's Cross Sermons, 1558–1642* (Oxford, 2011); Arnold Hunt, *The Art of Hearing. English Preachers and their Audiences, 1590–1640* (Cambridge, 2010), 396, 5. For the latest scholarship on early modern preaching, see *The Oxford Handbook of the Early Modern Sermon*, ed. Peter McCullough, Hugh Adlington and Emma Rhatigan (Oxford, 2011).

[28] For brief exceptions see James Rigney, '"To Lye upon a Stationers Stall, like a Piece of Coarse Flesh in a Shambles": The Sermon, Print and the English Civil War', in *The English Sermon Revised: Religion, Literature and History 1600–1750*, ed. Lori Anne Ferrell and Peter McCullough (Manchester, 2000), 188–207; Tom Webster, 'Preaching and Parliament, 1640–1659', in *Oxford Handbook of the Early Modern Sermon*, ed. McCullough, Adlington and Rhatigan; Green, *Continuity and Change*; and John Spurr's *The Laity and Preaching in Post-Reformation England* (Friends of Dr Williams's Library 66th lecture, 2013), consider the civil war period within their broader studies.

III

Recent studies of early modern preaching have made illuminating use of manuscript sermon notes made by hearers: 'Sermon noting is one of the keys to understanding how lay people "consumed" preaching in post-Reformation England', as John Spurr remarks.[29] Robert Baillie, one of the Scottish representatives to the Westminster Assembly, was rarely impressed by the religious practices he found in 1640s London, but he was nonetheless struck by the enthusiasm of the English for taking notes at sermons: 'the most of all the Assemblie wrytes, as almost all the people, men, women and children wryte at preaching', he declared in January 1644.[30] This was presumably an exaggeration of the literacy standards of Londoners as well as of their zeal for sermons but his opinion is supported by other witnesses, and by the survival of many contemporary examples of sermon notes.[31]

Note-taking was not an exclusively Puritan practice, as Spurr's recent analysis of John Evelyn's notes demonstrates, but in Alec Ryrie's words: 'the importance of sermon-noting for earnest, literate Protestants would be hard to exaggerate'.[32] Books of advice on listening to and noting sermons were a popular printed genre in seventeenth-century England; and training in the effective recording and memorialisation of oral discourse was an essential element in grammar school and university curricula. Printed shorthand manuals, a distinctive English genre, were targeted at conscientious sermon attenders.[33] Hearing the word preached was crucial to salvation; recalling, repeating and meditating on sermons heard was central to zealous Protestant sociability and piety. Notes come in many forms from brief summaries to very full reports, based on a prior short-hand record; some are barely legible, others finely written. Writers may be anonymous or known only by name, while others like Samuel Pepys and John Evelyn are very familiar. Most valuable for my purposes are notes by identifiable individuals about whom enough is known to assess how their sermon notes connect with other aspects of their lives and opinions. The following discussion is based on six examples, five men

[29] Spurr, *Laity and Preaching*, 10.

[30] *The Letters and Journals of Robert Baillie* (3 vols., The Bannatyne Club, 1841–2), II, 123.

[31] Hunt, *Art of Hearing*, 139–40, for the mid-seventeenth-century testimony of Ludovic Huygens.

[32] Spurr, *Laity and Preaching*, 22–4, 28–31; Alec Ryrie, *Being Protestant in Reformation Britain* (Oxford, 2013), 358.

[33] Valuable accounts of note-taking include Ann Blair, 'Note Taking as an Art of Transmission', *Critical Inquiry*, 31, 1 (2004), 85–107; Ceri Sullivan, 'The Art of Listening in the Seventeenth Century', *Modern Philology*, 104 (2006), 34–71; Hunt, *Art of Hearing*, 94–115; John Craig, 'Sermon Reception', in *Oxford Handbook of the Early Modern Sermon*, ed. McCullough, Adlington and Rhatigan, 178–97; Green, *Continuity and Change*, 19–25; Morrissey, *Politics and the Paul's Cross Sermons*; Spurr, *Laity and Preaching*.

and one woman, all broadly Puritan, with some sympathy at least for the parliament. Educated men from the middle and upper ranks of society predominate, predictably, given the value of a grammar school education to effective note-taking, but the most familiar example is socially the most humble: Nehemiah Wallington, who kept at least four notebooks of 'precious sermons' from the 'book with a black cover, which I have written many precious sermons, which I did give to my wife, 1636' to his fiftieth book, begun in 1654 of sermons heard at the Morning Exercise: 'the Lord make me humble and write it in my heart'.[34] Wallington's initial enthusiasm for parliament waxed and waned through the later 1640s and 1650s as his highest hopes of religious reformation were thwarted and opposed. My second example, Walter Boothby, like Wallington, was a supporter of Presbyterian initiatives in the city. Elected as a common councillor in 1642, Boothby was active in furthering parliament's war effort in the city, and although he was a Presbyterian activist in the mid-1640s, he accepted office as an alderman in 1652.[35] Boothby's massive commonplace book, 'A Nosegay of Everlasting Orificall Flowers Gathered out of Heavens Paradice' drew on city sermons, especially by Presbyterians, preached from the 1630s to the 1660s.[36] John Harper, a citizen and fishmonger, living in the small parish of St Margaret Moses, made notes on sermons he had attended throughout his adult life, and at some point in the mid-1650s, he created a further fair copy of his notes (or some of them) in a volume of almost 600 pages.[37] Harper was a conscientious servant of his company, his parish and his ward, but no parliamentarian zealot. Unlike Boothby, Harper refused to serve the republican regime as an alderman, although he acted as a common councillor for Bread Street Ward from 1658 until his death in 1667.[38] Finally, members of the provincial gentry, with parliamentary connections and London residences, kept volumes of sermons in the 1640s including fast sermons preached at Margaret's Westminster or in the Abbey church. Walter Yonge junior, the son and namesake of an MP and parliamentary diarist who noted sermons between 1642 and 1644, was from a committed Puritan and moderate parliamentarian family.[39] Successive generations of the Gells of Hopton, Derbyshire, were conscientious recorders of sermons

---

[34] Paul Seaver, *Wallington's World: A Puritan Artisan in Seventeenth-Century London* (1985), 200–2; *The Notebooks of Nehemiah Wallington, 1618–1654. A Selection*, ed. David Booy (Aldershot, 2007).

[35] Keith Lindley, *Popular Politics and Religion in Civil War London* (Aldershot, 1997), 197n, 229–30, 375.

[36] Bodleian Library, Oxford (Bodl.), MS Eng c 2693, discussed also by Spurr, *Laity and Preaching*, 18–19.

[37] William Andrews Clark Memorial Library MS B8535 M3.

[38] J. R. Woodhead, *The Rulers of London 1660–1689* (London and Middlesex Archaeological Society, 1965), 84.

[39] BL Add. MS 18,781–2.

in London and the country from the 1640s to the end of the century. Three volumes covering 1644–6, kept by John Gell, the son of the notorious parliamentarian commander Sir John Gell, and his wife Katherine, have been used in this analysis. Katherine Gell, the daughter of a leading Westminster Puritan and parliamentarian, John Packer, and her husband were noted patrons of Presbyterian ministers throughout their lives, and associated closely with political Presbyterianism in the 1640s and 1650s.[40]

The notes vary. There are summaries, apparently from memory, such as the five numbered paragraphs in which Boothby summed up a sermon by Edmund Calamy in 1646 on 'Whether Christs death be effectual to all', or the longer notes made by Wallington in November 1643: 'And because I would never forget it, I have here set down those few broken scraps which I brought home with me, the Lord of his mercy wright them with the finger of his holy Spirit in the Table of my heart.'[41] Both Gells and Yonge constructed relatively full accounts of many sermons in small notebooks apparently used in the church, Yonge occasionally resorting to a simple short-hand and idiosyncratic abbreviations. Harper's single, long notebook incorporates a variety of techniques: two of Harper's versions were paragraph-long summaries written from memory when he got home, while the lengthiest notes may depend on privileged access to the preachers' own texts, but most of the sermons are endorsed, 'Written this sermon from my note books from the mouth of him when he preached the same', indicating a prior short-hand record.[42]

There is a half-submerged tendency in some of the literature on preaching to assume that hearers' notes give a more authentic account of the sermon as preached, or at least a more accurate account than the printed text. But as John Spurr has cautioned, it is important to be clear about the 'original context' for note-taking. Although some took notes for directly instrumental purposes, such as to publish a printed version, with or without the minister's cooperation, for most lay people, the notes were part of a 'a personal regime of piety'.[43] Furthermore, all sermon

---

[40] William Lamont, 'Gell (nee Packer), Katherine (bap. 1624, d. 1671', *ODNB*; for their political sympathies, see, for example, Derbyshire Record Office (DRO), Papers of the Gells of Hopton, D258/10/9/9, a letter written by Katherine's mother Phyllis Packer on the plight of the MPs secluded at Pride's Purge. Some sixty volumes of sermon notes are in DRO D3287/boxes 24 and 25. D3287/24/1 is Katherine Gell's book; /25/5, 19 are John's.

[41] Bodl. MS Eng c 2693, 157; BL Add. MS 40,883, fo. 165r (and see *Notebooks*, ed. Booy, 207). In fact, Wallington left three pages of very coherent notes with numbered points and scriptural references, and the broken scraps were perhaps written notes rather than memories.

[42] Endorsement on notes from Richard Culverwell's sermon on the Protestation: Clark MS B8535 M3, second sequence, 113.

[43] Spurr, *Laity and Preaching*, 32; cf. Green, *Change and Continuity*. An earlier version of Marshall's 'Meroz Cursed', preached in Dec. 1641 at St Sepulchre's London, for example, was 'published in one sheet of paper (not by the Author) but by a lover of the truth, for their

notebooks have particular material forms, indicative of specific textual characteristics and histories.

Walter Boothby's notebook is the most generically complex. As Spurr has noted, it is 'in the process of mutating into a commonplace book', while the latter sections of the volume are a letter book. Notes from a November 1648 sermon by the eminent Presbyterian Edmund Calamy, 'How we may know our interest in Jesus Christ to be reall & good', are dispersed with much cross-referencing into sections on Christ, on love (of God), on Merit and so on. Notes from sermons are also deployed in Boothby's letters, sometimes decades after they were preached, Boothby reminding his sister in May 1662 of 'that grave advice which Mr Callamy gave you & I in a sermon preached 1641' in a letter dealing with their hopes of heaven, with sin and the need to avoid playhouses.[44]

The more conventional sermon notebooks reveal their enduring value for individual reflection. As John Harper noted from a sermon preached by William Jaggard at St Margaret Moses in February 1650, 'it is not how many sermons you heare, but what you remember at those sermons, and how you labour to work them upon your soul'.[45] Similarly, a Derbyshire minister counselling Katherine Gell on the spiritual distress to which she was too often subject, explained, 'the usefullest excercises of all piety, its a soules preaching to itselfe, without which the preacher from the pulpit doth little good'. Working through sermon notes helped a soul to preach to itself: 'to helpe you may use any book or sermon notes you have upon that subject you would meditate on'.[46] Katherine and John Gell often took notes on the same sermons; their books show signs of mutual checking and revision, and the couples' notebooks became precious and enduring family heirlooms. Their godly daughter Elizabeth read over her parents' notes in the 1670s, adding systematic lists of preachers. The volumes were listed in the inventory of her possessions taken after her death in 1705.[47]

Wallington's sermon notes were part of a life-long project, a perpetual construction, examination and renewal of his godly life, within his family and community, through an exhausting programme of writing, meditation, letter collections, tracts and treatises, frequently reread and

good especially that are not able to buy bigger books': *Meroz Curse* (1641), title page. When Simeon Ashe heard a shorthand note-taker was planning to publish a sermon delivered on the day of Charles I's attempt to arrest the five members, he decided to cooperate in its publication, clarifying and amplifying arguments and scriptural references: Ashe, *A Supporter for the Sinking Heart in Times of Distresse* (1642), A2r–v.

44 Spurr, *Laity and Preaching*, 18–19; Bodl. MS Eng c 2693, 4, 75, 834–7; Adam Smyth, *Autobiography in Early Modern England* (Cambridge, 2010), 123–58, on commonplacing as the appropriation of 'public texts' including sermons, for personal purposes.

45 Clark MS B8535 M3, second sequence, 151.

46 DRO D3287/47/7, 89–91.

47 DRO D258/38/1.

revised: 'my chiefe aime and ende of my writting of those books was for the praise and glory of my God'.[48] The notes served for personal reflection and for the characteristic practice of 'repetition' within Wallington's family, as with the 'broken scraps' of November 1643:

> This sweet word of God revived me and was profitable unto me: yet in the Afternoone I was somewhat barren & could get but little benifet by Gods Ordinance: yet at night when we ware all parting to our beds Some words of exortation I spake to my family not to forget the instructions which God hath made knowen to us but to remember them all the weeke Longe.[49]

Like the Gell's volumes, Wallington's notebooks passed down the generations. 'The groth of a Christian', a volume mostly of sermon notes focused on effective preparation for the sacrament was begun in January 1641 and completed in December 1643, read over in spring 1658, and in his son-in-law's possession after Wallington's death later that year.[50]

From internal evidence, Harper's volume was constructed from earlier notes in the mid-1650s, almost certainly in the early stages of hearing a long sermon series on 'severall heads of Divinity', the fundamentals of the Christian faith preached by his parish minister Benjamin Needler. A sense that these fundamentals were under attack in the 1650s seems to have prompted Harper to copy out the extensive notes he had made in his youth from the sermons of Needler's father-in-law and predecessor, the moderate Calvinist Richard Culverwell's, along with other 'brief notes' into a single book. The reassertion of his orthodox upbringing brought reassurance in a period of division and dispute.[51]

The sermon notes made by these conscientious hearers place the immediate, dramatic, polemical fast sermons, tied to particularly urgent conjunctures in the fortunes of the parliament and nation, within more personal, more enduring contexts. These hearers were not necessarily opposed or resistant to the more political or controversial messages of the sermons (although Harper probably was) but these were not necessarily

---

[48]'An Extract of the Passages of my Life or the Booke of all my Writting Books' (Folger Shakespeare Library MS V.a. 436), quoted in *Notebooks*, ed. Booy, 10.

[49]BL Add. MS 40,883, fo. 167v; Ryrie, *Being Protestant*, 359.

[50]*Notebooks*, ed. Booy, 47.

[51] Harper organised his notebook in distinct sections, some separately paginated. From the front, it begins with notes on a series of sermons by Richard Culverwell on the Lord's Prayer (1626–7) followed by a further Culverwell series on the Sacraments (1628–9); notes on sixteen occasional sermons heard between May 1641 and Feb. 1657, including one recorded from memory in Oct. 1656; Culverwell's sermons on the Creed (beginning in 1630); Benjamin Needler on 'severall heads of Divinity' beginning in Aug. 1655 and ending with his farewell sermon in Aug. 1662; and sermons by Needler's successor Charles Burke between 1662 and 1665. Another set of 'occasional sermons', from Aug. 1657 to May 1661, is written from the back of the volume: Clark MS B8535 M3. For a fuller account of Harper's notes, especially of the Culverwell sermons of the 1620s and early 1630s, see my 'A Moderate Puritan Preacher Negotiates Religious Change', *Journal of Ecclesiastical History*, 65 (2014), 761–79.

the most relevant elements for the purposes of personal note-taking.[52] Fast sermons were but part of the preaching available in London in the 1640s and 1650s. The notebooks of Harper and the Gells help us identify how listening to high-profile sermons on special public occasions took place within complex patterns of preaching attendance. It is not clear whether there was more preaching than ever in the city under Puritan rule. The usually gloomy Wallington was optimistic here, but modern scholars are more cautious. Against the regular fast days and the preaching exercises that flourished in some parishes, we must set the disruption of routine parish preaching in a city where 96 per cent of parish clergy were ejected in the early 1640s, and where revival of parochial religion was delayed and disrupted in many parishes by lack of ministers and increasing religious conflict and fragmentation.[53] The sermons Harper noted included thirty-four sermons preached on special occasions, including some dramatic fast days at St Paul's Cathedral (as he continued to call it) in the 1640s and 1650s: he heard William Gouge on heresy in March 1647, Stephen Marshall on peace negotiations in September 1648 and Edmund Calamy in March 1656 as the English fleet sailed to the Caribbean, but most of his notes are extended versions of more conventional, pastoral sermon-series preached in his own parish by Needler and Culverwell, the latter taking up more than half the volume. There is only one sermon from the parish noted between 1641 and 1650, whether this is because of disruption to parish life, or of Harper's choice of what to copy from earlier notes is impossible to say.

When in London, the Gells lived mainly in Twickenham, where they usually kept the major fast days, but they also spent time at Westminster with Katherine's parents. Stephen Marshall's preaching was precious to Katherine Gell in particular; as she explained to Richard Baxter much later, she had been converted by Marshall in the early 1640s and had subsequently 'received much comfort from him' through personal discussion and reading his books as well as through his preaching.[54] The three 1640s Gell volumes examined here confirm Marshall's reputation as an indefatigable preacher in and around Westminster, beyond the

---

[52] Walter Yonge is a partial exception, to be discussed below. The royalist historian William Dugdale's notes on the dramatic preaching of the fifth monarchist Christopher Feake in Aug. and Sept. 1653 offer another contrast. Dugdale's notes (without critical comment) concentrated on Feake's denunciations of earthly monarchy, suggesting a more directly political (and historical) motivation for note-taking: Merivale Hall, Dugdale MS HT 10/44.

[53] Cf. Ian Green, 'Preaching in the Parishes', in *Oxford Handbook of the Early Modern Sermon*, ed. McCullough, Adlington and Rhatigan, 137–54, at 150–1.

[54] *Calendar of the Correspondence of Richard Baxter*, ed. N. H. Keeble, and Geoffrey F. Nuttall (2 vols., Oxford, 1991), I, 185–6, July 1655. Included in the Gell Papers are full, fair copy notes from unpublished Marshall fast sermons that are perhaps taken from the minister's notes lent to John and Katherine Gell: DRO D258/34/14/1 (May 1646).

well-known fast days. But this was rarely the Marshall of *Meroz Cursed*, for the Gell notes (like some of Harper's) highlight rather his ability to deliver vivid and elaborate explications of biblical texts, and to present a sensitive pastoral message. In a volume covering November 1644 – May 1645, John Gell noted seventy-eight sermons, some three a week, almost half of them (thirty-three) given by Marshall. Some were fast sermons at St Margaret's, but more were from the pastorally focused morning lectures given in a rota by Marshall and other preachers at Westminster Abbey. In these weeks, Marshall was preaching on preparation for taking the sacrament from 1 Corinthians chapter 11.[55] Similarly, in two overlapping notebooks from 1645–6, Marshall is again a favourite. John's 'begun at Westminster June 27 1645 and ended at Wirksworth in Derbyshire Sept. 6 1646' records forty-five sermons; seven out of some twelve London and Westminster sermons were preached by Marshall – all but one on John 8.36. The sermon notes focus on salvation and on love of Christ.[56] Katherine's notebook ('begun at Westminster March 1 1645[/6] and ended at Darly in Darbyshire July 29 1646') includes notes on fifty-nine sermons in this shorter period; again there are twenty-four in Twickenham, against twenty-two in Westminster or London, with twelve in Derbyshire at the end. Over half (twelve) of the metropolitan occasions feature Marshall, and the majority (seven) look like a pastorally focused series on sanctification, based on 1 Thessalonians 5.23.[57] The most difficult issues indeed are noted from the provincial sermons of Martin Topham in Wirksworth, defending *jure divino* Presbyterian church government in the summer of 1646.[58]

Harper's notebook offers similar conclusions: the predominance in his notebook of parish-based sermon-series on the fundamentals of the Christian faith in itself suggests a relative lack of interest in doctrinal debate or overtly political preaching. Harper's notes on two unpublished fast sermons include controversial material within a broader, more conventional emphasis. His notes on Edmund Calamy's sermon in St Paul's Cathedral, at the fast to bless the expedition to the Indies (March 1656) registered Calamy's frank comments on the Lord Protector:

> As God tould David, Because he was a man of blood, that had made great warres, therefore he should not build him an house, 1. Chronicles 22.8. So it may be God hath not appointed this our Governour to setle a reformacon bec(ause) he hath shedd much blood, and hath made great warres.

But Harper was more concerned with sanctification (a preoccupation of the pre-war Culverwell notes), and with Calamy's exhortations to the city

[55] DRO D3287/25/19.
[56] DRO D3287/box 25/5.
[57] D3287/box 24/1.
[58] D3287/box 25/5, fos. 111v–115v.

magistrates (Harper amongst them) to religious and moral reformation.[59] Similarly, from the sermon Harper (on a rare visit to St Margaret's Westminster) heard Stephen Marshall give in August 1648 on Isaiah 28.29, 'to implore of God a blessing on the Treaty of peace, with the King', he did include a paragraph on 'the present business of our meeting' but most of the four pages of notes were taken up with Marshall's account of the Old Testament context, and more general pastoral and moral 'uses'.[60]

The early 1640s notebooks of Walter Yonge are more preoccupied with the political messages in monthly fast sermons and 5 November commemorations. In autumn 1642, an unnamed preacher at All-Hallows, Lombard Street, recalled the 'Egyptian darknes' when 'a tradesmans goods, a gentlemans lands, a ministers liberty to preach & to serve God, could never be exercised by reason of monopolyes, ship money, star chamber, high commission, popish superstitions, ceremonye'. The following spring a Mr Broom at St Peter's Cornhill insisted there could be no safety for those who wished 'all the Roundheads had but one neck to strike'. Perhaps Yonge was more interested in noting political allusions than Gell or Harper, or perhaps issues were more starkly expressed in the early 1640s when enemies were more easily identified and parliamentarian hopes undashed. Yonge 'gadded' to more parishes than the Gells or Harper. But Yonge's notebooks, like Gell's or Harper's, all made extensive notes on more conventional series of sermons, by the prominent future Presbyterians William Jenkins at Christ Church and James Cranford at St Christopher's, not here in polemical mode but preparing for the sacrament in Cranford's case and painstakingly interpreting the Song of Song in Jenkins'.[61]

IV

John Gell, Yonge and Harper all took notes on sermons that found their way into print, and their efforts confirm the recent studies that suggest a conscientious, trained hearer could produce a recognisable account of a sermon as delivered (or at least one that is recognisable from the

---

[59] Clark MS B8535 M3, second sequence, 156–8, examples include: 'unlesse you be justified and sanctified, all your services are abominable to God, your prayers are as the howlings of doggs'; 'If I could see the feilds empty one the Lords day, and his saboth day better kept; If I could see all the truly godly agree in doctrine, and united in love; If I could see the tavernes and alehowses lesse frequented, and the Churches more.'

[60] Clark MS B8535 M3, second sequence, 142–6: 'The present businesse of the Treaty is the occasion of our meeting this day, by fasting and prayer to implore of God his blessing upon, and a good successe to it. I know many are aweary of war, and many afraid of making an unsound peace.'

[61] BL Add. MS 18,781, fos. 134v, 28r. BL Add. MS 18,782 has Jenkins's regular sermons noted from the front, and fast sermons, also mainly at Christ Church from the back.

printed version). There was a productive interaction between preaching styles and note-taking culture, with the characteristic structure of sermons, organised around scriptural texts, doctrines and uses, facilitating concentration and effective note-taking.[62] Both contemporaries and modern scholars have pondered the complex relationship between hearers' notes, and a printed version, and the 'intractable' matter of how either version represents what was delivered.[63] Juxtaposing a manuscript and a printed version nonetheless offers some suggestive insights. One example must suffice here: John Gell's notes on Marshall's fast sermon, 30 April 1645, published shortly afterwards. Gell's is a decent summary in the main: he does not note a technical analysis of the Hebrew text (which might have been added for the press), and he drastically abbreviates the biblical stories which surely Marshall did give at length, confining himself to brief comments, such as 'thus David did'. More remarkably, however, he misses most of the overt contemporary references to England, Germany, Scotland and Ireland, to focus more specifically on the purposes of prayer in aiding reformation and comforting God's people in distress. Gell included Marshall's general exhortations on the necessity of the Saints' prayers to the building of Sion, but he was not struck by a passage in which Marshall bemoaned the lack of zeal in fast days: 'Thus follow him with a mourning heart, a melting eye, do it constantly, doe it daily, I confesse these monthly fasts are grown to a most wretched formality in many places, the Lord of heaven teach us how we may be more quickened in this great work of prayer.'[64] It would be odd for Marshall not to make this point to his immediate auditors; perhaps Gell did not see these remarks as applying to him.

---

[62] Hunt, *Art of Hearing*, 95–9; Spurr, *Laity and Preaching*, 12–13. Yonge, for example, took about 2,250 words of a sermon preached by Walter Bridges at the fast day 22 Feb. 1642/3, although he had not caught the preacher's name: BL Add. MS 18,781, fos. 10r–16r. The printed sermon, *Joabs Counsell and King Davids Seasonable Hearing It* (1643), is broadly similar although the notes stress more stridently the necessity for the king to heed good counsel. Thomason received his copy on 9 Mar. so there was, as usual, little opportunity for revision. Harper's notebook includes 1,500 words of notes on a sermon preached by Henry Hibbert at St Pauls on 29 May 1661 in celebration of Charles II's restoration, and his birthday: Clark MS B8535 M3, unpaginated section written from the back. It was published as *Regina Dierum or the Joyful Day* (1661). Again, the two versions correspond closely in structure and message.

[63] Hunt, *Art of Hearing*, 146–9, 155, 159–61, 352; Morissey, *Politics and the Paul's Cross Sermons*, 48–66; Spurr, *Laity and Preaching*, 26–7, are representative of subtle, wide-ranging scholarship. By the mid-seventeenth century, the prejudice against printed sermons had largely evaporated and hearing, reading and writing were seen as different valuable ways of apprehending sermons. Printed versions of sermons, as Hunt has explained, often presented illusions of immediacy and orality.

[64] *The Strong Helper or The Interest and Power of the Prayers of the Destitute for the Building up of Sion* (1645), 4, 53; DRO D3287/25/19, fos. 97v–102r.

V

The paradoxes of these years can be illustrated in conclusion by returning briefly to the initial broadside's evocation of the Morning Exercise, that itself attracted lively and often inter-connected manuscript and printed commentary. Founded by the Presbyterian Thomas Case in response to the royalist sack and capture of Leicester in spring 1645, the Morning Exercise might be seen as a pastoral alternative to the politically engaged sermons of parliamentary fast days, a programme that Elliot Vernon has described as a combination of 'evangelistic outreach and catechetical instruction', whereby over a whole month in a different parish a succession of ministers preached a brief early morning sermon.[65] The approach of the exercise to nearby parishes in March 1654 prompted Wallington to reflect enthusiastically on transformations in London preaching, on 'the many thousands of sarmons that have been preached and yet no lesse in this Fountain of the word which stremith forth so long as the world continueth'. He looked forward to the 'sweet profitabl veriety of the word' such an exercise afforded, and noted that the exercise would come in April 1654 to St Andrew Hubbard, 'a parish where my Father [lived] VIII yeers and never heard one sarmon where I here many a one in a weeke'.[66] Wallington's notes on the exercise have not survived, but three sets of notes (two of them known from printed books) suggest qualifications to Wallington's straightforward enthusiasm for their evangelical character. In 1648, a hostile hearer from John Goodwin's Independent church took notes of the Presbyterian ministers' denunciations of the army and the parliament during their preaching at the exercise, reproducing them in angry capitals in a printed pamphlet.[67] Presbyterians in response claimed that 'constant and conscientious hearers' found the sermons 'as hony to their tasts and marrow to their bones', rising early for them, 'winter and summer, wet and dry', while accepting that one of their aims was 'to discover the evills and errours of the times impartially, that Gods people may be humbled for them, and avoid them'.[68]

By the mid-1650s, Presbyterian hopes of a reformed national church were dashed, and even a man like Thomas Case, arrested for royalist plotting in 1651, had come to terms with the Cromwellian regime;

---

[65] Thomas Case, *The Morning Exercise or Some Short Notes Taken out of the Morning Sermons... Preached in St Giles in the Fields... May 1655* (1655); Nehemiah Wallington, 'A Record of Marcys Continued or yet God Is Good to Israel', Tatton Park MS 68.20, quoted from *Notebooks*, ed. Booy, 19–21; Elliot Vernon, 'A Ministry of the Gospel: The Presbyterians during the English Revolution', in *Religion in Revolutionary England*, ed. Christopher Durston and Judith Maltby (Manchester, 2006), 115–36, at 121–2.

[66] Folger MS V. a. 436, quoted from *Notebooks*, ed. Booy, 298–9.

[67] [John Price], *The Pulpit Incendiary* (1648); it was this sermon gadding and hostile note-taking that Walwyn denounced in *Walwyn's Just Defence*.

[68] *The Pulpit Incendiary Anatomized* (1648), 3–4, 8.

passions were less heated and to some extent Wallington's view of the Morning Exercise as a uncontroversial pastoral initiative focusing on personal reformation is supported by other evidence. Case published brief accounts of the sermons preached in St Giles in the Fields in May 1655, based in the main on 'notes being taken from the Pulpit to my hand', framed by his own introduction and a final sermon in which he offered 'a summary rehearsal' of the intervening ones (in the manner of pre-civil war Spital sermons).[69] In January 1659, the Morning Exercise finally arrived at John Harper's own small parish, St Margaret Moses, and in a manner characteristic of his moderate Puritan, parish-focused piety, Harper preserved his notes on at least six of them. Both Case's printed version and Harper's manuscript notes combine conventional, pastoral exhortations and references to God's providences with more pointed, controversial matter, unavoidable and unmistakeable traces of the divisions and perplexities of the times. In Case's concluding sermon, he insisted that amongst the dispensations of God was the sending of thirty properly ordained ministers to the parish to preach the word: 'he hath not sent gifted brethren among you, he hath not sent loose and debauched men of wretched principles, to speak to you the vision of their hearts'.[70] Harper's notes stressed the need for Christians to devote themselves to 'meditation of things above; examination of mans owne heart, mortifying of sinnes &c' and to avoid the hypocrisy of being 'a Saint in the Church and a cheate in his shop' . But he also recorded 'That it is the duty of Christians to have noe communion with hereticks, from such turne away' and warnings about the dangers of sinfulness amongst apparently godly 'professors'.[71]

It turns out that simple contrasts are unhelpful and that conventional, pastoral preaching and the set-piece, high-profile, controversial sermons are difficult to untangle in the records of hearers. Notes on fast sermons do not stress the immediate political imperatives of the day, whereas, particularly from the perspective of a very moderate hearer like John Harper, we can see that no routine, allegedly uncontroversial preaching could evade the religious conflicts and fragmentation of the 1640s and 1650s, as the dilemmas of a religious marketplace penetrated the most routine and didactic sermons on the fundamentals of the faith or at a Morning Exercise. It might be argued that that tendency of note-takers

---

[69]Michael Mullett, 'Case, Thomas (bap. 1598, d. 1682)', *ODNB*; Case, *Morning Exercise*, 86. For the Easter Spital sermons where a sermon preached at Paul's Cross on Good Friday and three sermons in Easter week at St Mary's Spital were commented on in a final sermon, see Morrissey, *Politics and the Paul's Cross Sermons*, 21–2.

[70]Case, *Morning Exercise*, A2r, 54–5.

[71] Clark MS B8535 M3, unpaginated section, written from the end; from the morning lecture preached on Saturday 15 Jan. by Mr Cooper. The previous day's lecture was on damnable heresies.

to underplay the more immediate, political references in the fast sermons is evidence for their overall failure as propaganda or inspiration, but this would be to ignore the specific character and lasting purposes of sermon noting. On the contrary, the dynamic parliamentary fast sermons of the revolution may well have worked to rally hearers to the parliamentary cause (or versions of it) precisely because they could also be absorbed and understood on a variety of levels, as enduring prompts to personal piety and reflection, or as arresting explications of biblical history. A distinctive revolutionary Puritan culture – the culture of fast days and *Meroz Cursed* – allowed for complex engagements and drew on long-standing practices of strenuous Puritan piety in hearing, recording, reflecting on and discussing sermons.

Transactions of the RHS 24 (2014), pp. 79–103 © Royal Historical Society 2014
doi:10.1017/S0080440114000048

'THE HONEST TRADESMAN'S HONOUR':
OCCUPATIONAL AND SOCIAL IDENTITY IN
SEVENTEENTH-CENTURY ENGLAND*

The Rees Davies Prize Essay

By Mark Hailwood

ABSTRACT. This paper starts from the proposition that historians of identity in
the early modern period have paid insufficient attention to the significance of
occupations and work. It demonstrates one possible approach to this topic by
exploring the social identity of a particular occupational group – tradesmen –
through a study of a particular source – printed broadside ballads. A number of
important conclusions result: it argues that historians have overstated the dominance
of craft-specific consciousness in the formation of early modern work-based identity
(a term that is offered as a more helpful alternative to that of occupational identity),
and suggests that broad-based identifiers such as 'tradesman' had a real purchase in
contemporary discourse. It also considers the extent to which broader changes in
the seventeenth-century economy – especially growing commercialisation and the
increasing complexity of credit relations – affected the identity of the tradesman.
Although the tension between the hard-working tradesman and the prodigal
gentleman in ballad portraits suggests a growing social confidence on the part of
the former, the marketplace is depicted to be as much a threat as an opportunity for
tradesmen given the fragility of credit relationships. Moreover, the paper examines
the gender dimensions of this occupational identity, arguing that a 'female voice'
was central to ballad discussions of masculine ideals, and that the tradesman's
patriarchal authority was generally portrayed as insecure. At its heart, the paper is
an exploration of the intersection of class, gender and occupational identities in a
period of economic change.

The understandings of the greater part of men are necessarily formed by their ordinary
employment.[1]

Adam Smith

* This paper is the product of an Economic History Society Tawney Fellowship. Earlier
versions were presented as a conference paper at the North American Conference on British
Studies (my attendance at which was generously funded by the Royal Historical Society),
and a seminar paper at the Institute of Historical Research. My thanks to the audiences
at both for their feedback, and to Henry French, Steve Hindle, Alex Shepard and Brodie
Waddell for reading and commenting on drafts of the paper.
[1] Adam Smith, *An Inquiry into the Nature and Causes of the Wealth of Nations*,
ed. R. H. Campbell and A. S. Skinner (Oxford, 1976), II, 781–2.

I am seeking to rescue the poor *stockinger*, the Luddite *cropper*, the 'obsolete' hand-loom *weaver*, the 'utopian' *artisan*... from the enormous condescension of posterity.[2]

E. P. *Thompson*

Fifty years on, Thompson's statement of intent to create a 'history from below' focused on labouring people in the pre-industrial world undoubtedly has a clichéd ring to it. The principle enshrined in these oft-cited lines has long been a fundamental driving force for historians writing the social history of early modern England.[3] It might seem, therefore, like an odd quote to deploy in calling for a new direction in that field. Yet, for all its familiarity, one of its key implications has been continually overlooked: the importance of occupational identity to the people at the centre of our studies.

When Thompson defined his intended subjects, the identifier he most often deployed was occupational: the stockinger; the cropper; the weaver, the artisan. The assumption was the same as that held by Adam Smith: men were what they did. For historians who have sought to rescue the experiences of non-elite men and women from the margins of sixteenth- and seventeenth-century English history, such an assumption has rarely been their starting point. In the best introduction to identity in this period, the question of 'the most important determining element of identity' – whether individual or collective – considers a range of possibilities: 'was it economic position or social power or cultural knowledge or religious opinion or regional origin or gender role or ethnic character?'[4] Whilst an individual's occupation may be connected to such factors, it is not accorded the status of a primary determinant of identity in the way it was for Thompson and Smith.

This may result from a perception that occupational identity in this period was relatively weak, 'frustrated by the tendency of so many individuals to combine different occupations or to move from one form of employment to another'.[5] There is evidence that attests to the contrary. The common use of an affix of occupation as a form of address and identification in the period – 'Arnold the Carpenter', 'Clarke the Mason', 'King the Thatcher' – can be seen frequently in account

---

[2] E. P. Thompson, *The Making of the English Working Class* (1963), 'Preface'. My italics.

[3] Although Thompson was writing about the eighteenth century, I am focusing here on his influence on the social history of the sixteenth and seventeenth centuries, which arguably has been more significant: see Mark Hailwood and Brodie Waddell, 'Plebeian Cultures in Early Modern England: 35 Years after E.P. Thompson', *Social History*, 34, 4 (2009), 472–6.

[4] Henry French with Jonathan Barry, 'Identity and Agency in English Society, 1500–1800 – Introduction', in *Identity and Agency in England, 1500–1800*, in Henry French and Jonathan Barry (Basingstoke, 2004), 1.

[5] Keith Thomas, *The Ends of Life: Roads to Fulfilment in Early Modern England* (Oxford, 2010), 106.

books and in particular as a way of denoting tradesmen, reminding us of the 'bygone equation of man and job'.[6] Contemporaries thought this equation determined more than just nomenclature: a man's occupation was thought to leave a physical imprint, and could be identified by the deformations it inflicted upon the body. Tailors and bakers could be identified by their legs, miners by the pallor of their skin and porters by their 'thick, strong and brawny' backs and shoulders.[7] Two recent books have drawn on such evidence to argue that occupation was indeed an important aspect of early modern identity. Given that work was expected to fill most of the daylight hours, Keith Thomas has suggested that it was 'almost impossible to throw off an occupational identity outside working hours' and therefore men 'usually looked to their work as the source of their sense of identity'.[8] Brodie Waddell has revived an older argument that far from being inherently weak, occupational identities in early modern England were so strong as to have created a sense of 'fraternal unity' within trades that served to inhibit 'inter-occupational solidarity' and 'disrupted the appeal of "class" identity' in the period.[9]

This paper starts from the proposition that historians therefore need to pay greater attention to the ways contemporaries understood the relationship between their occupation and their identity in seventeenth-century England. It does so by concentrating on a certain type of source – broadside ballads – and on a particular, albeit ambiguous, occupational group: tradesmen. The next section makes the case for using broadside ballads to investigate early modern occupational identity. The third section explains the focus on tradesmen, exploring definitions of this group and their changing role in early modern society. A longer fourth section offers an analysis of some of the key features of the tradesman's identity as represented by seventeenth-century ballads. These are examined in relation to the three contexts that John Tosh has identified as central to masculine identity: all-male association, work and the home, slightly reconfigured here as alehouse sociability, market exchange and marital relations.[10]

Within these parameters, the paper makes four main arguments. All of these may require revision when considered in relation to other occupations and alternative source material: indeed, it is my intention that they serve as an agenda for further research on this theme, rather

---

[6] David Postles, *Social Proprieties: Social Relations in Early Modern England, 1500–1680* (Washington, DC, 2006), 19–20; Thomas, *The Ends of Life*, 107.

[7] Thomas, *The Ends of Life*, 107.

[8] *Ibid.*, 106–8.

[9] Brodie Waddell, *God, Duty and Community in English Economic Life, 1660–1720* (Woodbridge, 2012), 205.

[10] John Tosh, 'What Should Historians Do with Masculinity?', *History Workshop Journal*, 38 (1994), 185–7.

than as definitive conclusions. The first is that historians' neglect of the influence of work on identity should not be overcompensated for by elevating occupation to the status of principle determinant in the way that Smith and Thompson did. It is neither possible nor appropriate to isolate occupational identity from other determinants such as gender, age or social status, and the call made here is to *integrate* occupation into our understanding of identity, and in particular to encourage historians to consider *how* occupation influenced identity, rather simply to assert its centrality. To this end, the second argument developed here is that occupational identity may not be the most fruitful category with which to think about the relationship between work and identity, if occupation is understood in narrow terms as relating to working in a specific trade or craft. Rather, broader categories such as 'tradesman', which demarcated a group with similar work experiences but made up of individuals working in a range of more specific occupations, had considerable influence on the way contemporaries understood the relationship between work and identity. It may be more appropriate to think of occupational identity in terms of broader 'work-based', rather than the narrower 'craft-specific', identities. The third key argument is that such work-based identities are best understood as a 'prism' through which early modern people sought to make sense of their experiences, rather than necessarily as a direct product of experiences that were peculiar to particular types of worker. Experiences that were in actual fact common to people in a diverse range of different types of work were often *understood* as being a product of engagement in a specific type of work: general experiences became particularised by individuals as part of a work-based identity. The fourth argument is that work-based identities were not always positive. As we will see, for many seventeenth-century tradesmen constructing and projecting a positive sense of identity would have proved a 'Herculean task'.[11]

Broadside ballads and social identity

Once described as 'one of the great neglected forms of evidence for early modern mentality', the seventeenth-century broadside ballad has now become widely regarded as a valuable source for social and cultural historians.[12] They are thought to represent the most popular form of print in early modern England, and were purchased by both gentlemen collectors and pasted on walls in the cottages of poor husbandmen. As

---

[11] This reflects a similar conclusion reached in relation to labouring men and women by Alexandra Shepard, in 'Poverty, Labour and the Language of Social Description in Early Modern England', *Past and Present*, 201 (2008), 95. My own conclusions here to some extent represent a caveat on those offered in my 'Sociability, Work and Labouring Identity in Seventeenth-Century England', *Cultural and Social History*, 8, 1 (2011), 9–29.

[12] Anthony Fletcher, *Gender, Sex and Subordination in England, 1500–1800* (1995), 'Preface'.

such, Tessa Watt suggests they are uniquely placed to provide historians with access to 'shared values', 'widespread attitudes' and 'commonplace mentalities'.[13] The fact that they were consumed across the social scale does not prove that consumers necessarily, still less universally, subscribed to the attitudes they expressed, however. Precisely how ballads and their meanings were received and understood by contemporaries will always remain to some extent an 'elusive quarry', and as such the conclusions that follow should be understood as suggestive rather than definitive.[14] Nonetheless, whilst the contents of any given ballad may have served alternatively to enrage, to amuse or perhaps even to flatter different readers and hearers, by paying attention to recurring themes and tropes across a number of ballads, we can begin to glimpse the contours of a cultural landscape that would have been familiar to a broad cross-section of contemporaries.

This potential has been recognised in recent work that has effectively mined ballads for contemporary discourses surrounding politics, religion, marriage, alehouse sociability, old age, economic morality, vagrancy and fashion.[15] They also represent an untapped resource for the study of work-based identity, as occupational groups were commonly chosen as a focus for ballads. Ballads celebrating the shoemaking trade were, for instance, particularly popular, describing this occupation as 'the gentle craft', and reciting the proverb that 'a shoemaker's son is a Gentleman

---

[13] Tessa Watt, *Cheap Print and Popular Piety, 1550–1640* (Cambridge, 1991), 3.

[14] For scepticism about our ability to 'recapture the way in which [printed ballads] might have been read or heard, internalized and appropriated', see Adam Fox, 'Ballads, Libels and Popular Ridicule in Jacobean England', *Past and Present*, 145 (1994), 47–8. For a study that looks to mitigate problems of reception through a close reading of ballad form and content, see Natascha Wurzbach, *The Rise of the English Street Ballad* (Cambridge, 1990).

[15] Angela McShane Jones, 'Roaring Royalists and Ranting Brewers: The Politicisation of Drink and Drunkenness in Political Broadside Ballads from 1640 to 1689', in *A Pleasing Sinne: Drink and Conviviality in Seventeenth Century England*, ed. Adam Smyth (Cambridge, 2004), 69–87; Angela McShane, '"Ne sutor ultra crepidam": Political Cobblers and Broadside Ballads in Late Seventeenth-Century England', in *Ballads and Broadsides in Britain, 1500–1800*, ed. Patricia Fumerton, Anita Guerrini and Kris McAbee (Farnham, 2010), 207–28; Watt, *Cheap Print*; James Sharpe, 'Plebeian Marriage in Stuart England: Some Evidence from Popular Literature', *Transactions of the Royal Historical Society*, fifth series, 36 (1986), 69–90; Elizabeth Foyster, 'A Laughing Matter? Marital Discord and Gender Control in Seventeenth-Century England', *Rural History*, 4 (1993), 5–21; Mark Hailwood, *Alehouses and Good Fellowship in Early Modern England* (Woodbridge, 2014); Alice Tobriner, 'Old Age in Tudor–Stuart Broadside Ballads', *Folklore*, 102 (1991), 149–74; Waddell, *God, Duty and Community*; David Hitchcock, 'The Experience and Construction of the Vagabond in England, 1650–1750 (Ph.D. diss., University of Warwick, 2012); Patricia Fumerton, 'Not Home: Alehouses, Ballads, and the Vagrant Husband in Early Modern England', *Journal of Medieval and Early Modern Studies*, 32, 3 (2002), 493–518; Angela McShane and Claire Backhouse, 'Top-Knots and Lower Sorts: Popular Print and Promiscuous Consumption in Late Seventeenth-Century England', in *Printed Images in Early Modern Britain: Essays in Interpretation*, ed. Michael Hunter (2010), 337–57.

born'.[16] Not all ballads dealing with shoemakers were so flattering. The ballad *The Shooemaker Out-witted* lampooned the celebratory self-image of the 'gentle craft', detailing how one over-proud shoemaker had sought a wife with a generous dowry to raise his fortune to a level fitting for a man of such noble calling. Yet, duped by a 'crafty lass of Surrey', who had simply borrowed money to make her appear affluent, the shoemaker was 'caught in a snare' with a penniless and disrespectful wife, who 'laughs in Derision and calls me her Fool, / And declares that I have but a pittiful Tool.'[17] The use of a favourite technique of occupational ballads – the reference to a tradesman's 'tool' as a euphemism for his sexual prowess – served to humiliate further the shoemaker, and hammered home the point that occupational pride was just that – the sin of pride – and usually precipitated a humbling. As the contemporary proverb put it: 'Look *high* and fall into a cowturd.'[18]

That ballads often characterised occupational groups gives them value as indicators of one of the key components of social identity identified by the sociologist Richard Jenkins: forms of external categorisation, or one of the ways in which social groups are defined by others.[19] Such definitions have utility for the historian of identity in two respects. First, although potentially pejorative or exaggerated, such categorisations of social groups tended to have some basis in the reality of how these groups were understood and encountered by their contemporaries: as Henry French has argued, printed stereotypes of social description only found purchase if they were 'sufficiently consonant with the lived experience of the literate public to appear to offer reliable characterisations of society'.[20] Second, external forms of characterisation had a significant influence on the ways in which social groups both acted and defined themselves. Indeed, French, with Mark Rothery, has recently suggested we see such stereotypes as 'bundles of experiences, prejudices, and assumptions' that exerted 'tremendous pressure' on social practice and 'imposed a deep psychological toll' on the individuals and groups subjected to them.[21] In short, external categorisations of social identity were both based in the

---

[16] For example *The Glory of the Gentle-Craft*, Pepys, 4.318 (1690); *The Shooe = maker's Triumph*, Pepys, 5.427 (1695). All ballads and collections cited in this paper were consulted via the open-access English Broadside Ballad Archive (http://ebba.english.ucsb.edu/). Dates provided are those given by EBBA, and relate to publication dates rather than dates of composition.

[17] *The Shooemaker Out-witted*, Pepys, 3.271 (1684–1700).

[18] John Ray, *A Collection of English Proverbs Digested into a Convenient Method for the Speedy Finding Any One upon Occasion* (1678), 13.

[19] Richard Jenkins, *Social Identity*, 2nd edn (2004), 21–3.

[20] Henry French, *The Middle Sort of People in Provincial England, 1600–1750* (Oxford, 2007), 15.

[21] See their *Man's Estate: Landed Gentry Masculinities, 1660–1900* (Oxford, 2012), 'Introduction'.

reality of social experience and identity formation, and consequent upon the same.

There is also an argument for seeing in ballads more than just external categorisations of occupational groups. They can provide access to the other side of Jenkins' equation for the formation of social identity: internal categorisation. They may not match up to the kind of 'personal documents' – such as diaries or personal correspondence – on which historians of identity prefer to rely, but they tell us something about how occupational groups liked to envisage themselves.[22] This is particularly so in relation to urban tradesmen, who represented a core section of the ballad-consuming market with their above-average levels of literacy, their significant disposable income, and their traditions of occupational sociability such as guild feasts, which provided the ideal context for the collective performance of ballads.[23] Many ballads were therefore directed at artisans and tradesmen, and sought to appeal to these groups by offering celebratory portrayals of particular occupations – such as blacksmiths, tailors and shoemakers – that were intended to 'flatter the heroic self-image' of these workers.[24] They therefore reveal something of the ways in which these occupational groups sought to define, or at the least liked to imagine, themselves. In sum, ballads allow us to reconstruct some of the most prevalent discourses about certain occupational groups, and to disclose assumptions which informed contemporaries' processes of identification, either in defining themselves or others. They permit us to identify some of the 'building blocks' out of which individual and collective identities were constructed.

Defining tradesmen

The ballad *Round Boyes Indeed, Or, The Shoomakers Holy-Day* offers a 'very pleasant new ditty' celebrating the coming together of fellow-shoemakers to 'drink strong beer, good ale and sack' in affirmation of occupational pride. It is a classic example of its genre, and many similar examples of what Samuel Pepys called 'good fellowship' ballads can be found for both this and other trades.[25] Of particular interest for the purposes of the argument developed here is the way the ballad deals with the relationship between the shoemakers and other tradesmen. Despite making lofty

[22] For a reliance on such personal documents see the essays in *Identity and Agency*, ed. French and Barry.

[23] Hailwood, 'Sociability, Work and Labouring Identity', 12–13.

[24] John Walter, 'Faces in the Crowd: Gender, Youth and Age in Early Modern Protest', in *The Family in Early Modern England*, ed. Helen Berry and Elizabeth Foyster (Cambridge, 2007), 107.

[25] *Round Boyes Indeed*, Pepys, 1.442 (1632); see also Hailwood, 'Sociability, Work and Labouring Identity'.

claims that shoemaking is a particularly noble craft – 'Shoemakers sonnes were princes borne' – this identity is not set up in opposition to the inferiority of those working in other artisanal trades: instead, the smith, weaver, tailor, carpenter, mason, bricklayer, costermonger, and a number of other tradesmen, are all described as being 'noe niggards of their chincke, / But with boone blades will sit & drinke.' These fellow-tradesmen are welcome drinking companions. Indeed, the shoemakers of the ballad declared: 'The gentle Craft doth beare good will, to all kind hearted tradesmen' that would join with them in bouts of good fellowship.

This highlights the existence of an occupational identity based on the more general marker, 'the tradesman', that encompassed something broader than a craft-specific consciousness: a marker that occurs regularly in reference to ballad characters. The ballad *The Honest Tradesmans Honour Vindicated* takes the form of a dialogue between a gentleman on the one hand and a non-craft-specific tradesman on the other.[26] The gallant blade and the London artisan take turns to trade insults about the negative characteristics of the other man's social type – gentlemen are accused of being sexually promiscuous, and in return tradesmen are derided as cuckolds – until the gentleman accepts that 'man is blest / that is the Tradesmans friend'. Here, the tradesman is identified as a broader social type, defined not by his specific craft and in opposition to other craftsmen, but by his involvement in artisanal work and his opposition to the idle and spendthrift gentleman.

This broader occupational-cum-social identity of 'the tradesman' raises questions about the extent to which narrowly conceived craft loyalty and consciousness cut across any wider sense of worker or 'class' identity in this period. That said, we do have evidence of conflicts and hostility between different crafts and guilds. Samuel Pepys recorded news in 1664 of a 'fray' on Morefields between the butchers and the weavers, 'between whom there hath been ever an old competition for mastery', with the butchers being 'soundly beaten out of the field, and some deeply wounded and bruised'.[27] There were also clearly defined hierarchies within crafts, with distinctions between masters, journeymen and apprentices being symbolically reinforced by each category using different drinking vessels and plate, dependent on their rank, at guild feasts.[28] It may be the case, then, that the inclusive category of 'tradesman' had little normative purchase with workers themselves, and was rather a fiction arising from the fact that it made better market sense to pitch a ballad at this broad

---

[26] *The Honest Tradesmans Honour Vindicated*, Pepys, 4.350 (1678–88).

[27] *The Diary of Samuel Pepys* (1906), 26 July 1664, 273.

[28] Jasmine Kilburn-Toppin, '"Discords Have Arisen and Brotherly Love Decreased": The Spatial and Material Contexts of the Guild Feast in Early Modern London', *Brewery History*, 150 (2013), 28–38.

category than at a specific trade. That said, the common occurrence of the marker of 'tradesman' in ballads at least shows that balladeers believed there were elements of identity common to all tradesmen that cut across or overrode differences and rivalries between and within trades. It is these areas of shared identity amongst the category of tradesmen that the remainder of this paper focuses on.

First, we need to define this category of 'tradesmen' for the seventeenth century. The issue is complicated by the fact that the term could carry a number of different meanings, as Daniel Defoe recognised in *The Complete English Tradesman*:

> in the north of Britain, and likewise in Ireland, when you say a tradesman, you are understood to mean a mechanic, such as a smith, a carpenter, a shoemaker, and the like, such as here [meaning England] we call a handicraftsman. But in England, and especially in London, and the south parts of Britain, we take it in another sense . . . in general, all sorts of warehouse-keepers, shopkeepers, whether wholesale dealers or retailers of goods, are called tradesmen . . . [men] who do not actually work upon, make, or manufacture, the goods they sell.

For Defoe, then, a 'tradesman' was one involved solely in the retail or wholesale of goods, whereas those involved in the manufacture of goods were better described as 'handicraftsmen'.[29] This was not the manner in which broadside ballads of the seventeenth century used the term tradesman. Instead, they used the term according more closely to the definition Defoe associated with Ireland and Scotland, to denote smiths, carpenters, shoemakers and so on. This difference between Defoe's definition and that prevalent in the ballads may reveal a shift in the meaning of the term over time: that in the seventeenth century the term was used throughout the British Isles to refer to a more artisanal conception of the tradesman, but by the early eighteenth century this was giving way – in England at least – to the term being used to refer specifically to retail tradesmen. This shift may be symptomatic of a growing occupational specialisation, with a clear distinction emerging between those involved exclusively in manufacture and those involved exclusively in retail that was not as pronounced in the seventeenth century.[30] Indeed, it is not a distinction that is present, let alone emphasised, in the ballad discourse, where grocers, shopkeepers, costermongers and sometimes even merchants might appear alongside smiths and carpenters in lists of tradesmen. It is in this more inclusive

---

[29] Daniel Defoe, *The Complete English Tradesman* (1726), 'Introduction'.
[30] Although it was a distinction that was sometimes made and probed in early seventeenth-century city comedies: Ronda Arab, *Manly Mechanicals on the Early Modern English Stage* (Selinsgrove, 2011), 130–1.

sense, meaning craftsmen and small-scale retailers, rather than that deployed by Defoe, that the category of tradesmen is understood here.[31]

If definitions of what constituted a tradesmen shifted over time, conduct literature suggests that so too did understandings of their social role. In the sixteenth century, the tradesman was seen as fulfilling an important function in society, but his was not an aspirational or prosperous calling. As the Aristotelian ethics that underpinned many household management manuals in the period would have it, a tradesman should manufacture goods which he could then exchange to obtain the things a household needed for its welfare that it could not produce by itself. This was 'a natural art', and was therefore 'necessary and honourable'. Producing goods to exchange for profit – or even worse buying and selling goods for profit – was to be 'justly censured; for it is unnatural, and a mode by which men gain from one another', and those that 'believe that getting wealth is the object of household management, and the whole idea of their lives is that they ought to increase their money without limit' were seen to corrode a sense of community.[32] A tradesman's calling was, ideally, a not-for-profit one. By the early eighteenth century, though, the conduct literature aimed at tradesmen appears to have adopted a dramatically different tone. Works such as Richard Steele's *The Tradesman's Calling* (1684), Daniel Defoe's *The Complete English Tradesman* (1726) and Benjamin Franklin's *Advice to a Young Tradesman* (1748) have been variously described as embodying the 'spirit of capitalism', or as speaking for a bourgeois 'social consciousness that had come of age'.[33] These interpretations suggest that the economic developments of the seventeenth

[31] This imprecise definition of the term tradesman for the seventeenth century is supported by the *OED*, which lists examples from across the century and later of 'tradesman' being used both to mean 'one who is skilled in and follows one of the industrial arts; an artificer, an artisan, a craftsman', and to mean 'one who is engaged in trade or the sale of commodities; *esp.* a shopkeeper'. Even here, it is not always clear from the examples offered that the term is being used to mean precisely one definition rather than the other, although more precise regional uses like those outlined by Defoe are noted from the nineteenth century. The same can be said of the earliest appearance of the term 'tradesman' in an ESTC title, a blank form of orders to check weights and measures from *c.* 1619, which is directed at 'Millers, Bakers, Brewers, Inholders, Vinteners, Mercers, Grocers, Drapers, Alehouse-keepers, Butchers, Chandlers, Smithes, Weavers, Farmers, Maltsters, Taylors, Glovers, Clothiers, Cloathworkers, Fullers, and generally all Artificers, Tradesmen or any other person or persons whatsoever . . . that useth or hath any Waight or Measures whatsoever'. Whether a distinction is being drawn between 'artificers' and 'tradesmen', or the terms are being used interchangeably, is not clear. This reflects the fact that if such a distinction was understood by contemporaries, it was rarely deployed with any precision.

[32] This section is based upon David Harris Sacks, 'Commonwealth Discourse and Economic Thought: The Morality of Exchange', in *The Elizabethan World*, ed. Susan Doran and Norman Jones (Abingdon, 2010), 392.

[33] Max Weber, *The Protestant Ethic and the Spirit of Capitalism* (1992), 51; Laura Stevenson O'Connell, 'The Elizabethan Bourgeois Hero-Tale: Aspects of an Adolescent Social

century – commercialisation and a growing demand for consumer goods – had tempted tradesmen to embrace market values and the pursuit of profit, and to play a key role as pioneers in the development of bourgeois capitalism.

Is this supposed shift evident in ballad discourses about tradesmen? If so, we would expect to detect a tradesman's identity reflecting a growing confidence, prosperity and embrace of the values of the market, that perhaps even exhibits the 'self-satisfied smugness' of caricatures of the 'middling sort' in this period.[34] Before turning to the ballads, we might consider two other hypotheses. Dramatic representations of tradesmen in Elizabethan drama, for instance, suggest an alternative perspective on their values. In her analysis of plays that depicted tradesmen, Laura Caroline Stevenson argues that playwrights increasingly came to recognise that this was a rising social group, and sought to offer a positive vision of tradesmen that would appeal to the growing numbers of such in their audiences. Before the eighteenth century, she suggests, these playwrights lacked the mental apparatus to understand this group's success in terms of bourgeois or capitalist values. Instead, she argues that positive depictions of tradesmen tended to fall back on elite 'chivalric' values that had little to do with tradesmen's actual social role.[35] We might therefore consider whether ballads echo the plays of the period in representing tradesmen as an increasingly self-confident and aspirant social group, but one that sought to appropriate the ethics of their social superiors rather than to forge an identity in relation to new capitalist values.

A third hypothesis emerges from Craig Muldrew's work on credit relations in early modern England. Muldrew reminds us that the growth in consumption and market exchange in the seventeenth century was not matched by sufficient growth in the supply of cash, and the majority of transactions that took place were therefore conducted on credit. As the number of such transactions rapidly increased, the networks of credit became more complex, more important and more precarious. Prosperity for individuals such as tradesmen did not take the form of money in the bank: any new-found wealth was far more mutable, tied up in multiple debt and credit relations, and vulnerable to rapid evaporation if a major debtor defaulted. Given the nature of this credit-based economy, Muldrew argues that we need to rethink some of the values historians have often associated with an emergent 'spirit of capitalism'. An increased emphasis

Consciousness', in *After the Reformation: Essays in Honor of J. H. Hexter*, ed. B. B. Malament (Manchester, 1980), 284–5.

[34] Craig Muldrew, *The Economy of Obligation: The Culture of Credit and Social Relations in Early Modern England* (Basingstoke, 1998), 274.

[35] Laura Caroline Stevenson, *Praise and Paradox: Merchants and Craftsmen in Elizabethan Popular Literature* (Cambridge, 1984).

on industriousness, diligence and thrift amongst the middling sorts were not for Muldrew about the desire for capital accumulation, but about the need to build reputation and credit. Far from embracing bourgeois individualism, tradesmen were seeking to demonstrate to their neighbours that they had working habits that would increase their capacity to pay their debts. These values were less a product of an inward-looking desire for social advancement than an outward projection intended to secure one's credit within the community.[36] This conclusion raises a third hypothesis: the prospect of identifying in the ballads a tradesman's identity founded on an engagement with the growing significance of credit relations, rather than an identity based on aping elite values, or on a warm embrace of a new spirit of capitalism. This type of identity would reflect the mutable and precarious foundations on which the prosperity of any tradesman stood in the seventeenth-century credit economy. As we will see in the following section, this more anxious identity was indeed the more prevalent in ballad discourse.[37]

Tradesmen in ballads

The ballad *Robin Hood and the Tanner* told the story of a 'jolly tanner of Nottingham', Arthur Bland. In defiance of nominative determinism, Bland had an adventurous streak that took him into Sherwood Forest, where he fought with Robin Hood: 'like two wilde Boars in a Chase: / Striving to aim each other to maim.' Ultimately, Bland was able to beat the folk hero into submission, forcing Robin to declare to Little John that 'the Tanner that stands thee beside / He is a bonny blade and a Master of his Trade, / for soundly he hath tan'd my hide.'[38] The values associated with the tradesman here were straightforward: he was strong, courageous and not lacking in martial prowess. Adventure ballads such as this were not uncommon, and the writers of such were reaching for a set of conventional elite values to flatter their tradesmen readers. It is clear that these values had little to do with the actual social role of a tradesman in the seventeenth century.

Even so, ballads did not invariably situate their positive portrayals of tradesmen within a fantasy world of chivalric adventure. Others celebrated the routine sociability of ordinary tradesmen. As we have seen above, 'good fellowship' ballads provide one example of a genre

---

[36] Muldrew, *The Economy of Obligation*.

[37] This emphasis on a more anxious identity can also be seen in Ronda Arab's more recent appraisal of dramatic representations of tradesmen, which focuses in particular on the masculinity of retail-only tradesmen in early seventeenth-century city comedies. There is, however, little emphasis on credit relations in her work: Arab, *Manly Mechanicals*, ch. 4.

[38] *Robin Hood and the Tanner*, Pepys, 2.111 (1681–4). See also *A New Song to Drive away Cold Winter*, Pepys, 2.107 (1684–6).

that articulated a collective identity on the part of tradesmen, depicting such workers joining together in a homosocial alehouse celebration of their occupations.[39] Such ballads provide the most positive portrayal of tradesmen, and offered an image that their authors hoped would strike a chord with the self-perception of potential buyers. The key principles underpinning the occupational pride expressed in these 'good fellowship' ballads – as I have elaborated elsewhere – were a commitment to drink heavily, and an ability to pay your share of the resulting bar bill, or 'shot'.[40] We might interpret this emphasis on liberal spending as a form of 'conspicuous consumption', with tradesmen using heavy alcohol consumption in alehouses to display in a public arena the new-found prosperity that many were enjoying in the seventeenth century. Was this another example of tradesmen mimicking the values of their social superiors, in this case their symbolic prodigality, in an attempt to show that they could now 'live up to the standards of the gentry'?[41]

Although ballad celebrations of good fellowship convey a strong sense of self-confidence and prosperity on the part of tradesmen, this was not achieved by drawing positive parallels between themselves and the gentry. On the contrary, ballads tended to contrast the behaviour of tradesmen with a negative critique of the prodigality of their social superiors. A social complaint ballad entitled *The Poor Man Pays for All* declared that whilst 'The rich men in the Tavernes rore' and 'The rich men eate and drinke the best', it was only through the labour of the poor man and the hard work of the tradesman that they could afford to do so.[42] Tradesmen's resentment of the conspicuous expenditure of the elite was also reflected in the exchange between the gentleman and the tradesman in *The Honest Trades-mans Honour Vindicated*. A key critique levelled at the gentleman focused on his gay apparel and love of sport and recreation, which he was able to indulge despite the fact that he 'scorned too much to toil'.[43] This dynamic is also evident in *Round Boyes Indeed*. Here, the shoemakers declare:

We get our livings by our hands,
Then fill us beare at our commands,

. . .

Whilst many gallants sell their land,
for money to serve their need.[44]

---

[39] Ballad depictions of alehouse sociability were not always exclusively male, although portrayals of occupational gatherings invariably were. See Hailwood, *Alehouses and Good Fellowship*, ch. 3.

[40] Hailwood, 'Sociability, Work and Labouring Identity'.

[41] O'Connell, 'The Elizabethan Bourgeois Hero-Tale', 284.

[42] *The Poore Man Payes for All*, Roxburghe, 1.326 (1601–40).

[43] Pepys, 4.350 (1678–88).

[44] Pepys, 1.442 (1632).

Again, this ballad sought to draw a distinction between the tradesman, who *worked* for his beer, and the rich gallant, whose prodigal spending was instead funded by the sale of his lands. The further implication of this was clear. The conspicuous consumption of rich gallants on fine clothes and bouts of feasting and drinking could be defined as reckless prodigality: it would stretch the resources of the gentleman, here his land, to the point that they would eventually be entirely consumed. Indeed, the gentleman in *The Honest Tradesman's Honour Vindicated* was lampooned as having such distorted principles, boasting that: 'Though I have neither House nor Land / I keep my self in good fashion.'[45]

Heavy alcohol consumption among the shoemakers was not, however, analogous with that of prodigal gallants. For when a tradesman needed more money to fund his good fellowship, he did not need to jeopardise his estate; he could work for more. As the Martin Parker ballad *The Three Merry Coblers* put it:

When all our money is spent,
We are not discontent,
For we can worke for more,
And then pay off our score.[46]

Ballad celebrations of tradesmen's good fellowship suggested that their liberality was based on much firmer foundations than was the prodigality of the gentry. They could always generate more income through their labour in order to serve their need.

In reality this was an idealised notion. As we have seen, the seventeenth-century tradesman was enmeshed in market transactions within a credit-based economy that meant that the fruits of labour were rarely delivered in hard cash that could then be immediately spent in the alehouse. The prosperity of the tradesman was not secured through a simple and direct relationship between labour and reward: it was entangled in complex relations of exchange and credit. Although drinking and good fellowship ballads tended to downplay the role of the tradesman in commercial relations, this theme was taken up in other ballad genres. Where this was the case, tradesmen were rarely portrayed in the positive light that bathes the drinking ballads. They tended to appear in social complaint ballads which looked to play on a common stereotype of the tradesman as a deceitful dealer. A common ballad type here was the satirical 'golden age' ballad, in which a new age of honesty, free from sin and deceit, was declared to have descended. The honest dealing tradesman invariably appeared alongside lawyers who had resolved to put justice ahead of

---

[45] Pepys, 4.350 (1678–88).
[46] *The Three Merry Coblers*, Pepys, 1.408 (1623–61).

financial gain, usurers who had given all of their money to the poor, and reformed drunkards now committed to a life of sobriety. These ballads proclaimed that now 'Tradesmen hate short measures, / false lights, and falser waights'; that 'All Trades-men grow weary, / of living by wrong'; and that 'The Taylor doth scorne to deceive any friend, / But unto plaine dealing his mind he doth bend.'[47] In each case, the proposed new golden age turned out only to be a fantasy. As one ballad character wryly put it, after hearing his friend describe this brave new world, 'But I will not beleeve it, / tis too good to be true.'[48] Other ballads dispensed with wishful thinking altogether and condemned the deceitful practices of tradesmen outright. The unambiguously titled *Knavery in All Trades* lamented that 'One tradesman deceaveth another, / and sellers will conycatch buyers, / For gaine one wil cheat his own brother.'[49] If the income-producing virtues of the craftsman-tradesman celebrated in good fellowship ballads were portrayed as a masculine trait, the vices of the retailing trader were seen to apply to male and female alike. Billingsgate oyster women and alewives were the two most prominent examples in a ballad literature that regularly portrayed market women as cunning, cozening and aggressive in pursuit of self-interest. It was a familiar complaint that 'The Ale-wives they go fine and gay, / Deck'd in their Silks and rich Array', on the basis of profits gained by selling short measures and frothy beer.[50] There was therefore a significant theme of ballad discourse in which the tradesman, along with the female trader, was portrayed as a deceitful dealer. The tradesman's role in retail was once again treated with suspicion, and any embrace of a 'spirit of capitalism' on their part was disdained.

Interestingly, though, another strand of ballad discourse depicted the sharp practice of tradesmen not as capitalistic, but as a response to the demands of the precarious credit networks within which they operated. The ballad *Poor Robin's Prophesy* was another satirical 'golden age' ballad, predicting a number of positive changes that would occur in society 'when the devil is blind' (an early modern equivalent to the modern idiom 'when hell freezes over'). One part of his prophesy is particularly striking:

And first for the Shopkeeper, this I can tell,
That after long trusting, all things will be well,

---

[47] *Newes Good and New*, Pepys, 1.210 (1623); *The Golden Age*, Pepys, 1.152 (1625–35); *The Honest Age*, Pepys, 1.156 (1601–40).

[48] *Newes Good and New*, Pepys, 1.210 (1623).

[49] *Knavery in All Trades*, Pepys, 1.166 (1632). For similar examples, see *Truth in Mourning*, Pepys, 2.52 (1687); *The Sorrowful Complaint of Conscience and Plain-Dealing*, Pepys, 4.354 (1671–1702).

[50] *The Carefull Wife's Good Counsel*, Pepys, 2.73 (1675–96). For more on representations of female traders, see David Pennington, '"Three Women and a Goose make a Market": Representations of Market Women in Seventeenth-Century Popular Literature', *Seventeenth Century*, 25, 1 (2010), 27–48.

The Gallant will pay him, what ever's his due,
And make him rejoyce when he finds it is true:
False weights, & false measures, he then will not mind,
But honest will prove, when the Devil is blind.[51]

Of course, this neat resolution was unlikely to occur, and although the equation of a tradesman with dishonest dealing is present here there is a further implication: the shopkeeper resorted to deceit to balance his books because the gallant was not paying his debts to him.[52]

It was a sentiment echoed in *The Country-Mans New Care Away*, a similar ballad-type listing remedies to social evils. The country man suggests that 'If Gallants poore Tradesmen / would honestly pay, / Then might they have comfort, / to sing, Care away.'[53] *The Honest Tradesmans Honour Vindicated* also picked up on the notion that tradesmen were as often victims of market exchange as they were deceitful beneficiaries of it, and again suggested that the prodigal gallant bore responsibility for this. The gentleman boasted about his fine apparel: 'a Rapier by my side, / A broad Hat and long curl'd Hair, / My Breeches at the knees so wide / that they would make four pair.' The tradesman retorted as follows:

Sir, if for your Rapier you had paid,
your Cutler would not frown,
Nor your Bever-maker have be[en] [a]fraid
of your riding out of Town.
Your Taylor he lamenteth still,
for a truth I heard it said
Oft viewing of his long Bill,
which you have left unpaid.[54]

The implication in each of these examples was that the prosperity of the tradesman rested on the willingness of their gentry customers to pay them their due and to do so promptly.

This could be taken to have a number of broader implications. We might read ballad attacks on the prodigal gentry who often failed to pay their debts as evidence of an increasingly assertive bourgeois voice, revealing a cultural aggression felt towards their social superiors by the tradesmen consumers of these ballads. Muldrew has suggested that seventeenth-century credit relations were increasingly based upon notions of equality that may have provided tradesmen with an opportunity to hold

---

[51] *Poor Robin's Prophesie*, Pepys, 4.304 (1674–9).
[52] For a similar argument relating to alewives see Pennington, 'Three Women and a Goose', 42.
[53] *The Country-Mans New Care Away*, Roxburghe, 1.34 (1635).
[54] Pepys, 4.350 (1678–88).

their social superiors to account for the failure to settle their debts.[55] This should not, however, be taken as evidence that tradesmen were adopting an assertive and confident *capitalist* identity. Attacks by tradesmen on the prodigality of the rich ultimately suggest that the growing levels of consumption of clothes and other material goods in the period were not seen by tradesmen as a fount of their own prosperity. There is no sense that tradesmen were embracing a consumer revolution for the opportunities for capital accumulation it might offer them. Instead, ballad discourse tended to invoke a rather more negative set of attitudes on the part of tradesmen towards the growing market in consumer goods. As *Knavery in all Trades* bemoaned: 'Some Rorers doe were gallant clothes, / for which they did never pay.'[56] Another social complaint ballad, *The Tradesman's Complaint*, elaborated on what the outcome of this failure to pay up on the part of the rich would be:

> The Courtier he complains for gold;
> To whom the tradesmen wares hath sold,
> And having run so on his score,
> He's forced alas to shut up door.[57]

Whilst the conspicuous consumption of elites may have provided demand for the wares of the tradesman, the growing number of transactions for such goods, conducted as they were on credit, left the tradesman in a particularly precarious position. Indeed, some ballads bemoaned that an aspirational desire for these goods had begun to filter down to tradesmen's own wives, which squeezed the tradesman further still. One London tradesman lamented that his wife was 'In debt with ev'ry Shop she runs / for to appear in gaudy Pride', with the consequence that 'To buy those Trinkets which they lack / Both Stock and Credit goes to Rack.'[58] As far as ballads reveal anything about the ways tradesmen understood the economic developments of this period, they suggest that anxiety, rather than smugness, was the more prevalent reaction to the growing demand for their goods.[59]

It was not just in the alehouse and the marketplace, but also in the household, that a tradesman's identity was forged – as the number of ballads exploring the role of the tradesman-as-patriarch attests to. In each

---

[55] Muldrew, *The Economy of Obligation*, 97, 253.
[56] Pepys, 1.166 (1632).
[57] *The Tradesman's Complaint*, Roxburghe, 2.454 (1662–92).
[58] *The Invincible Pride of Women*, Pepys, 4.153 (1675–96).
[59] This may have been changing in the late seventeenth century: McShane and Backhouse have identified the development from the 1680s of ballads in which workers in the textile trades voiced sentiments that endorsed luxury and fashionable consumption, in particular in relation to the wearing of top-knots, which were seen as a boon to tradesmen who produced the necessary ribbons: McShane and Backhouse, 'Top-Knots and Lower Sorts', 344–5.

of these contexts a tradesmen's self-perception was undoubtedly related to concepts of masculinity in early modern England, a component of identity that has received greater attention than occupational identity in the historiography. Alexandra Shepard's ground-breaking work in this area has suggested that contemporary codes of manhood based on alehouse sociability on the one hand, and upon patriarchal ideals on the other, were profoundly at odds in early modern English culture. It was men who were unable to reach the masculine ideal of a proficient head of household that looked instead to a form of 'anti-patriarchal' manhood that was articulated through acts of excessive drinking and bravado in the context of all-male alehouse sociability.[60] To some extent, this was about life-cycle stages, and the transition in status from apprentice to independent master would have been a stage in the life-cycle of the tradesman which coincided with that common shift from youthful, prodigal, 'anti-patriarchal' bachelorhood to the differing priorities of the married, patriarchal head of household. Yet, for the married tradesman-patriarch, there does not appear to have been a straightforward age-related shift away from alehouse sociability towards a greater focus on household management. Instead, ballad discourses suggest a tradesman-patriarch was still expected to engage in bouts of alehouse sociability with his fellow-workers to demonstrate his occupational pride and prosperity, but without jeopardising his duty of patriarchal provision.

Conduct literature of the period put great emphasis upon thrift as a principle essential for successful patriarchal provision. Yet, a tradesman who took this to mean that all alehouse sociability should be forsaken would end up labelled as a covetous miser. The ballad *A Health to All Good-Fellowes* derided those who refused to spend anything with alehouse 'good fellows':

The greedy Curmudgin, sits all the day snudging,
at home with browne bread and small beare,
To Coffer up wealth, he starveth himselfe,
scarce eats a good meale in a yeare.[61]

As another good fellowship ballad put it, 'The Miser that doth hoard his Coin' was 'a plague to thine and mine', because keeping wealth circulating was seen as good for trade more generally.[62] Nor was too strong a commitment to thriftiness conducive to one's creditworthiness:

---

[60]Alexandra Shepard, '"Swil-bols and Tos-pots": Drink Culture and Male Bonding in England, c. 1560–1640', in *Love, Friendship and Faith in Europe, 1300–1800*, ed. Laura Gowing, Michael Hunter and Miri Rubin (Basingstoke, 2005), 110–30.

[61]*A Health to All Good-Fellowes*, Roxburghe, 1.150 (1601–40).

[62]*The Careless Drunkards*, Pepys, 4.238 (1671–1702); see also *The Distruction of Care*, Pepys, 5.97 (1685–8).

no one wanted to be in a creditor or debtor relationship with a covetous miser. It was therefore essential for a tradesman to be seen to engage in alehouse sociability at least occasionally. Yet, there was also pressure on the tradesman not to over-indulge. Just as thriftiness could be seen to shade into miserliness, liberality and generosity were near neighbours of prodigality. *I Tell You, John Jarret, You'l Breake* offered a warning to those tradesmen who 'When you in your shop should be plying your worke, / In some scurvy blinde Alehouse you all day doe lurke', that they would end up bankrupt and broken: again, hardly desirable qualities in a creditor or debtor.[63] The household advice manuals of the period drew upon Xenophon and Aristotle to stress that it was important therefore to strike a balance of proper liberality, avoiding the extremes of miserliness and prodigality.[64]

The pressures upon tradesmen to steer such a steady course were not only a result of concerns about credit relations. The ability of a tradesman to manage his resources effectively was also central to broader notions of patriarchal prowess, a quality that was often judged in ballads not by one's male creditors, but by women. Indeed, a feature of ballads addressing the tradesman-as-patriarch theme that runs counter to trends in the historiography of masculinity is the prevalence of a female voice in dictating and upholding approved masculine values. As Jenny Jordan has argued, historians of masculinity often assume that the values associated with manliness were determined by men, to the exclusion of women.[65] Yet, in many ballads, women assume the mantle of judging the masculine, and in particular the patriarchal, capacities of a tradesman. Sandra Clark has argued that we should see the strong presence of a female voice in ballad literature as evidence that this was a genre that articulated ideas and values held by women as much as by men.[66] Whilst this may apply to some extent to those ballads about alehouse sociability and market exchange, it is most clearly evident in a genre of ballads that weighed up the relative merits of potential husbands from the perspective of a female ballad voice.

Much of the attention here focused on a husband's capacity to provide for a family economically, and in some ballads the tradesman fared well in comparison to other social types. For instance, in *The Maidens Delight*, a young maid by the name of sweet Betty rejects the advances of a finely attired young gallant, despite the fact that he had employed that

[63] *I Tell You, John Jarret, You'l Breake*, Pepys, 1.170 (1630).

[64] Muldrew, *The Economy of Obligation*, 159.

[65] Jennifer Jordan, 'Her-Story Untold: The Absence of Women's Agency in Constructing Concepts of Early Modern Manhood', *Cultural and Social History*, 4, 4 (2007), 575–83.

[66] Sandra Clark, 'The Broadside Ballad and the Woman's Voice', in *Debating Gender in Early Modern England, 1500–1700*, ed. Cristina Malcolmson and Suzuki Mihoko (Basingstoke, 2002), 103–20.

fail-safe wooing technique of adorning his cod-piece with ribbons. Instead, echoing the sentiments of many a 'good fellowship' ballad, the maid asserted that she would rather marry a tradesman:

A spendthrift that consumeth
And sells his land for gold
Is very like to live in want
Or beg when he is old
But the noble-minded tradesman
His work goes forward still
For he hath meat and drink enuf
And all things else at will.[67]

Other ballad females were more sceptical of the tradesman's capacity to act as a reliable provider, and cautioned against tradesmen as marriage choices. One ballad explained that the tailor, for example, 'For making clothes, is paid with oathes', and was unable to maintain his charge and pay his house-rent and would end up as a broken beggar. Here, we see the recurrence of the notion that it was unreliable debtors who placed tradesmen in a precarious economic position: he was paid in 'oaths', promises which did little to help him provide for his family. The same ballad once again pointed the finger for this at the prodigal gallant:

The joviall neate Shooe-maker
is on the Tanners score
By giving [t]rust to gal[a]nts,
a meanes to make him poore;
And when he can no longer trust,
unkindly they forsake him,
Which grieves his heart, and breeds his smart,
come take him beggar, take him.[68]

The fact that a tradesman's prosperity was embedded in uncertain networks of credit was therefore perceived to diminish his ability as an economic provider, and undermined his reputation as an effective patriarchal male. So too could attempts to display his economic prowess in bouts of alehouse sociability: the warning about the impact of alehouse sociability on economic fortunes delivered in the story of John Jarret was voiced by Jarret's wife, and ballad wives urging their husbands to forgo alehouse sociability were a market staple.[69] Historians of the period have arguably overlooked the extent to which judgements about men's

---

[67] *The Maidens Delight*, Euing, 205 (1623–61).
[68] *Sure My Nurse Was a witch*, Pepys, 1.204 (1630).
[69]Pepys, 1.170. See, for example, *A Caveat for Young Men*, Pepys, 2.22 (1678–88); *Wades Reformation*, Pepys, 2.90 (1684–6).

fulfilment of masculine ideals in this society were formulated in a dialogue conducted between men *and* women, rather than being judged by men alone.

If both men and women contributed to the process of defining masculinity, we also know that both made crucial contributions to household economies which did not in reality rely solely on the capacity of a patriarchal 'bread-winner'. In fact, recent work by Amy Erickson has suggested that the prosperity of tradesmen-households in particular often rested on husbands and wives working closely together, running joint businesses or complementary enterprises from the same premises.[70] Some ballads painted a rather different picture of the tradesman's wife as one who does 'rise about the hour of Noon', 'Then goes she to a Ball or Play', and runs up debts for the household purchasing 'lofty Topknots' and 'Powder'd Hair'.[71] Others more readily acknowledged the important role played by the tradesman's wife in the household economy. Wives were depicted selling their husbands' goods in shops or from stalls in the market, and one ballad maid in search of a tradesman husband emphasised the contribution she could make to his work: 'if a Shoemaker me wed, / his Shop-Thread I can spin', or:

> If I should a Weaver have,
> either of Silk or Linnen;
> This can I do, and Money save,
> which is a good beginning:
> Either wind Silk, or fill his quills
> tis either I can fit.[72]

Indeed, a wife who was an effective spinner was often depicted as a particularly attractive prospect for any man, and it was perhaps here that women's work came closest to achieving something like the appreciation directed at men's productive artisanal work that was celebrated in good fellowship ballads.[73] A tradesman-patriarch was not then always portrayed as a munificent patriarchal provider, and there was recognition in ballad discourse that a prosperous tradesman-household needed a significant contribution from both husband and wife. Indeed, a tradesman's wife who did not work was not celebrated as a symbol of

---

[70] Amy Erickson, 'Married Women's Occupations in Eighteenth-Century London', *Continuity and Change*, 23, 2 (2008), 267–307.

[71] *The Invincible Pride of Women*, Pepys, 4.153 (1675–96).

[72] *The More Haste, the Worst Speed*, Roxburghe, 4.62 (1672–96). For wives selling goods, see Pennington, 'Three Women and a Goose', 38

[73] On the importance of spinning to household economics, see *The Knitters Jobb*, Roxburghe, 2.244 (1672–96), and Craig Muldrew, '"Th'ancient Distaff" and "Whirling Spindle": Measuring the Contribution of Spinning to Household Earnings and the National Economy in England, 1550–1770', *Economic History Review*, 65, 2 (2012), 498–526.

the new-found prosperity of these workers and their subsequent ability to support a leisured and fashionable wife – instead, they added yet another layer to the anxiety of the tradesman who was seeking to steer a steady course through the challenging economy of seventeenth-century England. A tradesman relied on a working wife.

Whilst some ballads ruminated on the abilities of the tradesman as provider for the household economy, others adopted a female voice to consider other aspects of his husbandly capability: sexual prowess was another important 'building block' of a tradesman's masculine identity. *The Wanton Maidens Choice* placed a man's sexual appetite above his economic standing as a criterion for selecting a partner. Here, the farmer was rejected because: 'He is so weary all the day, / with holding of the Plow / He is no sooner got to Bed, / but he is fast asleep.' The preferred choice was instead the tinker: 'He shall be welcome day and night, / into my Company: / He has a Bag of Tools I swear, / and bravely he can them use.'[74] Another ballad female was similarly impressed by the abilities of 'William the Joyner', and again capitalised on the opportunity for an occupationally themed pun in recalling the 'pleasure' derived from their 'wanton and wild' sexual adventure: for William was a 'young Spark' who 'can handle his Tools'.[75]

Whilst ballads such as these touched on the sexual prowess of tradesmen in a playful and jocular tone, contrasting ballad discourses probed at the tensions and anxieties of tradesmen-patriarchs. Indeed, tradesmen are commonly portrayed as cuckolds in ballad literature, and whilst this was of course not a sleight directed only at tradesmen, there do appear to have been particular associations between tradesmen and that fate. In the ballad *The London Cuckold*, the unfaithful wife of a tradesman explained her behaviour to her husband as follows:

> 'Tis (quoth she) you were so busie,
> I was loath to trouble you.
> You love Business as your Life,
> but ne'r mind to kiss your Wife,
> You leave me to lye alone,
> All night long to sigh and moan,
> And therefore when you took the Air,
> there came a Colt that back't your Mare.[76]

This was not an untypical story, and ballads could side-line the fact that tradesmen and their wives often worked together, and suggest that

[74] *The Wanton Maidens Choice*, Pepys, 3.190 (1671–1702).
[75] *The Buxome Lass of Bread-Street*, Pepys, 3.295 (1675–96).
[76] *The London Cuckold*, Pepys, 4.122 (1685–8). See also *An Answer to the London Cuckold*, Pepys, 4.123 (1685–8).

tradesmen were cuckolded while they were away in their workshops. As a turner in one ballad complained 'To my work straight I go where I labour and toyl', leaving another man to 'turn up my wife the mean while'.[77] Alternatively, engagement in alehouse sociability could create a window for cuckoldry, and whilst a tradesman was at 'the pipe and the pot', even his own apprentice might take the opportunity of some 'sweet Recreation' with his mistress.[78] Ballads depicting apprentices as protagonists sought to probe the tradesman-patriarch's anxieties both over his ability to command the obedience of his wife and his servants, and tapped into a discourse about the sexual threat young men posed to older married men. *The London Cuckold* had an 'antient' tradesman cuckolded by a 'coltish-spark', and in one amorous encounter between a mistress and an apprentice the former complained of married men that there were 'Not ten in fifteen that do lie with their Wives', leaving such wives to seek out 'a mettle-some Lad'.[79] Alongside the apprentice, a regular character to fulfil this role, as in the case of both the London cuckold and the turner, was a finely dressed young 'gallant': here, as in the world of credit relations, the gallant was the perennial bogeyman that undermined the tradesman's capacity to stake out a positive and assured sense of masculine identity.

This context allows us to see with clarity the resonances of the ballad *The Honest Tradesmans Honour Vindicated*. Its juxtaposing of the values of the prodigal gallant with those of the hard-working tradesman reflect a wider discursive trope, but more than that its title reveals the crucial point that a tradesman's honour was something that needed to be vindicated: it was not a given. It came under pressure on a number of fronts: from their operation in the unstable world of credit relations; from the judges of a tradesman's patriarchal and sexual prowess; from the challenges presented by steering a course between miserliness and prodigality when it came to engaging in the seemingly escapist world of alehouse sociability. To assert a positive identity in the face of such pressures was undoubtedly one of the most testing dimensions of the tradesman's calling.

Conclusions

These broadside ballads reveal some of the discourses, stereotypes and values – sometimes positive, other times negative and oftentimes humorous – that were associated with a particular occupational-cum-social group in a cultural landscape that would have been familiar to a wide range of early modern English men and women. The ballad

---

[77] *The Catologue of Contented Cuckolds*, Pepys, 4.130 (1651–86).
[78] *An Amorous Dialogue between John and his Mistris*, Roxburghe, 2.12 (1672–96); *A Pleasant Jigg betwixt Jack and his Mistress*, Pepys, 3.14 (1675–96).
[79] *An Amorous Dialogue between John and his Mistris*, Roxburghe, 2.12 (1672–96).

discourses reconstructed here represent some of the 'building blocks' out of which the identity – whether external or internal, individual or collective – of seventeenth-century tradesmen could have been constructed. This is not to say that this work-based identity was the only, or even the primary, form of identity for those who could be classed as tradesmen. Yet, it seems unlikely that anyone working as a tradesman in this society would have been able to construct a sense of identity that was not in some way influenced by the various discourses discussed here. As such, work-based identity needs to be recognised as one of the many components of identity in this period.

How did this influence manifest itself though? We might suggest that some of the defining features of being a tradesman were not specific to being a tradesman at all. Concerns with patriarchal provision, with sexual prowess, with networks of credit, were surely central tenets of the lives of workers in a range of occupations, and could apply to men – and to some extent women – across the social scale. The experiences from which these preoccupations grew were not necessarily specific to certain types of workers. This does not mean, however, that work was not fundamental to notions of social identity. In fact, what the ballad evidence suggests is that broader aspects of social experience in this society, such as credit relationships, or fears of cuckoldry, were often interpreted by contemporaries as aspects of their particular type of work. General, common concerns were made specific and personalised by reaching for work-based contexts as a narrowing framework through which to organise social experiences that were in reality more widely shared. The job may not have made the man, but it did provide a lens through which he could make sense of the world.

What sort of identity did a tradesman develop by viewing the world through the lens of his working experiences? We set out with three possible hypotheses. One was that although tradesmen were a prospering and aspirant social group in the seventeenth century, there did not yet exist a set of positive values that accurately reflected upon their social role, and they were accordingly left to express their identity by mimicking the values of their social superiors. Whilst some ballads associated tradesmen with chivalric qualities, others made very clear distinctions between the values of tradesmen and those of their social superiors, especially in relation to forms of consumption. Ballad literature tended to contrast the reckless prodigality that underpinned the consumption of the rich with the more sustainable alehouse liberality of the tradesman, which was in turn founded upon an ability to turn to labour in order to fund such consumption. This unease about the ability and willingness of those who were driving the demand for consumer goods actually to pay for their wares has implications for another of our hypotheses: that tradesmen in this period were enthusiastically embracing the development of the market. Whilst some ballads implied that tradesmen sought to gain profit through dishonest dealing in market exchange, any suggestion that they saw the market as a friend was countered by others. There were constant complaints that tradesmen struggled within the economic climate of the seventeenth century because their wealth was dependent on networks of credit, credit that was often extended to social superiors who did not or could not pay their bill. The tradesman's relationship with the growth of consumer demand and the expansion of market exchange was not treated in the ballads as one of affection, but rather as one of precarious and anxious dependency.

This conclusion chimes with our third hypothesis: to understand the identity of tradesmen in this period we need to acknowledge the significance of a credit economy in which 'household wealth was seen primarily as a social relationship, and not as a thing'.[80] It would be misguided to assume that the economic developments affecting tradesmen is the period would necessarily lead to their emergence as an increasingly prosperous and self-confident bourgeois class. As Craig Muldrew puts it, 'it is too simple to think of early modern society as divided into "classes" of wealthy and poor. Wealth was not so much a state of being, or inclusion in a privileged group, as a continual *process* of ethical judgement about credit'.[81] Wealth and prosperity were mutable relationships rather than things, and for the tradesman they could very easily and very suddenly be lost – this was self-evidently not a situation about which to feel smug. Tradesmen's anxieties about credit relations also informed their concerns about their capacity to function as patriarchal providers. And as tradesmen spent long hours in their workshops trying to demonstrate to their wives and neighbours that they were diligent, productive and creditworthy, ballads preyed on their insecurities about fulfilling patriarchal ideals by depicting tales of cuckoldry, with carefree gallants, dressed in clothes obtained on credit, sneaking into their homes and marital beds. Within this economic and cultural context, many seventeenth-century tradesmen would no doubt have struggled to find the necessary tools to construct, project and maintain a positive self-image or sense of 'honour'.

[80]Muldrew, *The Economy of Obligation*, 328.
[81] *Ibid.*, 303.

Transactions of the RHS 24 (2014), pp. 105–25 © Royal Historical Society 2014
doi:10.1017/S008044011400005X

ANDRES BELLO AND THE CHALLENGES OF SPANISH AMERICAN LIBERALISM

By James Dunkerley

READ 8 FEBRUARY 2013

ABSTRACT. Andrés Bello (1781–1865) is generally reckoned to be the foremost intellectual amongst opponents of the Spanish empire in the Americas after the Napoleonic Wars. This paper provides a synoptic account of Bello's development as a scholar, politician and statesman from his early career as a servant of the crown in colonial Caracas, through his nineteen-year exile in London, to his prominent role in the institutional design and management of the young Chilean republic. The paper traces the historiographical treatment of Bello and the application of his cosmopolitan learning to the tasks of nineteenth-century state-building. It is suggested that his trajectory reflected a successful adaptation of liberal precepts to a conservative local social setting within a world order dominated by British promotion of free trade.

A serious historiographical regeneration certainly attended the series of bicentennial anniversaries that began in 2009 with those celebrating the *juntas* of La Paz and Quito. Ranging from Jeremy Adelman's strategic inter-continental history, which asks 'how colonists disidentified with empires and monarchies', to Guadalupe Soasti's biography of Carlos Montúfar that provides a cogent and even chilling case-study of precisely that experience, this advance in historiography has moved us beyond a rather empty dichotomy of talismanic *historias patrias*, on the one side, and the revisionist school of imperial implosion, on the other.[1] Moreover, as the reception of John Lynch's studies of Bolívar and San Martín has shown, biography has retrieved regional academic acceptance. It is now much easier to depict the process of independence and the early republican period of Spanish America with all due sensitivity to the subjective and emotional worlds as well as the economic structures and social systems that are more familiar features of the scholarly literature.[2]

It may seem paradoxical – even perverse – to suggest that a reassessment of Andrés Bello needs to be made part of that process. After

---

[1] Jeremy Adelman, *Sovereignty and Revolution in the Iberian Atlantic* (Princeton, 2006), 9; G. Soasti, *El Comisionado Regio Carlos Montúfar y Larrea* (Quito, 2009).

[2] John Lynch, *Simón Bolívar. A Life* (New Haven, 2006); John Lynch, *San Martín: Argentine Soldier, American Hero* (New Haven, 2009).

Figure 1 Andrés Bello by Raymond Monvoisin, 1843. Courtesy of Unidad de Fotografía, Archivo Central de la Universidad de Chile.

all, he is such an established icon of the independence and early republican eras, and we have Iván Jaksic's outstanding intellectual biographical study that sets the documentary record as straight as one might hope for.[3] Written very much in the style of its subject – diligently detailed and scrupulously discerning at every turn – Jaksic's study has properly dominated the field for over a dozen years.[4]

Yet Bello's name still remains more widely recognized than his personality and it is his ideas that are appreciated. Moreover, since those ideas have been lionized by 'official Latin America' for the better part of 200 years, it has often been hard to discern their complexities and links with his character and experience. He has long served as a

3 Iván Jaksic, *Andrés Bello. Scholarship and Nation-Building in Nineteenth-Century Latin America* (Cambridge, 2001).

4 See, most recently, Iván Jaksic, *The Hispanic World and American Intellectual Life, 1820–1880* (2007).

classic target for positivist and progressive-left schools in search of a foundational reactionary figure to attack, despite the fact that his political conservatism was underpinned by personal liberalism and undying attachment to the rule of law. Bello's profile, then, has suffered from a laudatory and denunciatory pincer-movement. His formidable record as a philologist and his accomplishment as a poet complicate the picture further, introducing jealous lines of disciplinary demarcation just when the understanding of Bello's trajectory as a historian, statesman and thinker depends vitally on the other, private or 'cultured' side of his life.[5]

When teased out a little, however, this is a figure on the margins of glory. He is Bolívar's tutor, but not his real mentor – that role belongs to Simón Rodríguez. In his London years, he deciphers Bentham's appalling handwriting alongside James Mill, but debates with neither.[6] He is said to have met Humboldt as a young man and Darwin in his middle age, and yet we have no contemporaneous and reliable record from them of these encounters.[7] Bello is a lodger of Miranda in London, but his signature appears nowhere in the documents of the Venezuelan mission of 1810 seeking British support for self-government, just as he is not identified in the May 1810 declaration of the junta in Caracas that it had no less a right than the Regency in Cádiz to uphold the rights of King Ferdinand VII. Yet it was Bello, on his own account, who wrote all those words.

He was counselor to the Chilean dictator Portales, but always behind the scenes, appearing only a handful of times in the three volumes of Portales's correspondence and being sharply shut-down when he had the very occasional temerity to voice criticism in public. For over twenty years, Bello directed the ministry of foreign relations of Chile but little of the diplomatic correspondence he drafted went out under his signature and he consistently resisted meeting foreign diplomats in person. Likewise, he was an adviser on the Constitution of 1833 and wrote the country's Civil Code of 1855, the most influential and enduring in regional history. For decades, he drafted the presidential messages. Everyone who mattered knew it, but these were anonymous enterprises, services rendered to the

---

[5] One signal multidisciplinary exception is *Andrés Bello y los Estudios Latinoamericanos*, ed. Beatriz González Stepan and Juan Poblete (Pittsburgh, 2009).

[6] *Cartas a Bello en Londres, 1810–1829*, ed. Sergio Fernández Larraín (Caracas, 1968), 77; Barry L. Velleman, *Andrés Bello u sus libros* (Caracas, 1995), 221–2.

[7] Alexander von Humboldt makes no mention of Bello in his *Personal Narrative* when relating his stay in Caracas, and particularly the ascent of the Silla de Avila on 2 January 1800, although it seems that Bello accompanied him and Bonpland on the climb until exhausted, returning to the city with carriers sent back to fetch food. Over fifty years later, Humboldt recalled advising the Bello family to moderate his dedication to study in order to preserve his health. M. L. Amunátegui, *Vida de don Andrés Bello* (Santiago, 1962), 18. For Darwin, see G. Whittemberg, K. Jaffé, C. Hirshbein and D. Yudelivich, 'Charles Darwin, Robert Fitzroy and Simón Rodríguez met in Concepción, Chile after the Earthquake of February 20 1835', *Interciencia*, 28, 9 (2003), 549–53.

state by an assiduous and retiring public servant who refused payment beyond his stipulated salary.[8] Bello, one might say, was the ghost-writer of the emergent republican state of Chile.[9]

As already indicated, one key reason for Bello's most uncertain place in popular consciousness derives from what Iván Jaksic calls his 'crystallization', which impedes us from getting to the mind behind the name. Bello himself favoured monuments, which he saw, drawing on the Roman tradition, as guarantors of historical memory, and far from un-republican in quality. In the days of limited mechanical reproduction, he spent a whole newspaper article describing for the people of Santiago a statue of Bolívar in Bogotá that he himself had not seen. But it is not for nothing that his great-grandson Jorge Edwards Bello wrote of a 'Bisabuleo de piedra', a great-grandfather of stone, for statues and busts abound.

It is, then, something of a mystery that is there not one mention of Bello in David Brading's otherwise magisterial study *The First America, 1492–1867*, which carries as its subtitle *The Spanish Monarchy, Creole Patriots, and the Liberal State*[10], with its chronological terminus placed at 1867, two years after the death of Bello – a man who earnestly served the monarchy through to 1810, who must stand as the quintessence of creole patriotism, and who was a leading architect of the subcontinent's remarkable liberal state. One might ask the same question of Adelman, who name-checks Bello just once, for accompanying Bolívar to London in 1810, in *Sovereignty and Revolution in the Iberian Atlantic*. That fine study has the great merit of breaking precisely with the parochialism of the nation-state paradigm but it passes over one of the very, very few individuals of the age who was capable of doing that himself in real-time.[11]

Luis Castro Leiva, the late Venezuelan political philosopher, devoted considerable energy to his brilliant deconstructions of the myth of Bolívar and what has now become a Chávez-fuelled *Bolivarianismo*, but in doing so Castro entirely ignored the constitutional critique of *caudillismo* offered by Bello, who equally dismissed the Liberator's 1826 charter for Bolivia.[12] From the Chilean perspective, Patricio Silva understandably mentions Bello in his recent study *In the Name of Reason. Technocrats and Politics in*

---

[8] According to Guillermo Feliú Cruz, 'Personality disappears in this very broad concept of what service to the country meant. And it is precisely in this that we can explain the scarcity within Chilean literature of memoirs, autobiographies, and intimate revelations to newspapers.' *Obras completas de Andrés Bello* (hereafter *OC*), XII (Caracas, 1981), ccxxxiii.

[9] I owe this phrase to Antonio Cussen, *Bello and Bolívar. Poetry and Politics in the Spanish American Revolution* (Cambridge, 1992), 70. The best synthetic appraisal of Bello's contribution to the creation of a stable republic in Chile is Jaime Concha, 'Bello y su Gestión Superestructural en Chile', *Revista de Crítica Literaria Latinoamericana*, 43/4 (1996), 139–61.

[10] David Brading, *The First America. The Spanish Monarchy, Creole Patriots, and the Liberal State, 1492–1867* (Cambridge, 1991).

[11] Adelman, *Sovereignty and Revolution*.

[12] *Obras de Luis Castro Leiva*, I: *Para Pensar a Bolívar*, II: *Lenguajes Republicanos* (Caracas, 2005).

Chile, which provides a compelling survey of the technical specialists and intellectuals who have provided different scientific rationalities for state management. With his concentration on the twentieth century, Silva's story understandably focuses on groups such as the 'Chicago Boys' behind Sergio de Castro's conduct of the economy for Pinochet and the post-structuralists at CIEPLAN who played a similar role for liberal democratic governments.[13]

But Silva starts this story precisely with Bello's prize pupil and leading critic Lastarria, not least because of Lastarria's explicit embracing of positivism and the language of science as a critique of a Chile, where he claimed there still prevailed in social life the theological and metaphysical ideas of the Middle Ages. Bello is thereby morphed into the antediluvian regime, precisely where Lastarria sought to consign him, but less for what he did in terms of state-building and management than for his insistence upon an empirical and documentary core to history-writing. Lastarria was never reconciled to Bello's embracing of science but refusal of scientism, which he disliked for its rhetorical hubris, even as he read Darwin closely, and even came to appreciate the merits of the railway.[14]

Bello's 'ghostliness' is a general pattern, but it is still subject to signal interruption. The 'Cláusula Bello' marked his personal commitment to Spanish American community by ensuring that Chile always offered commercial treaty terms to other regional states that improved upon Most Favoured Nation status. His decade-long campaign in the columns of *El Araucano* for peace and reconciliation with Spain was unsigned but known to all, bearing uncontroversial fruit in 1844.[15] And, of course, on 17 September 1843, this severe and decidedly reticent man stepped forward to deliver the inaugural address of the University of Chile, of which he was the founding rector, before the president of the republic, members of congress, leaders of the armed forces, the church and the diplomatic corps as well as the faculty. He was sixty-one years old and at the peak of his intellectual powers, deferred to even by the radical liberals who sought to tarnish him as the intellectual author of dictatorship but whose critiques reveal him to be the architect of a far more consequential conservative hegemony.

On that day, Bello spoke out firmly in his own name, and his lecture was a critical moment in the intellectual life of the nineteenth-century American world. It is fully comparable with Newman's *The Idea of a University*, which postdated it by a dozen years, and it is still salient today

[13] Patricio Silva, *In the Name of Reason. Technocrats and Politics in Chile* (University Park, 2008).
[14] Nearly 100 of the 2,000 books of Bello's library at his death were devoted to medicine and science. Velleman, *Bello y sus libros*, 65–70.
[15] *OC*, x, 543–62.

for its anti-positivist treatment of the relationship of reason and logic, on the one hand, and morality and faith, on the other.

In the *Philosophy of Understanding*, Bello upholds the tenets of what today would be dubbed 'intelligent design': 'We believe . . . that the whole search for the reason for first principles and the logical bases of the confidence we place in them, is nothing but plunging into a sphere which is beyond the reach of human faculties.'[16] And at the same time, drawing directly on the Scottish Enlightenment, he calmly notes that

> The primary elements of reason, axioms, truths that have a complete certainty and which are found within the reach of all, are the peculiar objects of common sense, a denomination to which some give a more extensive meaning than others and which has been much abused in modern times.[17]

Always mindful of the needs of present public policy, he drove his empirical explorations deep into the past, back through the *Siete Partidas*, the voluminous legal instruments of Alfonso X, beyond the medieval epic *Poema de Mio Cid*, through to Virgil and Homer, whose verses he learned as a child and recited on his deathbed, to the Roman Law that he prized as the basis for modern jurisprudence, and to the Latin which he so loved but which he energetically rejected as a model for Spanish syntax.

An empirical pragmatist, Andrés Bello clearly knew that he was party to a changing world in which history and culture needed to attend to the claims of the future. If his research was meticulous, it was self-consciously at the service of design for future generations. And it is as much a mark of his inner tenacity as of his faith that he consistently pursued those tasks even though nine of his fifteen children predeceased him.

The portrait before you, by Raymond Monvoisin, is of Andrés Bello in the dress of the Founding Rector of the Universidad de Chile and with all the gravitas of a senior figure in an oligarchic society, but upon closer inspection you might appreciate that it is also of a grieving father, who has lost his seven-year-old daughter Dolores a few weeks earlier. That event prompted one of Bello's finer poems, 'La Oración por Todos' (A Prayer for All), where, having recognized the reality of death and asked Lola, as the family called her, to pray for them and humanity as a whole, he anticipates joining her before too long:

I will also – the day is not far off –
Inhabit the house of darkness
And I will ask for a pure soul
To give me consolation for my long suffering.[18]

---

[16] *Filosofía del Entendimiento*, in *OC*, III.

[17] *Ibid.* English translation here is from O. Carlos Stoetzer, 'The Political Ideas of Andrés Bello', *International Philosophical Quarterly*, 23, 4 (1983), 399.

[18] This translation is from Jaksic, *Andrés Bello*, 193.

A secondary figure

In case you think I am set fair to do nothing but write this man up, let me reiterate straightaway that he has been treated as a figure of secondary order for some very understandable reasons, not just at the caprice of posterity. First, Bello was a scribe, not a warrior, at a time of war in a heroic age. Whilst his student Bolívar led successive armies in a twelve-year continental 'war to the death', he was bottled up in north London, for half of his time here scraping a living through translation, tutoring, and even assisting his tailor in order to pay off the family clothes bill.[19] His own trade was pen and ink, his posture sedentary, and although his gait was rapid, there is no evidence he ever rode a horse in adulthood. That did not look too good in the age of Byron and Bolívar.

Secondly, Bello was certainly a conservative and legalist state-builder, not a proclaimer of popular programmes. He stood for many admirable things, but 'order' – that most mercurial constituent of Liberalism, and nowhere more so than in Spanish America – is in ordinary times a vote-winner only with a minority.[20] His insistence that 'freedom' was not synonymous with 'licence' pleased neither those who disdained every form of change nor those who sought it any cost, and today it still resonates of *Pinochetista* prescription.

Thirdly, Bello belonged to everyone and yet to nobody. In nothing was his identity so fragile than in response to history's insistence that identity be place-based. Born in 1781 a subject of the king of Spain, he descended from Canary Islanders. A colonial servant in the Captaincy General of Venezuela, his first political initiative upon the collapse of the Spanish monarchy is to uphold the rights of Caracas within an international royalist confederation. At no stage did he live as a citizen in the Republic of Venezuela, which country he left in 1810 and to which he never returned.

With the rapid defeat of the cause of self-government, for the promotion of which he travelled with Bolívar to London, Bello entered – in law and to some appreciable degree also in psychological condition – into the status of exile. He spent almost twenty years in London, married an Irish Londoner, raised three children, lost his wife (at the age of twenty-six) and his youngest boy here; remarried, again to a woman of Irish descent, with three further children born as Londoners. Yet Bello, who for fifteen years worked his British Museum reader's ticket for every waking minute it was worth, never felt himself a Londoner or British or even European, despite his profound respect for Spanish history and culture. He closely studied and profoundly admired British politics, law and civic culture, but only to

---

[19] *Andrés Bello. The London Years*, ed. John Lynch (1982).

[20] Ana María Stuven, *La seducción de un orden. Las elites y la construcción de Chile en las polémicas culturales y políticas del siglo XIX* (Santiago, 2000).

seek out suitable applications for the Americas, where he ardently wanted his children to grow up. During the 1820s, Bello often described himself as 'Colombian', and he did so with palpable pride, but by the end of the decade Gran Colombia, which then included Venezuela and Ecuador as well as present-day Colombia, had come to an end. This time, the nation left the man.

After apparently settling the issue with his move to Chile in 1829 (he was naturalized in 1832), Bello wrote, 'here I am, a Chilean citizen by law, a father of Chileans, and employed by the Chilean government for more than ten years... and yet in the opinion of most Chileans, just as alien as the day I arrived'.[21] This was not self-serving. The oppositional Liberals readily drew attention to Bello's foreignness, the old federalist José Miguel Infante in defiantly xenophobic terms, and even Bello's student José Victorino Lastarria was not above giving the issue an airing with menace.

In a way it is surprising that more scandal was not attached to an act for which we do have hard documentary evidence – Bello's supplication of June 1813 to the Spanish regency to be included in an amnesty, deploying what might now be thought a thoroughly craven apology.[22] Such a move can certainly be explained by developments in Spain, where the defeat of the French and the promulgation of a charter of liberalism unprecedented in world history provided probably all of what Bello sought in terms of constitutional monarchy, to which he cleaved until at least 1821.

But Bello refused a fate of mute marginality. The application for amnesty having been rejected by the Spanish liberal authorities – Ferdinand VII was still imprisoned in France – his own exile status was confirmed. Now he becomes a regular reader in the warmth of the British Museum, legwork on the origins of the *Poema de Mio Cid* being undertaken in these severely lean years, Bello's discovery of lost stanzas and his deconstruction of the complexities of the work's metre constituting what he and his family considered his greatest scholarship. The letters of his son Carlos, one of only two to visit Europe, frequently described the Spain of the 1840s in terms of the *Cid*, and it must have been a particularly bitter blow for Bello to learn – at the age of eighty-two and from an aside in a letter from Lastarria of all people – that the Spanish Royal Academy had declined on completely non-academic grounds to publish his edition of the epic.[23]

---

[21] To Felipe Pardo, 26 July 1839, *OC*, XXVI, 55.
[22] 'The supplicant took no part whatsoever in the movements and plotting that preceded the Revolution – no intelligence with those planning the First Junta, no slippage, not even of the slightest nature, whilst a legitimate Government stood in Caracas'. *OC*, XXV, 55–7.
[23] *Archivo Epistolar de Don Miguel Luis Amunátegui* (Santiago, 1942), 155–6.

I think that Antonio Cussen is right to see Bello's identification of the missing scene of the *Jura de Santa Gadea* – when the Cid obliges King Alfonso to swear himself innocent of the death of King Sancho – as emblematic of an accountability deep in the Spanish monarchical tradition, perhaps comparable to that celebrated by Burke in Britain and definitely in need of promotion in 1823, when Ferdinand VII was restored by French troops to absolute power and the constitution of 1812 swept away.[24] Whatever the case, the question of monarchism continued to cause Bello trouble into the 1820s, and nothing stirred things up so much as a letter of November 1821 he wrote on this subject to Fray Servando Mier, that erratic radical priest and recidivist jail-breaker. Mier, who was then in Philadelphia, never received the letter, which unaccountably fell into the hands of the republican ministry in Bogotá for which Bello now worked as a diplomat and which was less than thrilled to learn of his view – soon to be dropped for ever – that monarchy was the only reasonable system of government for Spanish America.[25]

The Liberals, of course, had only momentarily regained power in Spain, but at no stage did policy towards the Americas undergo major alteration. Indeed, these were the years of fiercest warfare. Moreover, Bolívar did not seem particularly dismayed by Bello's views. After all, he would himself soon write a quasi-monarchical constitution for Bolivia, and once out of power he confided in General O'Leary that the region would be better administered under the aegis of the Koran than anything resembling the US Constitution.[26]

It is probable that Bolívar felt slighted by the faintness of the praise offered by Bello's 1822 epic poem on the struggle for independence *Alocución a la Poesía*, and Bello's claim that he lacked the literary skills to celebrate the magnitude of the Liberator's achievement does seem disingenuous. Yet more than that, or any memory of the early years, it appears to have been Bolívar's loss of office that complicated relations between the two men, the soldier because he became disorientated and careless of detail, the intellectual because he could not quite grasp that the hero now lacked unquestioned executive authority, and was unable to deliver on simple requests such as paying the London embassy.

Thus, it was over the tiresome sale of a Venezuelan mine on the London market that Bolívar miscalculated, irritably chastising Bello in May 1827 for what he deemed slackness. Perhaps more than any other event, this

[24]Cussen, *Bello and Bolívar*, 53–7.
[25]*OC*, XXV, 114–18. It was probably Mier's name that attracted one of several agents sifting through the international mails in that period, but letters were generally vulnerable.
[26]Bolívar to O'Leary, 13 Sept. 1829, quoted in I. Jaksic and M. Leiras, 'Life without the King. Centralists, Federalists, and Constitutional Monarchists in the Making of the Spanish American Republics, 1808–1830', Working Paper no. 255, Kellogg Institute, University of Notre Dame (1998), 13.

determined that Andrés Bello would never return to Venezuela, choosing instead the country which Bolívar, when he realized the mistake he had made, dubbed the 'land of anarchy'.[27] In April 1829, he wrote from Quito to the Colombian ambassador in London, Fernández Madrid, urging him to persuade Bello that 'Colombia is the least bad of the countries of America', and that he would be given a good post there:

> I know the superior talents of this native of Caracas who is my contemporary; he was my teacher when we were of the same age; and I loved him with respect. His reticence has kept us apart to a certain extent, and because of that I want to be reconciled with him.[28]

It was, as Iván Jaksic says, too little, too late. Bello, his second wife Elizabeth and their five children had boarded the brig *Grecian* at Gravesend two months earlier, their voyage paid for by the Liberal government in Santiago de Chile, which had long since matched Bolívar's job offer. At dawn on the day of their departure, Bello dashed off an affectionate note to Fernández, noting that London was 'in so many ways hateful to me, and in so many other ways the object of my love'.[29]

On the second and final journey of his life, Andrés Bello took with him the saddest of personal memories, a fount of practical experience in international diplomacy, and 400 books. Today, it is easy to forget that this most domestic and cautious man, close to fifty years of age had not just opted against going 'home'. He had also chosen to spend the rest of his life in what was then a desperately unstable country, currently ruled under a constitution that had been devised by his friend José Joaquín Mora but that took federalism and the division of powers to lengths that Bello thought absurd and destructive.

The scribe finds his place

The country he reached on 25 June 1829 was, however, about to change decisively. Within ten months, the Liberals were decisively defeated at the Battle of Lircay (17 April). Many of the problems that Bello had anticipated were now emphatically removed from the political realm, his intellectual peers finding frightened and often resentful refuge in the academic arena.

At Lircay, the battle-cry of the Conservative troops led by Diego Portales was 'no dejar gringo vivo' ('Leave no Gringo alive'), few prisoners were spared, and a young London friend of Bello's, William Tupper, was subjected to an almost ritualistic and cruelly protracted death by sabre-blows on the field. One of Elizabeth Bello's early tasks in Santiago

---

[27] Bello to Gual, 6 Jan. 1825, *OC*, XXV, 142–3.
[28] Bolívar to Fernández Madrid, 27 Apr. 1829, *Cartas del Libertador*, VII (Caracas, 1969), 127–8.
[29] *OC*, XXV, 408–9.

was to support Tupper's widow Isidora Zegers and her newborn son.[30] Bello himself now confronted the formidable prospect of dealing with Portales, the deeply feared victor, a coldly violent man who despised all foreigners but, as an international merchant, considered the English at least practical and reliable. And although he had been contracted by the despicable Liberals, in Bello Portales smelled the blood of an Englishman.

José Victorino Lastarria, who bitterly resented Bello's decision to collaborate with 'the dictatorship', tellingly describes him at home one night in a fit of giggles, holding onto a pillar and fighting back the tears as the elderly and deadpan Simón Rodríguez recounted how some years earlier in La Paz he had been anxious to throw a banquet for Marshal Sucre and his entire staff after the Battle of Ayacucho. However, at the last minute he found he lacked sufficient crockery and so was obliged to buy some chamber pots from a store down the street in order to serve all the officers.[31] Perhaps predictably, relations between Sucre and Rodríguez soured thereafter. Here, of course, we find the pleasures of self-mockery among intellectuals, but there is also a deeper, nervier element, of which Rodríguez was acutely aware: 'The Independence of America is due to the use of Arms . . . and it is with them that it will have to be maintained; those who have not been able to take them up have worked under their protection or lived in their shadow.'[32]

Chile adopted as its national motto 'Por la razón o la fuerza' in 1834, when Portales was not in ministerial office, but it was precisely Portales's preferred form of exercising power to occupy subordinate positions and threaten the use of force against those located in the commanding heights of reason if they exceeded their brief. Portales did not exclude the possibility of development and even of some future democracy, he simply believed, not unlike Bolívar, that it would be long delayed by 'el peso de la noche' ('the weight of the night') or that assemblage of historical backwardnesses to which, of course, he himself made such a singular contribution.[33] Bello did not stand outside this equation – after all, he had asked Portales to be the godfather of his daughter María Asención

<hr />

[30] F. Encina, *Resumen de la historia de Chile*, II (Santiago, 1954), 827; L. Bocaz, *Andrés Bello. Una biografía cultural* (Santa Fé de Bogotá, 2000), 207; T. Sutcliffe, *Sixteen Years in Chile and Peru: From 1822 to 1838* (1841), 245–6.

[31] *Literary Memoirs* (New York, 2000), 34–5.

[32] Simón Rodríguez, *En defensa del libertador del mediodía* (Arequipa, 1830), 152, cited in L. Castro Leiva, 'El Historicismo Político Bolivariano', *Revista de Estudios Políticos*, 42 (1984), 100.

[33] 'The democracy that is so urged by the deluded is absurd for countries like the Americas, full of vice and where citizens are entirely bereft of virtue, which is necessary for the instituting of a true republic. Neither is monarchy an American ideal; we emerge from one terrible condition to enter into another, and what have we gained? Republicanism is the system we should adopt, but do you know how I understand it for these countries? A strong government, centralized, whose members are true models of virtue and patriotism . . . When

six months earlier, and had received a box of cigars from the governor when he could not attend the baptism. Much of Lastarria's critique must stand.

Yet, whatever the trauma of Lircay and the temporising with Portales, Bello's political strategy for the new republican order was clear from his first months in Chile and consistently upheld until his death thirty-five years later:

> The form of government is not itself the primordial cause of the wealth of nations. Rather, it is the consonance between the institutions of the state and the character and morality of the populace. So long as a society is in conflict with the laws under which it subsists, and whilst these provoke disturbances as well as impeding the supreme power from suppressing them, there will always be instability. [34]

For Lastarria, the young ideologue, this was to borrow the authority of Montesquieu for a cause that Portales imposed as if it were a state of nature. But Bello was far from alone in his incrementalism. Domingo Fausto Sarmiento, a friend of Lastarria during his long exile in Chile, later president of Argentina, and arguably the only figure of nineteenth-century Spanish America to match's Bello's intellectual influence, took the same route. Sarmiento supported Lastarria's repudiation of Spain but could not abide his corollary sympathy for indigenous America, which he found utterly barbarian, and when he returned to Chile in 1841 Sarmiento took only a week to accept the conservative regime's offer of work because,

> We ... had to prove to America that it was not in the name of some utopia that we were suffering persecution, and that, given the imperfection of American governments, we were disposed to accept them as facts, with the firm intention, at least on my part, of injecting them with progressive ideals. [35]

Such a strategy of pragmatism in pursuit of modernity was, as you might expect, much easier to proclaim than to implement. The six volumes of Montesquieu possessed by Bello were themselves prohibited, as was Vattel's *Le droit des gens,* the primary inspiration for his own treatise on international law, the first book he published in Chile and the most influential throughout the continent. A comparable paradox lay in the fact that Bello's only platform for denouncing censorship was *El Araucano,* the paper of the very government that refused to confront the church and dismantle the mental world of the Inquisition. [36] As a corollary, Bello

---

the citizenry has been moralized, then let completely liberal government prevail.' *Epistolario de Portales,* ed. G. Feliú Cruz (Santiago, 1936), I, 176–8.

[34] *El Araucano,* 27 Nov. 1830, cited in Stuven, *La seducción de un orden,* 51.

[35] Domingo Fausto Sarmiento, *Recollections of a Provincial Past* (New York, 2005), 188; Norman Sacks, 'Lastarria y Sarmiento: El Chileno y el Argentino Achilenado', *Cuadernos Americanos,* 2, 62 (1997), 491–512.

[36] *El Araucano,* 23 Nov. 1832, cited in Margaret Campbell, 'Education in Chile, 1810–1842', *Journal of Inter-American Studies,* 1, 3 (1959), 366; Simon Collier, *Chile: The Making of Republic 1830–1865* (Cambridge, 2003), 29.

apparently never saw anything amiss in editing a paper of that title whilst persistently ignoring the condition of the contemporary indigenous people of Chile. There are just two references to indigenous figures – Atahualpa and Moctezuma – in Bello's epic poem *La Agricultura en la Zona Tórrida*. Equally, Catherine Davies has argued convincingly that there and in his other poetical works he effectively 'troped women out of history'.[37]

There is something of this, too, in Bello's Civil Code of 1855, where the effort to promote modernity through Lockean contract chafed badly against the need for laws to chime with social mores. For just as Bello was opposed to idealist legislation, so also did he believe that 'laws that empower [citizens] to take part in public affairs are infinitely less important than those that secure one's person and property'.[38] But since his prescription for this was formal process rather than custom and practice, the instruments for dealing with legitimacy and inheritance effectively 'stripped everyday acts that were socially indicative of paternity of their legal significance'.[39] Out went scandalous gossip and dodgy legal reasoning, and up went the liberties of fathers as a levelling civic democracy was crushed by formalized bureaucracy.

Bello produced a more efficacious result for the vexed question of entail, or *mayorazgos*, since entailed estates had been at the heart of the liberal-conservative ideological conflict from independence, with the latter successfully beating off efforts to abolish them, albeit at the considerable cost of impeding the development of markets in land and mortgages. Here, Bello's mercantilist pragmatism succeeded by converting such estates into rent-bearing assets and thereby assuring the owners that their inheritance remained valorized.[40]

The picture, then, is distinctly mixed. It would not be until 1865, the year of Bello's death, that religious tolerance was introduced to Chile, and even then such was the opposition that this could not be by amendment of the Constitution but only through an interpretative law. There is perhaps a tragic echo of such engagement between tradition and modernity in the destruction of the Santiago Church of the Compañía de Jesús in December 1863, when the great majority of a congregation of 2,000, overwhelmingly women and children, expired in a conflagration caused

[37] Ruth Hill, 'Entre lo transatlántico y lo hemisférico: los proyectos raciales de Andrés Bello', *Revista Iberoamericana*, LXXV (2009), 730; Catherine Davies, 'Troped out of History: Women, Gender and Nation in the Poetry of Andrés Bello', *Bulletin of Hispanic Studies*, 84, 1 (2007), 99–111.

[38] 'Civil Code. Presentation of the Bill to Congress', *Selected Writings of Andrés Bello*, ed. I. Jaksic (New York, 1997) (hereafter *SW*) 271.

[39] Nara Milanich, *Children of Fate. Childhod, Class, and the State in Chile, 1850–1930* (Durham, NC, 2009), 58.

[40] Arnold J. Bauer, *Chilean Rural Society from the Spanish Conquest to 1930* (Cambridge, 1975), 20–1.

not by the 7,000 candles but by a leaking gas canister used to illuminate a colossal image of the Virgin Mary. The elaborate crinolines worn by the doomed celebrants apparently accelerated the fire, which, in turn, provoked the establishment in the capital of a volunteer fire service – including Bello's eighteen-year old son Emilio – that would become a core element in twentieth-century democratic culture.[41]

Ventriloquism (and vehemence) in foreign policy

Like Rodríguez, Bello recognized the primacy of force, and in public he neither contradicted any government nor engaged in partisan politics, but privately he continued to argue cases, even with Portales. For Iván Jaksic, the only time that the Venezuelan intellectual seriously considered leaving Chile was in late 1836, when Portales was set upon destroying the new Peru-Bolivia Confederation set up by Marshal Santa Cruz.[42] Now serving as minister of war, Portales wrote to Admiral Blanco Encalada,

> I have argued a thousand times with don Andrés, against his opinions on the blockade etc., but he keeps on putting texts in front of me, and I have to shut up. Today I had him come back . . . and he replied that there never has been an instance of a conditional blockade being ordered, and still less one declared by higher law of the nation, which would not be respected by neutrals.

But then, predictably, Portales instructed his commander to open hostilities.[43] A month later, the government reserved the right to remove any citizen to any point in the republic, and two months after that permanent courts martial were instituted, any returning exiles being subject to a mandatory death penalty to be executed within twenty-four hours with no right of appeal.[44] Even Pinochet stopped short of such public instruments.

Bello had held firm on the issue of hostilities because he neither shared Portales's 'realist' conviction about the need to remove the Confederation nor was he convinced that the facts – too labyrinthine to recount here – justified a *causus belli*.[45] Yet, it is notable that after Portales was killed in June 1837, Bello continued to support the conflict, which now had widespread popular approval. Henceforth, his settled policy – and it was tested more than a few times – was to ascertain whether parties or individuals were

[41] Benjamín Vicuña Mackenna, *El incendio del templo de la Compañía de Jesús: fundación del Cuerpo de Bomberos de Santiago* (Santiago, 1971).

[42] Jaksic, *Andrés Bello*, 120.

[43] Portales to Blanco Encalada, 17 Oct. 1836, *Portales pintado por si mismo* (Santiago, 1941), 115–16.

[44] D. Barros Arana, *Un decenio de la historia de Chile, 1841–1851*, I (Santiago, 1905), 77.

[45] According to Portales, 'Chile's position in relation to then Peru-Bolivia confederation is untenable. It cannot be tolerated neither by the people nor by the government, for it would be equivalent to suicide'. *Epistolario*, ed. Feliú Cruz, II, 452.

disturbing the affairs of their neighbours and whether crimes had been committed or were being planned.

In 1844, the Confederation defeated and Santa Cruz now held prisoner in Chillán, Bello argued precisely on such grounds for detaining a former head of another state. Having been an exile himself, he was most mindful of their rights, but Santa Cruz, although a foreigner, was still subject to municipal law, even if the crimes, including murder, he planned or committed were in another jurisdiction.

> When has International Law protected this class of criminals? Does it not, rather, group them as enemies of the human race which every nation can properly try and punish? Which moral code justifies clandestine conspiracy in which assassination is an instrument?

> If a Chilean were to be confined and punished with corresponding severity for activities like those we have described... Chile would have no grounds upon which to protest.[46]

If that observation by Chile's foremost scholar of jurisprudence had been to hand in London a decade ago, the defence of General Pinochet in the House of Lords would surely have been spoiled rather more rapidly than was the case.

Chile has always had to 'speak to power' internationally, and for that it possessed a remarkable early tutor in Andrés Bello, who understood the difference between a message sent and one received, between mere expression and true communication. In his approach to international relations, Bello might be described as both a realist and an idealist. Louise Fawcett has recently made a compelling case for his contribution to international thought being a singular blend of 'Western' and 'non-Western' approaches.[47] In London, he had learned from Irisarri that even the greatest asymmetry in power need not obviate just treatment of weak states, provided they conducted their affairs prudently.[48] And in *Principios* he goes straight to the point:

> in issues between the weak and strong, the strong state is effectively judge and jury... That is the condition of the world and that is also the value of supposed international equality, which in each era can only correspond to the prevalent intellectual and moral culture. This is where we can progressively move towards the ideal.[49]

---

[46] *El Araucano*, 25 Oct. 1844, in *OC*, XI, *Derecho International*, II, 271–2.

[47] Louise Fawcett, 'Between West and Non-West: Latin American Contributions to International Thought', *International History Review*, 34, 4 (2012), 679–704.

[48] According to Irisarri, 'it is not weakness but imprudence that has caused the poor outcome of relations between strong and weak states, because when the just cause of the weak is made plain, the strong cedes'. Quoted in G. Feliú Cruz, *Andrés Bello y la redacción de los documentos oficiales, administrativos, internacionales y legislativos de Chile. Bello, Irisarri y Egaña en Londres* (Caracas, 1957), 229–30.

[49] *OC*, XI, 31–2.

On one occasion, in a piece of diplomatic *jiu-jitsu*, Bello wrote to Henry Walpole, 'The British government is strong enough to be unjust with impunity, but hitherto the benign effect of her serious and generous conduct has been palpable.'[50]

We already know that Bello was something of a ventriloquist, and he certainly seemed to have a European-style balance-of-power approach to Spanish American relations. But if there is a sort of subalternity in substance as well as form, we should be mindful of the constraints: in 1836, the Chilean foreign ministry employed just four diplomats abroad – the chargés in Paris, Washington, Lima and Central America – on a budget of less than 20,000 pesos. Under such circumstances, it was vital to 'get the record straight', maintaining scrupulous records of past treaties – until Chile signed new ones, she effectively inherited international commitments from Spain – as well as keeping up to speed with legal and political developments across the globe. A compulsive collector of detailed accounts, and ever attentive to the issue of sequencing, Bello went so far in 1849 to have Congress publish an entire volume providing in minute detail the unravelling of the notorious 'Seth Barton Case', in which the US ambassador of that name sought to create an international crisis over his marriage to a Chilean Catholic under the Protestant rite in the American legation. Barton's claims collapsed in the face of one triangulated fact after another.[51]

Sometimes, however, empirical precision was simply not enough. In the prolonged case of the *Jeune Nelly*, a French craft from which the Valparaiso authorities confiscated some cargo in 1833, Bello made little headway with Chargé Ragueneau de la Chainaye under Article 5 of the Treaty of 23 May 1769 between France and Spain, and was then stung by the unbridled insolence of a letter from Paris's vice-consul.[52] He duly drafted for Minister Tocornal a reply that must have been most satisfying:

> In that memorandum the familiar charges are repeated, albeit sometimes expressed in more pungent and offensive terms than before; resort is even made to sarcasm, and with respect to most of the accusations . . . no proof is offered beyond the exceptionally weak claims already made; but a new charge is made – more despicable, if that were possible, than the others, but this time unsupported by any factual evidence at all. I am interrogated; I am admonished for sophistry in what was a full, frank and unambiguous explanation; I am charged with a distortion, which, had I made it, would have rendered me unworthy of the office I hold.[53]

---

[50] *Ibid.*, xlv.

[51] *Memoria sobre las incidencias ocurridas en el matrimonio del Honorable Señor Barton, Encargado de Negocios de los Estados unidos de América, con doña Isabel Astaburnaga* (Santiago, 1849).

[52] It is unclear to me if this is the same vessel as the *Jeune Nelly* which featured in 'United States v. Guillem, 52 U.S. 47 (1850)', an important Supreme Court case relating to the rights of neutrals during naval blockades.

[53] Tocornal to Ragueneau, 7 Dec. 1833, *OC*, XII, 88.

Bello's Pan-American vocation is undeniable. After all, this was a man who wrote to his brother Carlos,

> I cannot express to you the melancholy that now, more than ever afflicts me because of the distance between us. Caracas is in my thoughts at all times; Caracas is in my dreams. Last night I dreamt of being in the company of some beloved people from that wonderful time of our childhood.[54]

A dozen years before, Bello had thanked Carlos for a print of Caracas, 'which is hung opposite my bed, and will perhaps be the last object that my eyes will perceive before I depart this earth'.[55] For Bello, then, this was naturally a family affair. Spain was the 'madre-patria', and he told his biographer,

> Nature gives us one mother and one mother-land...In vain we try to adopt a new country; the heart gives itself but once. The hand may wave a foreign flag...and strangers call you fellow-citizen, but what does that matter? The land of our birth lives on in the human breast.[56]

Here, we find the familiar blend of sentiment and practicality, and it is correspondingly expressed in the foreign policy of Chile during the Bello years, when the country seeks close relations, 'with all the states that form this great family of free peoples' and which 'have the same origins, speak the same language, profess the same religion, and . . . have the same customs'.[57]

Yet, Santiago did not favour grand multilateral declarations or region-wide treaties, which carried the inescapable risk of binding her to commitments she could not fulfil, particularly over defence. Rather, the approach – then as now – was through a succession of bilateral trade treaties, not least because it was Bello's firm conviction that 'trade has done more to facilitate international relations than all other factors combined' – a belief that complemented his local view that participation in political affairs was less important to the citizenry than the security of their life and property.[58]

The institution of reason

Bello's incrementalism, his evolutionary and empirical approach to these big questions, is also to be found in the inaugural lecture of the University of Chile. There, he affirms, in another domestic turn of phrase, that 'the diffusion of knowledge involves one or more hearths from which light is emitted and spread; and this light, expanding little by little through the

[54] To Carlos Bello, 30 Dec.1856, *OC*, XXVI, 345.
[55] To Carlos Bello, 30 Apr. 1842, *ibid.*, 78.
[56] *El Araucano*, 13 Nov.1844, *OC*, XII, li; Amunátegui, *Vida*, 301.
[57] Tocornal to Mexican foreign minister, 17 June 1836, *OC*, XII, 103.
[58] *Ibid.*, 644.

intervening spaces will, at last seep into the furthest levels of society'.[59] And that is now assuredly where Bello wanted reason to be. He sought a 'gente educada', who would lift themselves out of Portales's 'weight of the night'. And he was now reconciled to this in a republican setting: 'In no type of association is education more important than in a republic.'[60]

The university would not have its own buildings or even teach students directly for a number of years, but it was charged, under Bello's self-imposed mandate, to oversee Chile's entire educational system and so may properly be seen as 'one of the first truly national projects undertaken by the emerging Chilean state'.[61] Bello's rectorship might seem a shoe-in nowadays, but it was controversial enough at the time – first because he was up against the conservative priest who had directed the old college of San Felipe, which was now to be incorporated into the University, and then because, breaking with the French tradition, he included a faculty of theology and so infuriated the energetically anti-clerical opposition.

The university could not, of course, replace the church, but, Bello declared, 'Morality (which I consider inseparable from religion) is the very life of society.' Like Newman, he did not see how an intellectual training of the whole mind could exclude this branch of learning, but he wanted to create a practical institution of learning, in the vernacular tongue and a secular setting.

Here, he is in Kantian mode, with 'God as the moral author of the world', although at the time this was taken by some as simply a craven capitulation before the *status quo*. Yet, Bello's approach defies simple forward–backward linkages, just as it escapes any easy right–left spectrum. These issues are to the fore of philosophical debate today over ethics, and particularly the qualities of evil. Terry Eagleton and Peter Dews would have had no trouble with this side of the new university's mission, or indeed with Bello's insistence that teachers undertake research and his celebration of inter-disciplinarity that likewise remain high on the agenda of higher education.[62]

Here, we might draw assistance from our second Nelly–la Nelly avant-garde, Nelly Richard, who stands opposed to Bello in many aspects, not least his repudiation of Romanticism and licence as 'an orgy of the imagination' and his promotion of clarity in speech and written

---

[59] *SW*, 124–37.

[60] 'On the Aims of Education' (1836), *SW*, 110; *OC*, XXII, 658.

[61] I. Jaksic and S. Serrano, 'In the Service of the Nation: The Establishment and Consolidation of the Universidad de Chile, 1842–79', *Hispanic American Historical Review*, 70, 1 (1990), 139.

[62] T. Eagleton, *Trouble with Strangers: a Study of Ethics* (2009); P. Dews, *The Idea of Evil* (Oxford, 2008).

expression, which she takes to have long since mutated into the local hegemonic voice.[63]

Richard makes a densely worded but perfectly reasonable claim for a post-modern perspective in that 'Tradition and modernity... cease to be in opposition under an axis of antagonism between the old (repetition) and the new (transformation): post-modernity disorganizes and reorganizes the procedure of phases thanks to transverse connections that intercalate pasts and presents disturbed by the operation of historical referencing.'[64]

That is pretty much what Bello gets up to in the inaugural lecture, giving most public expression to his own imagination. Mid-way through the talk, he takes his disquisition at the birth of a new seat of learning to the very point of death, or, rather, to the point of preparing for death. 'Letters and science', he told his distinguished audience, 'are the best preparation for the moment of death':

> On the eve of drinking the hemlock, Socrates illumined the cell with the most sublime speculations on the future of human destinies that have been left to us by pagan antiquity... Chenier wrote his last verses while awaiting death within instants, leaving them unfinished when he went to the scaffold.

And, just for once, he puts himself in the picture:

> Letters adorned the morning of my life with joyous bursts of light and still retain some glimmerings in my soul, like a flower that lends beauty to ruins... Letters... have sustained me in my long pilgrimage and guided my steps to this soil of freedom and peace, this adoptive country that has offered me such benevolent hospitality.[65]

We know, of course, that Lola's recent death will have been to the fore of his mind when composing these lines, which came to be tested over the next dozen years as a further six children, aged between twenty-three and thirty-nine, were felled by TB or childbirth. Suffice it to say, then, that Andrés Bello believed in ghosts with reason.[66]

---

[63]'Her texts have insisted on micropractices of difference and an aesthetic of the fragmentary, partial and oblique as opening new discursive and artistic possibilities for contesting hegemonic discourses.' Nelly Richard, *The Insubordination of Signs* (Durham, NC, 2004), xiv–xv. In a debate included in this volume, Germán Bravo declared, 'I think that just as Portales can be seen as a kind of paradigm for the político-institutional, Andrés Bello appears as the paradigm of the notion of culture based on the prevention of "orgies of the imagination".' *Ibid.*, 87.

[64]'Latinoamérica y la posmodernidad', *Escritos*, 13–14 (Jan.–Dec. 1996), 276.

[65]*SW*, 128.

[66]In the *Filosofía* he states, 'There is for man a future destiny capable of satisfying his aspirations. The human soul survives death', *OC*, III, 221. Lastarria ridiculed Bello for his conviction that a wealthy merchant and his new young spouse had seen the ghost of his first, murdered wife at a banquet, saying he had heard it as evidence in their subsequent trial. Bocaz, *Andrés Bello*, 204.

I have left somebody out. The very person who must have preyed on Bello's mind the most – his mother. Ana Antonia López de Bello, who had been born in 1764, lived until the age of ninety-four, hearing this story in fragments from afar. The first of a sparse but emotional fifty-year series of letters from her son never reached Doña Ana because the mail it was contained in was seized by the Puerto Rican pirate ship *Valiente Rovira* in 1812. That does seem to have been something of an ill omen, first with respect to her belief in Bello's promises of impending return home; secondly for her love for her grandchildren, only one of whom she ever met and so many of whom died before her; and thirdly for her son's exceptional waywardness – she chided him that several years had passed and he had still to reveal the name of his second wife.[67]

I have to say that I am generally unpersuaded by Karen Racine's explanation of Bello's London identity in terms of Jungian psychoanalysis, but one does have reason to pause when severe homesickness is explained in terms of 'unresolved problems arising from a conflict relationship with the mother'.[68]

'Read these lines to my mother', Bello wrote to his sister-in-law in 1847. 'Tell her that her memory never leaves me, that I am not capable of forgetting her, and that there is neither morning nor night when I do not remember her.'[69] Ana Antonia died just seven years before Bello himself.

He, we know, was too blind to see the etching of Caracas in his final hours, but he had correctly predicted the solace of letters, mumbling muddled verses from the *Iliad* and the *Aeneid* which he thought he saw half-erased on the walls.[70] And the man who had affirmed that animals possessed souls beyond the sphere of materialism could only be separated from his cat, Misifuz, when the coffin containing his mortal remains was removed to the nearby cathedral.[71]

Andrés Bello is buried in Santiago's Cementerio General. He is also commemorated in the National Pantheon in Caracas. Yet, it is an engaging mark of this complex man, who lived in time and thought so resolutely outside of it, that he believed that his true *Patria*, like that of all civil persons, lay not in any given place but in the embrace of the

[67] Ana Antonia López de Bello, Caracas, to Bello, 17 Sept. 1826, *OC*, XXV, 201.

[68] L Racine and R. Grimberg, *Psycholanalytic Perspectives on Migration and Exile* (Yale, 1989), 20, cited in K. Racine, 'Evolution of Andrés Bello's American Identity in London', in *Strange Pilgrimages. Exile, Travel and National Identity in Latin America 1800–1990s*, ed. I. Fry and K. Racine (Wilmington, 2000), 7–8.

[69] Bello to Concha Rodríguez, 27 May 1847, *OC*, XXVI, 153.

[70] O. Sambrano Urdaneta, *Cronología de Andrés Bello 1781–1865* (Caracas, 1990), 64.

[71] 'Animals have a sort of intelligence in which sensitivity enters as one of the elemental faculties'. *Filosofía*, quoted in Rafael Caldera, *Andrés Bello: Philosopher, Poet, Philologist, Educator, Legislator, Statesman* (1977), 63.

law.[72] His reputation may not deserve some Soviet-style 'rehabilitation', but it certainly merits some prising away from the teleologies imposed by the mental world of 'modernity'. His legacy for Spanish America has certainly not yet crystallised two centuries after its liberal possibilities first took constitutional form. Today, whether tested in the Venezuela of a once-boisterous Hugo Chávez or in the nervous conservatism of Chile, it retains all the validity and disconcertedness of profound statesmanship.

[72] 'Our true *Patria* is that rule of conduct indicated by the rights, obligations and functions that we have and that we owe each other; it is that rule which establishes public and private order, which strengthens, secures and imparts all their vigor to the relationships that unite us, and forms that body of associations of rational beings in which we find the only good, the only desirable thing in our country. Therefore that rule is our *Patria*, and that rule is law, without which everything disappears'. 'On the Observance of the Laws' (1836), *SW*, 263.

Transactions of the RHS 24 (2014), pp. 127–48 © Royal Historical Society 2014
doi:10.1017/S0080440114000061

SKILL, CRAFT AND HISTORIES OF INDUSTRIALISATION IN EUROPE AND ASIA*

By Maxine Berg

READ 10 MAY 2013

ABSTRACT. It is time to reexamine craft and small-scale manufacture within our histories of industrialisation, both West and East, and to reflect on the long survival and adaptation of artisanal production even within our globalised world of production and consumption. Historians since the 1950s have addressed craft, skill and labour-intensive production in historical frameworks such as 'the rise of the factory system', 'proto-industrialisation' and 'flexible specialisation'. More recently, they have devised other concepts which include labour and skill-intensive production such as 'industrious revolution', 'the great divergence', 'knowledge economies', 'East Asian development paths' and 'cycles of production'. This paper surveys this historiography of craft and skill in models of industrialisation. It then reflects on small-scale industrial structures in current globalisation, emphasising the continued significance of craft and skill over a long history of global transitions. It gives close examination to one region, Gujarat, and its recent industrial and global history. The paper compares industrial production for East India Company trade in the eighteenth century to the recent engagement of the artisans of the Kachchh district of Gujarat in global markets. It draws on the oral histories of seventy-five artisan families to discuss the past and future of craft and skill in the industry of the global economy.

Introduction

Today, a global story of industry and manufacturing presents us, on the one hand, with China's huge factory regions where whole cities manufacture buttons or zips, or, on the other, with unregulated clothing factories such as Bangaladesh's, feeding the cheap clothing consumer cultures of the West. When I wrote my first book, *The Machinery Question*, manufacture was perceived as a history of factories and machinery.[1] Its depiction in the early nineteenth century was not so different, but included the role of sweated labour. Cruikshank's 'A Tremendous Sacrifice' showed cheap female labour being ground up in a mill, while women in shopping

* The author wishes to thank the European Research Council, under the European Union's Seventh Framework Programme (FP/2007–2103) ERC Grant Agreement no. 249362.
[1] Maxine Berg, *The Machinery Question and the Making of Political Economy 1815–1848* (Cambridge, 1980).

emporia not so far away declared 'I don't know how they can possibly make them so cheap'.[2] What came before this factory labour was assumed to be craft and artisan manufacture with some household domestic industry.

It is time to reexamine craft and small-scale manufacture within our histories of industrialisation, both West and East, and to reflect on the long survival and adaptation of artisanal production even within our globalised world of production and consumption. Historians since the 1950s addressed craft, skill and labour-intensive processes within frameworks such as 'the rise of the factory system', 'proto-industrialisation', flexible specialisation'. More recently, they have devised concepts such as industrious revolution, the 'great divergence', knowledge economies, East Asian development paths and cycles of production. These frameworks have, in some cases, charted stages by which skilled labour arose, flourished, declined and disappeared; in others, they have found conditions under which alternatives to large-scale mass production seemed viable for a time; in yet other frameworks we see a role assigned to craft labour undermined, yet subsequently to reemerge in changing market conditions. Whatever the frameworks of our analysis, there is also an empirical point. The crafts and skilled labour have survived over our long world history of industrialisation and global transitions. They challenge our models of industrialisation; they have survived, as we will see from the oral history accounts in the later part of the paper, because they have innovated and adapted to new markets.

The rise of globalisation from the 1990s demanded we turn to the resurgence of Asia as a manufacturing power house as we watched manufacturing in Europe and the US decline. It also demanded that we rethink our own histories of industrialisation – they were not a separate European miracle, but connected to wider world trade and Asian industry. Existing alongside and connecting with the large-scale factory sectors in East, South and Southeast Asia is an extensive domestic, small-scale and craft sector. This runs against the grain of the modernisation theories and theories of industrialisation of many of the twentieth-century theories which placed industrialisation in the factory system, with an output directed at standard and mass products.

In the later twentieth century, many historical theories frame debate on this alternation between factories and small-scale production along

---

[2] The image 'A Tremendous Sacrifice' by George Cruikshank was published in *Our Own Times* in 1846. The illustration was accompanied by the text: 'The monster steam swallowed up whole districts of spinners and weavers as he strode over the land. Every sort of manufactured article fell in price as the great magician . . . caused the supply to exceed the demand . . . A very large class of the public, therefore, eagerly demand products from human labour at prices as low as those sent forth by machinery.'

with the technologies which fostered this. But few have addressed this within a global history framework. Such an approach will also help us to understand present-day characteristics of manufacture in the framework of globalisation.

Skill, craft, small-scale and labour-intensive processes inform the different histories of industrialisation in Europe and Asia. Comparing these theories provides a first stage in raising new questions from global history. Empirical investigation based on historical theories, especially those of proto-industrialisation, flexible specialisation and industrious revolution, showed multiple paths or outcomes; they became regional theories. Does comparison with histories of Asian industrialisation also reveal such multiple and regional outcomes? Can global history frameworks change our perspectives? Can we draw parallels between the impact of globalisation now on skilled craft workers and small-scale manufacture and the impact of global trade in the past?

Drawing on the methods of global history directed at a 'different scale', 'a different point of view', I consider a region, Gujarat and Kutch, within its global setting.[3] This region of long-standing skilled artisan manufacture in India contains many such skilled manufacturers today engaging with the new challenges of globalisation. Oral histories of these craftspeople allow insight into their sense of place in the long manufacturing history of their region, and also the opportunities they see in the impact of globalisation on this place. The regional approach both links us to the deep history of manufacture for global trade in a specific place; it also allows us to engage with the complex experience of globalisation on small-scale manufacture in the region today.

Global economic history, industry and the 'great divergence'

Global history, which most directly emerged ten years ago with the debate on the 'great divergence' between China and Europe, strikingly avoided the contrasting paths of technology and industry between East and West. Pomeranz's explanation for divergent paths of economic development which he dated from the eighteenth century lay instead in Europe's advantages in resources and geography: coal and the ghost acres of colonial and New World territories.[4] More recently, technology, small-scale industry and industrialisation have been central to historians debating wage differences between East and West. They have charted the great decline in the share of world manufacturing produced by India

---

[3] Maxine Berg, 'Global History: Approaches and New Directions', in *Writing the History of the Global: Challenges for the Twenty-first Century*, ed. Maxine Berg (Oxford, 2011), 1–18, at 11.

[4] Kenneth Pomeranz, *The Great Divergence: China, Europe and the Making of the Modern World Economy* (Princeton, 2000). Also see Jan de Vries, '*The Great Divergence* after Ten Years: Justly Celebrated yet Hard to Believe', *Historically Speaking*, 4 (2011), 10–25.

and China in the eighteenth century, and its resurgence since the 1980s. Robert Allen has argued that high real wages in the West spurred the way to mechanisation.[5] Low real wages in India and China, and the high capital costs of mechanisation, account for the slow rate at which they have adopted Western technologies of the twenty-first century.[6] Parthasarathi challenged the evidence for low real wages in India and argued that the key divide between East and West in the eighteenth century was not based on ecology, but on technology. It was not high wages, but the need to out-produce not just the quantity, but the quality of Indian textiles which prompted the innovative activities of British cotton producers, and subsequently mechanisation and the factory system.[7]

Other histories of an 'East Asian development path' highlighted the space for small-scale and labour-intensive technologies, one which accords with the labour and resource endowments of Japan and much of East Asia. Large populations and relatively small amounts of land entail a focus on increasing land productivity. This yields labour-intensive technologies and labour-absorbing institutions in agriculture and proto-industry. Labour-intensive industrialisation in Japan was also followed by China in the interwar period and by other Southeast Asian countries after the Second World War.[8]

Recent globalisation has brought to the fore new consideration of the different trajectories of manufacture in the East and the West. It has also brought new attention to knowledge economies, the role of specific skills and the networks and nodes for fostering these. How did these issues of skill, scale and craft feature in our earlier histories of industrialisation, in the West and the East, and how has globalisation changed our perspectives?

The transition from feudalism to capitalism

The long-standing debate on the transition from feudalism to capitalism sought a clear pathway through stages of economic transition to an ultimate goal of industrialisation. Industrialisation was associated with modernisation, both with high capital intensity and the shift to the factory system. A dynamic capital-intensive and mechanised factory sector contrasted with old unchanging pre-industrial handicrafts. These assumptions about the characteristics of industrialisation were common

---

[5] Robert Allen, *Global Economic History: A Very Short Introduction* (Oxford, 2011), 37.
[6] *Ibid.*, 51.
[7] Prasannan Parthasarathi, *Why the West Grew Rich and Asia Did Not* (Cambridge, 2011).
[8] Kenneth Pomeranz, 'Is there an East Asian Development Path? Long Term Comparisons, Constraints and Continuities', *Journal of the Economic and Social History of the Orient*, 44, 3 (2001), 322–62; Kaoru Sugihara, 'The European Miracle in an East Asian Perspective', in *Writing the History of the Global*, ed. Berg, 129–44.

to liberal and Marxist approaches. Rostow and Kuznets, writing their broad comparative studies of economic growth and productivity change, showed little interest in small-scale production and labour-intensive technologies.[9] Rostow gave priority to high capital investment, leading sectors and rapid and fundamental transitions.[10] David Landes whose text on European industrialisation, *The Unbound Prometheus* dominated historical interpretation from the 1960s through the 1980s, defined industrialisation as the transformation of handicraft to modern industry. This meant the factory, a new system of production which created a 'new breed of worker'.[11]

The Marxist perspective on the transition to capitalism became a debate on the 'rise of the factory system' and subsequently on the labour process under capitalism.[12] The factory system arose, according to these theories, as a means of controlling labour, and extracting the highest labour power and labour productivity. Stephen Marglin's 'What Do Bosses Do?' set an agenda focused on a clear divide between traditional artisan, guild-controlled manufacture or rural, labour-intensive domestic manufacture on the one hand and capitalist-controlled factory production on the other.[13] Marxist historians associated the rise of the working class with the rise of the factory.

A turning from the 1970s to what Cannadine termed a 'limits to growth' perspective on the Industrial Revolution also entailed more research on the longer taproots of industrialisation, and into the complexities of the transition from feudalism to capitalism. Among these were novel and distinctive features of manufacture as trade expanded. A new debate on 'proto-industrialisation' focused on small-scale domestic industry, the spread of rural manufacture and especially export-orientated industry. Analysis of mixed agricultural and industrial occupations, of the division of labour and of advanced putting-out systems that yielded a surplus for merchant manufacturers appeared to offer a possible path

[9] David Cannadine, 'The Present and the Past in the English Industrial Revolution 1880–1980', *Past and Present*, 103 (1984), 131–72, at 132.

[10] *Ibid.*, 154. See Simon Kuznets, 'Towards a Theory of Economic Growth', in *National Policy for Economic Welfare at Home and Abroad*, ed. Robert Lekachman, Columbia University Bicentennial Conference Series (New York, 1955); W. W. Rostow, *The Stages of Economic Growth* (Cambridge, 1960).

[11] David Landes, *The Unbound Prometheus: Technological Change and Industrial Development in Western Europe from 1750 to the Present* (Cambridge, 1969).

[12] See Paul Sweezy *et al.*, *The Transition from Feudalism to Capitalism*, introduction by R. H. Hilton (1976).

[13] Stephen Marglin, 'What Do Bosses Do', *Review of Radical Political Economics*, 6, 2 (1974), 60–116; Part II, *Review of Radical Political Economics*, 7, 1 (1975), 20–37.

to industrialisation.[14] While the debate focused to a great extent on the demographic consequences of different regimes of proto-industry, regional studies revealed no clear results over paths to industrialisation.[15]

The theories of proto-industrialisation like those of the 'rise of the factory system' which had gone before were teleological. Indeed, after nearly two decades of case-studies, Schlumbohm argued, there was nothing definite in research findings up to 2000 to support a history of industrialisation as a great line of development from dispersed small-scale manufacture to more centralised and mechanised production. 'Is it more appropriate', asked Schlumbohm, 'to speak of a series of cyclical fluctuations between centralized and de-centralized – and between smaller-scale and larger-scale production?'[16]

While much research on proto-industrialisation was focused on Europe, the model also prompted historians of China, India and Japan to look at their labour-intensive industrial history in new ways. Most of this research, like that on Europe, however, remained focused on specific regions within national historical frameworks. India's experience of colonialism drove some of her historians, such as Frank Perlin, to investigate connections between India's commercial manufacture in the seventeenth and eighteenth centuries to European developments. He compared manufactures in Bengal and the Coromandel coast to those described by Arnŏst Klima in Bohemia. In both places, Dutch and English merchants penetrated textile regions, controlling markets and production networks, and gaining greater supervisory control over spinners and weavers. He showed us how that phase of proto-industrialisation was entangled in large-scale inter-regional connections and world commerce.[17]

Consumer cultures

The wide spread of proto-industrial manufacture across north-west Europe shaped new labour supplies dependent on a restructuring of the family division of labour. Women and children committed more of their time to the production of manufactured goods for the market, and less for household services and production. This became the 'industrious revolution' which Jan de Vries linked to the stimulus of new consumer

[14] See Maxine Berg, Pat Hudson and Michael Sonenscher, 'Manufacture in Town and Country before the Factory', in *Manufacture in Town and Country before the Factory*, ed. Maxine Berg, Pat Hudson and Michael Sonenscher (Cambridge, 1983), 1–32.

[15] Sheilagh Ogilvie and Markus Cerman, 'The Theories of Proto-industrialization', in *European Proto-industrialization*, ed. Sheilagh Ogilvie and Markus Cerman (Cambridge, 1996), 1–11, at 9–10.

[16] Jürgen Schlumbohm, 'Proto-industrialization – A Balance Sheet', in *European Proto-industrialization*, ed. Ogilvie and Cerman, 12–22, at 21.

[17] Frank Perlin, 'Proto-industrialization and Pre-colonial South Asia', *Past and Present*, 98 (1983), 30–95.

demand for goods from outside the region. These novelties, luxuries, fashionable and addictive goods changed consumer and household practices, on the one hand yielding a large labour force for labour-intensive handicraft production, and on the other spreading new cultural and social practices from coffee house and tea culture to rapidly changing dress fashions through the lives of ordinary people. In north-west Europe, such 'industriousness' coincided with a newly available global trade in New World and Asian foodstuffs and luxury goods.[18] In Japan, such an industrious revolution occurred without such a wide expansion of foreign trade; indeed many such new consumer goods were internally generated, what Eric Jones called 'clever, inventive commodities'.[19]

Much of the historiography of 'industrious revolutions' has focused on household behaviour and demand, the commercial and capitalist social environment in which people used their goods. A parallel historiography on the supply of new products and fashion goods explored dynamic craft and design-intensive economies. My own work on smaller-scale industries, especially in the metal trades, investigated product innovation and new technologies developed to underpin these. A dynamic small-scale and skill-intensive sector developed in the metal trades and many other industries alongside the rise of the factory system in some parts of the textile industry.[20] Equally, the fashion economies developed from the later seventeenth century in the textile and other industries were design-intensive, and developed sectors of enhanced skills. France's workshop and artisan-produced silks, printed cottons and fine woollen goods outcompeted Britain's on quality and fashion.[21]

Flexible specialisation

Some of Europe's and North America's regions, like the Lyon silk region, had strongly embedded nodes of crafts and skills. These yielded many externalities, and such regions seemed for sociologists and historians of the 1980s to offer an alternative historical path to the large factories and mass production which seemed at the time to have had their day as new technologies offering dispersed units connected by ICT and 'just-in-time solutions' came on stream. Current possibilities then for small-scale units deploying flexible skills stimulated a new historical investigation of potentials offered in the past for small-scale production.

---

[18] Jan de Vries, *The Industrious Revolution: Consumer Behavior and the Household Economy 1650 to the Present* (Cambridge, 2008).

[19] E. L. Jones, *Growth Recurring: Economic Change in World History* (Oxford, 1988), ch. 9.

[20] Maxine Berg, *The Age of Manufacture: Industry, Innovation and Work in Britain 1700–1820* (1985; 2nd edn, Oxford, 1994).

[21] William Sewell, 'The Empire of Fashion and the Rise of Capitalism in Eighteenth-Century France', *Past and Present*, 206 (2010), 81–120, at 101–4, 110–13, 116.

Debate first centred on the persistence of small firms; they were clearly evidence of 'industrial dualism', where craft sectors and small units of production responded to surges of demand or provided the varieties tacked onto main production lines. But, asked Piore, Sabel and Zeitlin, had there once been and indeed was there still a real possibility of a craft alternative to mass production? To answer this question, they sought out industrial districts – such as Emilia-Romagna – which appeared to offer an alternative of a dynamic region of many small producers.[22]

Their historical enquiries turned to the Lyon silk and hardware industries; to cutlery and specialty steels in Solingen, Remscheid and Sheffield; to calicoes in Alsace, woollens in Roubaix, textiles in Philadelphia. There, small-scale producers had used multi-purpose machines and skilled labour to make a changing assortment of semi-customised products. Their eventual decline, these historical sociologists argued, was not due to their model of technological development, but to political, institutional and economic factors.

The backdrop for these histories was a utopian vision during the 1980s of alternative economic development, based in regions, in cooperative institutions and small in scale. The widespread transfers of industrial production back to Southeast and South Asia, Turkey and Latin America with the onset of globalisation swept away the prospects for many of these vaunted European specialist manufacturing regions. A corresponding sociological investigation also in the 1980s of 'the new international division of labour' found a new phase beyond centralised factory processes in a subdivision of production processes between parts of the developed and less-developed world. Transport and communications improvements created the conditions for a new de-centralisation of production on an altogether different spatial scale than in the past.[23]

Skill and knowledge economies

The skill nodes and regions highlighted in the debates over flexible specialisation led into new questions focused on 'knowledge economies'. Not just labour, but skills have returned to a central place in discussion of industrialisation. Skill and the 'tacit knowledge' underlying it have been central to the concept of 'useful knowledge' as developed by Joel

---

[22]Charles Sabel and Jonathan Zeitlin, 'Historical Alternatives to Mass Production: Politics, Markets and Technology in Nineteenth Century Industrialization', *Past and Present*, 108 (1985), 133–76; M. J. Piore and C. F. Sabel, *The Second Industrial Divide: Possibilities of Prosperity* (New York, 1984).

[23]Folker Frőbel, Jűrgen Heinrichs and Otto Kreye, *The New International Division of Labour: Structural Unemployment in Industrialized Countries and Industrialization in Developing Countries* (Cambridge, 1980).

Mokyr.[24] 'Local knowledge' and 'nodes of craft skill' were vital to the artisans that the late Larry Epstein followed across Europe as they carried and reconfigured knowledge sets, and brought technological leadership to new regions of early modern Europe.[25]

The turning of European historians in recent years to such knowledge economies also raised this as an issue in the divergence debate. Both Epstein and Mokyr claimed that adaptable skills and technological innovation were what the West had and Asia did not. Prasannan Parthasarathi, Tirthankar Roy and David Washbrook debated the extent and direction of an Indian dynamic culture of technical knowledge.[26] Sugihara contrasted an East Asian development path, innovative in its intensive use of labour and resource and energy-saving techniques with the West's capital and resource-intensive path.[27] Studies in comparative economic development assessed the rapid manufacturing development in parts of East Asia, South and Southeast Asia, Latin America and Turkey against the historical backdrop of France's path of economic development in the nineteenth century, to emphasise niche markets, mid-range technological innovation and manufacturing experience.[28]

Craft and small-scale manufacture in East Asia and India

The East Asian development path, as historicised by Sugihara for Japan, the Lower Yangzi and other parts of East Asia focuses on resources and energy-saving, labour-intensive adaptations of Western technologies and labour-absorption possibilities in different organisational forms of manufacture. This was also a path that described the development of mid-range labour-intensive technologies in Southeast Asia during the later decades of the twentieth century, technologies described in the new international division of labour.

[24] Joel Mokyr, *The Gifts of Athena Historical Origins of the Knowledge Economy* (Princeton, 2002); Joel Mokyr, *The Enlightened Economy: An Economic History of Britain, 1700–1850* (New Haven, 2010).

[25] S. R. Epstein, 'Craft Guilds, Apprenticeship and Technological Change in Pre-industrial Europe', in *Guilds, Innovation and the European Economy, 1400–1800*, ed. S. R. Epstein and M. Prak (Cambridge, 2008), 52–80.

[26] Parthasarathi, *Why the West Grew Rich*, 187; Tirthankar Roy, 'Knowledge and Divergence from the Perspective of Early Modern India', *Journal of Global History*, 3 (2008), 361–87; David Washbrook, 'India in the Early Modern World Economy: Modes of Production, Reproduction and Exchange', *Journal of Global History*, 2 (2007), 87–112.

[27] Kaoru Sugihara, 'The East Asian Path of Economic Development: A Long-Term Perspective', in *The Resurgence of East Asia: 500, 150 and 50 Year Perspectives*, ed. Giovanni Arrighi, Takeshi Hamashita and Mark Selden (2003), 78–123. Also see Sugihara, 'The European Miracle in an East Asian Perspective'.

[28] Alice Amsden, *The Rise of 'the Rest': Challenges to the West from Late-Industrializing Economies* (Oxford, 2001), 1, 15–16, 32.

Some economic historians have seen these innovative labour-intensive processes as temporary expedients. Summed up by Robert Allen, they describe a history of increasing employment relative to capital in a low-wage economy to cut costs. And the real industrialisation of Japan took place in the steel mills and automobile factories whose exports to the US soon led to the collapse of the US steel and car industries.[29]

The historiography of small-scale manufacture in India's economic history stands apart from this East Asian historiography of labour-intensive development paths and dual economies. For much of the debate on craft and small-scale industry in India's history arises out of the framework of the history of colonialism. Craft has been a key issue of national identity, and lies at the heart of a long-standing debate on India's 'de-industrialisation'. Abigail McGowan's *Crafting the Nation in Colonial India* (2009) and Douglas Haynes's *Small Town Capitalism in Western India* (2012) outline how artisans became a political symbol of India's fate under colonialism. British colonisers perceived them as indicators of India's economic backwardness. The British and other Europeans also collected India's unique and beautiful products for museum collections that orientalised not just the goods, but the artisans themselves. The discourses ossified and homogenised widely geographically dispersed and very distinctive groups of artisans.[30]

Equally, the nationalists in their turn saw craft producers as a trope for the self-sufficient society that they thought India had once been before the disruption of colonialism and industrialisation. These historical perspectives were as utopian as were those of the flexible specialists; in this case, the artisan and her craft represented autonomy. The discourses also informed the writing of Indian economic history for the generations after Independence as economic historians of India debated the de-industrialisation thesis.[31]

---

[29] *Ibid.*, 135–8.

[30] Abigail McGowan, *Crafting the Nation in Colonial India* (New York, 2009); D. Haynes, *Small Town Capitalism in Western India: Artisans, Merchants, and the Making of the Informal Economy, 1870–1960* (Cambridge, 2012); Dutta, *The Bureaucracy of Beauty*, 136–44. Also see the discussion of displaying and collecting Indian craft skills in silk manufacture in international exhibitions from the mid-nineteenth century in Brenda M. King, 'Exhibiting India', in *Silk and Empire* ed. Brenda M. King (Manchester, 2005), ch. 6.

[31] See P. Parthasarathi, 'The History of Indian Economic History', unpublished paper, 2012, to be published in *Globalizing Economic History. Multiple Roads from the Past*, ed. Francesco Baldizzoni and Pat Hudson, forthcoming; M. D. Morris, 'Towards a Reinterpretation of Nineteenth-Century Indian Economic History', *Indian Economic and Social History Review*, 5 (1968), 1–15; T. Raychaudhuri, 'A Reinterpretation of Nineteenth-Century Indian Economic History?', *Indian and Economic and Social History Review*, 5 (1968), 77–100; C. Simmons, '"De-industrialization", Industrialization and the Indian Economy, c. 1850–1947', *Modern Asian Studies*, 19 (1985), 593–622.

The strongest statements on the decline of artisan and small-scale industry in India were offered by A. K. Bagchi in his paper, 'De-industrialization in Gangetic Bihar 1809–1901', where he compared data on craft employment in some Bihar districts in Buchanan's surveys of the 1820s with data in the 1901 Census. He found a contraction of the craft population of these districts from 18.6 per cent to 8.5 per cent. Irfan Habib's extended review of the *Cambridge Economic History of India* added to this that as early as 1837 Indian textile cloth exports had been eliminated, and English imports had replaced c. 6 per cent of Indian cloth production.[32] Parthasarathi drawing on Sumit Sarkar places the strong consensus in much Indian history over the great decline in Indian handicraft production with the context of the Left–Nationalist–Marxist consensus in Indian middle-class intellectual life over this period.[33]

Recent research has certainly challenged this consensus; small producers have continued as a major feature of industrial production right across India over the whole period from 1870. Tirthankar Roy's study, *Traditional Industry in the Economy of Colonial India* (1999), focused on the late colonial period, and covered broader areas of India over the period 1870–1930. In the period since 1947, small-scale industrial production increased its share of waged employment; indeed, there was staggering growth in the towns and informal industrial labour in the crafts he studied: handloom weaving, gold thread, brassware, leather, glassware and carpets.[34] Roy concluded that artisan industry 'has not just survived, but shaped the character of industrialization both in colonial and post-colonial India'.[35]

Some of India's historians writing in the 1980s were already challenging the extent and finality of the decline of craft industry. Rajnarayan Chandavarkar's 'Industrialization in India before 1947' argued that though there was general agreement on the decline of handicraft industries from the nineteenth century, this decline was uneven, and handloom weaving expanded in areas such as Tamil Nadu from the later nineteenth century. Indeed, forms of industry that seemed traditional survived and adapted. Some non-factory forms to be found in the jute industry showed dynamism and innovation between the 1830s

---

[32] A. K. Bagchi, "De-industrialization in India in the Nineteenth Century: Some Theoretical Implications'. *Journal of Development Studies*, 12 (1976), 135–64; Irfan Habib, 'Studying a Colonial Economy – Without Perceiving Colonialism', *Modern Asian Studies*, 19, 3 (1985), 355–81, at 360–1.

[33] Parthasarathi, 'The History of Indian Economic History'. See Sumit Sarkar, 'The Many Worlds of Indian History', in Sarkar , *Writing Social History* (Delhi, 1997), 1–49, at 37.

[34] Tirthankar Roy, *Traditional Industry in the Economy of Colonial India* (Cambridge, 1999), 3–6, 232–5.

[35] *Ibid.*, 7.

and 1880s.[36] It was only with this discussion that debate moved on from assumptions of a technologically static craft sector undermined by colonialism, or facing extinction in face of new factory mechanised processes. Chandavarkar investigated processes of diversification in cotton textiles, and investment strategies as a hedge in uncertainties of trade. There were many common features between the formal and the informal sectors. They often produced similar products, made use of labour-intensive techniques and responded to market fluctuations to set output levels.[37]

Chandavarkar writing in the early 1990s of the rise of the factory system in Bombay contrasted what he saw as a Marxist analysis of the rise of the working class in Britain as a trajectory from small peasant to factory proletarian with the complexities of India. India's history of differentiation of the peasantry, the expansion, decline and stabilisation of artisanal industry interconnected with the emergence of factory production.[38] His analysis of dynamism in the informal sector and rigidities and undercapitalisation in the factory sector in early twentieth-century India ran parallel to new histories of European industrialisation focusing on the alternative pathways of flexible specialisation. The regions of Europe that were crucial for flexible pathways and local knowledge economies had their parallels in India, as conveyed in Chandavarkar's 1990s history of Bombay's industry, and Douglas Haynes's recent study of Surat and Gujarat.[39]

Bombay and Gujarat

What Chandavarkar found for Bombay and Haynes for Gujarat was a history of cycles of industrial production, production passing into and out of factories, workshops and domestic production as world and domestic markets changed. Investment strategies kept all these organisational forms in play. Early twentieth-century Bombay held little distinction between formal and informal sectors of industry. Smaller enterprises in some industries were more capital-intensive than the cotton factories which used a great deal of labour-intensive technology. The interwar years saw a steady expansion of small industrial units; indeed, a whole range of these serviced the textile industry. Engineering, dyeing and printing

---

[36]Rajnarayan Chandavarkar, 'Industrialization in India before 1947: Conventional Approaches and Alternative Perspectives', *Modern Asian Studies*, 18, 3 (1985), 623–68, at 640–1, 668.

[37]*Ibid.*, 638–9.

[38]Rajnarayan Chandavarkar, *The Origins of Industrial Capitalism in India: Business Strategies and the Working Classes in Bombay 1900–1940* (Cambridge, 1994), 20.

[39]*Ibid.*; D. Haynes, *Small Town Capitalism in Western India: Artisans, Merchants, and the Making of the Informal Economy, 1870–1960* (Cambridge, 2012).

processes using chemical works, leather works supplying bands and belts for machines, and woodworking factories manufacturing spindles and bobbins supplied the textile factories. There was, furthermore, a whole host of 'craft industries' and artisanal workshops, handloom weaving, silkweaving, dyeing and printing, wire, tinsel and kincob workers, brassworkers, blacksmiths and potters, goldsmiths and jewellers.[40]

The cotton industry, especially its factory sector, expanded and contracted with domestic and international markets. The boom in mill building from the 1870s was stimulated by Chinese demand for yarn. From 1890 to 1914, new fluctuations arose from the growth of the industry in Ahmedabad and the new challenge of Japanese exports to China.[41] But the swadeshi campaign did increase consumption of Indian cloth. Tariffs in the early 1930s provided a niche to enable some mills to diversify into higher counts of yarn and finer varieties of piece goods.[42] At the end of the 1930s, the industry was facing overproduction, but the war brought new demand, and removed Japanese cottons as a threat for a time. Between 1940 and 1952 the Bombay mills made a big shift to fine counts and varieties, and diversified into bleaching, dyeing and printing.[43]

Bombay's story of flexibility and adaptation was based on old business strategies of responding to market fluctuations by expanding or retrenching on labour, or reducing wages. Manufacturers continued with the investment strategies they had started in the nineteenth century of spreading risk and diversifying business interests.[44] Bombay's story of diversifying over scale and quality of production finds its parallel in Haynes's recent study of Surat and the small textile towns of Gujarat.

Douglas Haynes, in his *Small Town Capitalism in Western India* (2012) researched in depth the textile economies of Western India and Gujarat over the period 1870 to 1960. He analysed cycles of small-scale industry over this long period, arguing a case for the rise of 'weaver capitalism' in small manufacturing centres; the old handloom towns renewed their cloth manufacture with small producers using electric power. A small-scale powerloom industry in *karkhanas* or workshops with multiple looms from the 1940s diversified output and adopted electric or oil powered looms.

At the end of the twentieth century, Western India's small weaving towns became large urban agglomerations with structures that included a wide variety of small and large firms, and skilled artisans working

[40] Chandavarkar, *The Origins of Industrial Capitalism*, 74–9.

[41] *Ibid.*, 245–9.

[42] *Ibid.*, 261–5.

[43] *Ibid.*, 267–71.

[44] *Ibid.*, 277, 271.

alongside pools of casual labour.[45] Both Chandavarkar in the case of
Bombay and Haynes for Surat and Gujarat take us well beyond the
binaries that inform the historiographies of India's de-industrialisation:
handloom and powerloom, craft and industry, artisan and factory work,
and informal and formal sectors of the economy.[46] The factory textile
industry of Bombay and Ahmedabad that disappeared did not, as we
have seen, mean the end of the textile industry. Haynes recognised that
the cycles of small producer capitalism he charts over the nineteenth and
twentieth centuries had deep historical roots in a wide Indian Ocean and
global trade, and versions of the mixed workshop and family economy
embedded in networks of middlemen and sub-contractors in eighteenth-
century Surat and other textile towns of Gujarat.[47]

  Cycles of production provide one context in which small-scale
manufacture reemerges and even flourishes. The new international
division of labour and globalisation provided further opportunities for
such expansion. For craft and small workshop manufacture, globalisation
in particular has provided new scope, and especially lucrative Western
and Middle Eastern markets. Liebl and Roy's assessment for India as
a whole in 2003 found a large dynamic handicrafts sector, employing
approximately 9 million, and gaining under freer markets, but needing
sophisticated adaptation to new consumers.[48]

Craft and skilled labour in Kachchh (Kutch)

The closest comparison to this recent expansion of small industrial
production is the period when these industries provided for the East India
Company trade to Europe. I, therefore, turn to a section of the paper
focused on one region, Kachchh,[49] where the crafts face globalisation
today, and which had such a trade to Europe in the seventeenth and
eighteenth centuries. A focus on a region such as this connects the
historian to the regional frameworks of earlier models of industrialisation
and small-scale industry such as proto-industrialisation and flexible
specialisation. It connects also to issues arising out of 'the local' and
the 'global'. A local focus allows insight into the heterogeneities arising

---

[45] Haynes, *Small Town Capitalism*, 265, 272–7, 311.
[46] *Ibid.*, 6.
[47] *Ibid.*, 24–36.
[48] M. Liebl and T. Roy, "Handmade in India: Preliminary Analysis of Crafts Producers
and Crafts Production', *Economic and Political Weekly*, 37 (27 Dec. 2003), 5366–76.
[49] The current name of the region is Kachchh. The name during the colonial and early
post-colonial period was Kutch. Both names are used here; Kachchh when referring to the
region now, and Kutch when referring to it in the colonial period.

out of global connections.[50] More significantly for a study of manufacture, a focus on a region or locale allows the detailed research on production, and the impact that global connections and wider world trade have on the people there.[51]

Turning to the early history of Kutch, we find little written account of its manufactures and their adaptation to Western trade, but examples remain today in museum collections and country houses. The Newberry Collection of 1,200 pieces of printed cotton textiles in the Ashmolean Museum attests to an extensive world trade in printed cotton textiles from wider Gujarat, including Kutch, going back to the tenth century.[52] Fine mochi embroidery was made for generations of the Maharaos of Kutch and it was also traded from Cambay and Surat. Prototypes were sent from Europe to India to be copied for embroidered hangings that would coordinate with chintz fabric sets brought from the Coromandel coast.[53] The English East India Company traded over twenty different fabric types from Surat in 1708 in fifty-three different colours, patterns and lengths. The Company was already well aware of the textiles of Kutch by 1710, and directed its officials in Surat to give special attention to the trade.[54]

Few British East India Company officials or travellers wrote about the manufactures of the region, though several among them described the varieties of peoples, and in some cases provided an outline of the castes, including some of the crafts.[55] One amongst these, Marianna Postans, the wife of an army officer who spent five years in Kutch, noted in the 1830s the cotton cloth 'woven of various colours, and eminently fanciful designs', and she praised craft abilities of 'imitation' and the 'fame their

[50] Arjun Appadurai refers to this in his more recent work. See, for a brief introduction, 'How Histories Make Geographies: Circulation and Context in a Global Perspective', *Transcultural Studies*, 1 (2010), 4–13.

[51] See Anne Gerritsen, 'Ceramics for Local and Global Markets: Jingdezhen's Agora of Technologies', in *Cultures of Knowledge: Technology in Chinese History*, ed. Dagmar Schaefer and Francesca Bray (Leiden, 2011), 164–86.

[52] Ruth Barnes, *Indian Block-Printed Textiles in Egypt: The Newberry Collection in the Ashmolean Museum* (Oxford, 1977).

[53] The Ashburnham hangings at the Victoria and Albert Museum, London, and embroideries at Hardwick Hall are examples. See Rosemary Crill, *Indian Embroidery* (1999), 8; Rosemary Crill, *Textiles from India: The Global Trade* (2006); Eliuned Edwards, *Textiles and Dress of Gujarat* (Ahmedabad, 2011), 162–9.

[54] Order Lists of the English East Indian Company: E/3/96/18, India Office Records, British Library. Derived from Europe's Asian Centuries EIC trade database, see www2.warwick.ac.uk/fac/arts/history/ghcc/eac/.

[55] J. Tod, *Travels in Western India Embracing a Visit to the Sacred Mounts of the Jains . . .* (1839), 449.

beautiful work has acquired, both in England, where it is now well known, and also in all parts of India'.[56]

The crafts of Kutch and wider Gujarat readily adapted to their markets among a wide range of indigenous tribes people, and to those for its court in Bhuj especially from the early seventeenth century; they also adapted to the diverse tastes of wider world markets. The rich legacy of those crafts has remained today. As in other parts of India, producers have faced a decline in traditional domestic markets with the new competition of factory-made goods, synthetic fabrics, screen-printed prints and mass-produced bandhani or tye dye. The state and NGOs have played a part, especially since the 1980s, in supporting what they see as India's distinctive craft tradition: building infrastructure, business aid and programmes of national craftsman awards and support for travel to international exhibitions. The crafts did survive over the nineteenth and twentieth centuries, serving then more localised markets. But above all the crafts and small producer sectors of Kachchh are now part of a new story of globalisation, one, however, which connects with that earlier story of craft production and global history in the region.

In a region such as Kachchh with its long history of craft production, it is possible to investigate its current globalised context as well as its history through interviews and oral histories among the craftspeople now. Such interviews were conducted among the manufacturers and workers of Gujarat and Surat by Douglas Haynes as a source base for his recent history of the region.[57] Interviews and oral histories also take us into the methods of archaeologists; they are a way of accessing local material cultures and technologies, not just for the present day, but for the past. Archaeologists have used analogical reasoning, observing and interrogating living communities in the regions where they seek to reconstruct material cultures of pre-historic production centres. Other archaeologists practice a method of 'experimental archaeology', reconstructing technologies from site findings. Likewise, historians of science have reworked historical experiments to understand the 'tacit' aspect of the experimental process. Such methods of talking to craftspeople today and observing current industrial practices help us to gain insight into the challenges faced in the past, even a past going back to that of the East India Companies.[58]

[56]Marianna Postans, *Cutch or Random Sketches Taken during a Residence in One of the Northern Provinces of Western India Interspersed with Legends and Traditions* (1839; new edn, New Delhi, 2001), 173.

[57] Douglas Haynes, 'Just like a Family? Recalling the Relations of Production in the Textile Industries of Surat and Bhiwandi, 1940–60', *Contributions to Indian Sociology*, 33, 1–2 (1999), 141–69.

[58]M. Jones *et al.*, 'Food Globalization in Prehistory', *World Archaeology*, 43, 4 (2011), 665–75; H. O. Sibum, 'Reworking the Mechanical Value of Heat: Instruments of Precision and

I have, therefore, led a project to collect the oral histories of a number of craftspeople and their families. Working with two assistants, Mohmedhusain Khatri and Dr Chhaya Goswami Bhatt, over the past two years, we have collected approximately seventy-five sets of interviews, deposited these on a website and summarised them in written English. The web resource is both a source for historians' research, and a public record of the family histories of the region's skilled workforce, and one to which they can continue to add.[59]

I will draw on the interviews to show the strong perspective provided by the prospect of new and especially international markets, and what needs to be done to access these. Most recount challenges they have experienced of labour supply, the division of labour and new and older technologies. Many conveyed the deep history of their crafts in the region going back many generations, or they had learned their skills from parents and grandparents.

The ajrakh printing artisans from the villages of Damadka and Ajrakhpur, Abdul Jabbar Khatri and Ismail Khatri, claim ancestors in the trade going back nine to ten generations, and arriving then in Kutch from Sindh.[60] The bellmaker, Kanji Devji Maheshwari, spoke of his work as an early medieval craft also originating in Sindh.[61] Haroon Ibrahim Maniyar, from a family of banglemakers, and now aged eighty-three, cited seven generations of his family in the craft. His father, grandfather and great grandfather made their livings in the trade, and now so too do his sons. Rameez Imtiyaz Maniyar, another of the banglemakers set out his family tree going back six generations.[62] The quiltmakers had also migrated from Sindh, settling first in Banni, then in other parts of Kutch. The family of Ramji Devraj Marwada had practised the craft for over a hundred years.[63] The batik workers too looked back to a long ancestry. Shakeel Ahmed Mohammed Qasim Khatri, aged thirty is in the fifth generation of his family's work in the trade.[64] The weaver from Sarli, Danabhai Samatbhai Bhadru, had a family history of four generations in

Gestures of Accuracy in Early Victorian England, *Studies in the History and Philosophy of Science*, 26, 1 (1995), 73–106.

[59] An Oral History of the Crafts in Kachchh: www.warwick.ac.uk/go/eac/oralhistoryproject. The interviews cited in this section of the paper are all summarised on this website.

[60] Interview with Dr Ismail Khatri, Ajrakhpur, 15 Feb. 2012; interview with Abdul Jabbar Khatri, Dhamadka, 8 Nov. 2012.

[61] Interview with Kanji Devji Maheshwari, Zura, 26 May 2012.

[62] Interviews with Haroon Ibrahim Maniyar and Rameez Imtiyaz Maniyar, 25 May 2012.

[63] Interview with Ramji Devraj Marwada, Hodko, 29 May 2012.

[64] Interview with Shakeel Ahmed Mohammed Qasim Khatri, Mundra, 28 May 2012.

the trade; so too did the leather workers, Patthubhai and Umara Kana Marwada.[65]

All of those claiming these generations in the trades learned their crafts from parents, in-laws and uncles and aunts. Julekha Hussain Khatri, a highly skilled bandhani worker, watched her maternal grandparents doing very fine work, and started to learn from them. This was a generation when men of the Khatri community also did tying work, and her grandfather, Osman Hasam, was famous for bahdhara work.[66] Likewise, Maghibai Manodiya a sixty-year-old weaver in Bhojodi learned his craft from his parents and maternal in-laws.[67] The batik printer, Shakeel Qasim Khatri, learned batik printing from his father and maternal and paternal uncles. The bellmaker, Sale Mohammed Jacab, now in his sixties, was also trained by his father and grandfather.[68]

Practices of mixing agricultural and craft work and of peddling goods are very familiar to European historians of proto-industrialisation. The older craftspeople in Kachchh today remember peddling their goods. The weaver, Samatbhai Karsanbhai Vankar, aged seventy-five, and father of the now highly successful Kantilal Vankar, remembered days as a peddler selling his goods.[69] The leather worker, Umara Kana Marwada Kharat peddled leather shoes for Muslims village to village, and the banglemakers sold bangles house to house and village to village at 10 rupees a pair. After six days on the move, carrying one bag of bangles and the other with food and other goods for their subsistence, the banglemakers could earn 400 rupees.[70]

Many practising these crafts also still combine their work with agriculture in much the same way as practised by the proto-industrial workforces of early modern Europe; others have lost their land, and find their survival much more precarious. Farm workers seek work with craftsmen such as the ajrakh printers when the farming season is over; that is for eight months of the year, or they seek work in the crafts as former camel grazing land is bought up.[71] Sisters Hanifa and Jamila Khanna came in to Mandvi from an outlying village to bring their completed bandhani work into the putting-out shop of the merchant manufacturer. They combine tying with agricultural and domestic labour; 'weeding,

[65] Interviews with Danabhai Samatbhai Bhadru, Sarli, 27 May 2012, and Patthubhai and Umara Kana Marwada, 29 May 2012.

[66] Interview with Julekha Hussain Khatri, Bhuj, 26 May 2012.

[67] Interview with Maghibai Khimoo Manodhiya, Bhujodi, 30 May, 2012

[68] Interviews with Shakeel Qasim Khatri, Mundra; Sale Mohammed Jacab, Zura, 25 May 2012.

[69] Interview with Samatbhai Vankar, Sarli, 27 May 2012.

[70] Interview with Umara Kana Marwada Kharet, no date or place, and Haroon Ibrahim Maniyar, Bhuj, 25 May 2012.

[71] Interview with Abdul Jabbar Khatri and Usman Musa, Dhamadka, 8 Nov. 2012.

harvesting and picking cotton'. It takes them five days to complete a piece of work for which they might earn 1,500–1,800 rupees a month. They describe their work as like a habit; they never sit empty-handed.[72] Bandhani is like the hand spinning of early modern Europe. It is widely practised by the women of farming families, and those other craftspeople; the batik workers and the cutlers among them. The cutler from Mota Reha, Abdul Rashid, described the precarious state of the cutlers' villages; in the last generation, they had small farms or did farm labour to make up their earnings. 'Now there are no farms left', and he 'supports his four children hand to mouth'.[73]

Newly emerging national and international markets in the past ten years have transformed prospects for some craftspeople. They have seized opportunities to adapt designs and techniques, and to draw on the rich heritage of skilled labour in the region. Among the most successful are the families of the ajrakh printing artisans in Ajrakhpur and Dhamadka, Ismail, Razzaque and Abdul Jabbar Khatri, and the high-quality bandhani makers of Bhuj, Jabbar and Abdulla Khatri. They have both developed designs and technology to meet the tastes of Western markets. They have accessed international buyers, craft exhibitions and lucrative markets among tourists visiting the region. The Vancouver firm Maiwa and India's Fab India buy 30–5 per cent of the output of these printed fabrics of this family of ajrakh producers. They have developed new designs attractive to elite Indian and to Western markets, and make these in a range of fabrics. Ismail Khatri argued that focusing on a high-quality product brought a better future for the business.[74] Both Abdul Jabbar and Ismail Khatri spoke of their history of transferring from the use of chemical to natural dyes. Maiwa insisted on natural dyes, and helped to finance workshops and training. Both have had problems adapting to the urgent demands of Fab India, but are developing successful commercial ties.[75]

Jabbar Khatri, a very successful bandhani producer in Bhuj, leading the family firm Sidr Craft, has recently developed a connection with Maiwa. Now thirty-four, he learned the craft from his mother as a way of earning extra money while at school. He then built up a business supplying cotton dupattas and sarees for the local market, later expanding this to a national level, and selling to dealers in Delhi, Mumbai and Ahmedabad. He was curious about his community's craft, and sought ways of reviving it to a new standard. He attended design workshops run by the National Institute of Design at different occasions over a five-year period, and developed

---

[72] Interview with Hanifa Yusuf Sumra and Jamila Ramju Sumra, Mandvi, 16 Feb. 2012.
[73] Interview with Abdul Rashid and Osman Abdulla Bhatti, Mota Reha, 17 Feb. 2012.
[74] Interview with Ismail Khatri, 15 Feb. 2012.
[75] Interviews with Ismail Khatri, 15 Feb. 2012, and Abdul Jabbar Khatri, 8 Nov. 2012.

contacts with designers. One of these connected him with an American company that brought a contract for dupattas, scarves and stoles for the fashion market in 2002. He produced for the NGO, Khamir, and received a UNESCO seal of excellence. He has sold regularly since then at the Santa Fe folk art festival. He has not only developed designs to use the most highly skilled and intense bandhani, but in the past two years has turned to the use of natural dyes to meet the demands of Maiwa.[76]

Both firms employ a range of skilled workers, many of whom have worked for them for many years. Sugrabai Khatri has worked for Jabbar Khatri for six years, and does her work in the interstices of the domestic duties of bringing up five daughters in a relatively poor household. She can earn 2,000 rupees a month as against others who can earn 5,000 rupees working throughout the day.[77] Julekha Khatri also uses her earnings from fine bandhani to support her three sons and three daughters. Her domestic demands also limit the amount she can do, and she both trains other women and outsources her work.[78]

The weavers of Sarli and Bhojodi have also made great gains from new international and national markets. Kantilal Samatbhai Vankar got his first foreign contract in 1994, and now sells his cloth to Malaysia, Brazil, Milan, Paris, London, Colombo and Singapore. The bulk of his orders arise from exhibitions. He sees the only prospect for the 700 handlooms in these villages in partnerships with foreign importers. The weavers need expertise to match international standards; they find great challenges in meeting the strict quality controls of Fab India, and responding to large bulk orders with tight time constraints.[79]

The quiltmaker, Ramji Devraj Marwada, and four of his five brothers, saw the opportunity in the work of the women of the village of Hodko. The women of the village traditionally made fifteen to twenty quilts for their wedding trousseaus. The brothers saw the market potential in this, and turned these skills to quiltmaking for export and for Fab India. They used design catalogues written by an American and natural dyed fabrics, focusing on design and quality, and selling through exhibitions such as that in Santa Fe and wholesale to partners in Ahmedabad, Bangalore and Bombay.[80] Surprising crafts such as the bellmakers of Zura, from the Lohar, or ironmaking caste, for generations met the local demand of cattle herding communities, producing bells of different pitches for

[76] Interview with Jabbar Mohammad Hussain Khatri, Bhuj, 20 Feb. 2012.
[77] Interview with Sugrabai Mohhamed Farooq Khatri, Bhuj, 9 Nov. 2012.
[78] Interview with Julekha Khatri, 26 May 2012.
[79] Interview with Kantilal Samatbhai Vankar, Sarli, 27 May 2012.
[80] Interview with Ramji Devraj Marwada, Hodko, 29 May 2012.

different tribes and communities, but access to international exhibitions opened a new set of lucrative customers in the Danish dairy industry.[81]

The quality demands of those international markets have thwarted some such as the batik printers. Shakeel Ahmed Qasim Khatri from Mundra did the design courses at the NGO Kalaraksha, and engaged four members of his family in making, marketing and supervising other workers. But he has been unable to adapt the batik wax processes to natural dyes, and because of this cannot access those lucrative foreign markets.[82] All those who have accessed these international markets have worked to improve the quality of their products. The weavers of Bhojodi adopted the hand fly shuttle to increase their productivity, and improved their markets by shifting during the 1960s to a softer weave; but powerloom cloth from the Punjab flooded their markets in the 1990s; they again had to improve further the fineness of their fabrics, and embroidered affects. The ajrakh printers made the difficult transition back from chemical to natural dyes, as more recently have the bandhani makers at Sidr Craft in Bhuj. The batik printers, despite their design initiative, have not achieved that crucial technical transition back to the use of natural dyes. In the words of Shakeel Khatri, 'the chemical-based paraffin wax reacts to the acetic natural dye substances such as alum. The herbal colours absorb the wax in the fabric, and it becomes impossible to remove the wax.'[83]

The place of these crafts and small industries in the Kachchh region of Gujarat convey an aspect of globalisation that falls outside our models of industrialisation. The deep roots of these crafts in a long global history of external trade provide historical parallels in the challenges faced by these craftsmen today. Even more striking is the survival of this node of craft skill through the many phases of Indian de-industrialisation and industrialisation over the course of the later nineteenth and twentieth centuries. As we have seen, globalisation and the external markets it has brought for fine craft, high design and high-quality products has rapidly advanced the lives of those families able to seize the opportunities offered. Others, unable to do so, are at some extremes struggling for survival, and at others expanding on low-wage labour. Jabbar Khatri's Sidr Craft enterprise has expanded from very small-scale production for the local market to high design goods in natural dyes for fashion outlets, international craft fairs and international buyers such as Maiwa. On the other side, the fine cutlers of Mota Reha have watched their historic trade decline from 100 shops in the village to eight or ten. Wholesalers purchase

[81] Interview with Jan Mohammed and Kanji Devji Maheshwari, Zura, 26 May, 2012.
[82] Interview with Shakeel Ahmed Mohammed Qasim Khatri, 28 May 2012.
[83] *Ibid.*

their knives in bulk, leaving minimal profit, and a hand to mouth existence for the uneducated workforce.[84]

Conclusion

Interviews and oral histories among the craftspeople of Kachchh today convey to us a world of high-quality goods produced within strong craft communities and providing both goods for local sumptuary and everyday use in the region as well as products for globalised markets. The region provides a unique setting for investigating the impact of globalisation and new technologies on embedded craft skills. The deep history of this craft economy also makes it a place for the use of analogies between the present and the past. The things carried out of the region as fine art objects by merchants and the East India Company into Europe's domestic interiors and later museums were most likely made in small village workshops or in outwork or proto-industrial settings.

What will the future hold for these people? Will they go the way of some of Europe's proto-industrial workforces into the factory, for example into the chemical factories setting up nearby? Or will they go to cheap garment factories such as those of Bangaladesh, or will its young people leave for Mumbai's streets? Or will the variety and quality they can produce contribute to enlarged global markets which seek differentiation as well as standardised goods? We do not yet know.

But thus far, these crafts have survived over our long world history of industrialisation, and of India's colonial, national and global transitions. They challenge our models of industrialisation; they have survived because they have innovated and adapted to new markets. And they have been supported by family groups and communities strongly conscious of their long craft histories. They form part of the history of cycles of production and of small-scale industry in India. The region's highly localised skills over a long history from the early modern world to the present provide a distinctive opportunity to compare the craft products and their manufacture traded to the West through the East India Company trade to those trading in the world's globalised markets today.

[84]Interviews with Abdul Rashid and Osman Abdulla Bhatti, Mota Reha, 17 Feb. 2012.

Transactions of the RHS 24 (2014), pp. 149–64 © Royal Historical Society 2014
doi:10.1017/S0080440114000073

CHRISTENDOM'S BULWARK: CROATIAN IDENTITY AND THE RESPONSE TO THE OTTOMAN ADVANCE, FIFTEENTH TO SIXTEENTH CENTURIES

By Norman Housley

READ 27 MARCH 2013 AT THE UNIVERSITY OF LEICESTER

ABSTRACT. Croatia's entry to the EU in July 2013 signalled an association with Europe which was anticipated in the fifteenth and early sixteenth centuries in the regular use of *antemurale* (bulwark) rhetoric. This rhetoric was one of the salient characteristics of the period's crusading discourse, as the task of mobilising Christian assistance for regions confronting the Ottoman advance, and in so doing defending the faith as a whole, created a two-way traffic of information and arguments between the embattled frontline states and centres of power in the European interior. This paper investigates the distinctively Croatian features of *antemurale* language. The exposition of Croatia's role as an *antemurale* reveals the extent of the country's embrace of humanist ideals and techniques, enabling prominent lobbyists like Tomaso Negri to convey Croatia's plight with finesse in orations delivered at Rome, Venice and elsewhere. The written output of the humanists also shows that Croatia's dismemberment occurred at a time when national identity was forming, and the emphasis placed on the country's relationship with fellow-Catholics reinforced the tendency to look westwards. In addition, Croatia provides a telling example of the tension between centre and periphery in the person of Andrija Jamometić. When he dramatically called for the deposition of Sixtus IV in 1482, Jamometić included neglect of the crusade against the Turks amongst the accusations directed against the pope.

There can be little doubt that the principal shaping force in Croatia's history in the fifteenth and sixteenth centuries was the Ottoman advance, and the response to that advance by Croats and their neighbours, Hungary, Venice and Habsburg Austria. Borislav Grgin has recently provided an admirable overview of the Ottoman impact on the Croatian lands. Even before the battle of Mohács and the Ottoman/Habsburg dismemberment of Croatia that followed, the medieval polity was subjected to extraordinary strain. Much of the country became in effect a war zone, and agricultural and commercial activity had to be radically adjusted to cope with the ever-present threat of raids, and the need to take shelter at short notice in Croatia's fortresses and walled towns. As Marko Marulić noted in 1526, it was only behind stone walls that a Croat could feel even reasonably safe.[1] Long-established social structures came close to collapse as archives were lost, with the result that legal decisions and tenurial relationships became unenforceable. There was considerable migration. Nobles fled from the more vulnerable southern regions to the safer north, while skilled commoners crossed the Adriatic to Venice and the Marche in search of security and work. The need for coordinated defence managed by the single governor (ban) appointed by the king of Hungary from 1476 onwards challenged the autonomy traditionally enjoyed by the constituent *regna* of Croatia, Slavonia and Dalmatia.[2]

These pervasive and often catastrophic developments are clear, though the loss of so much important evidence makes precise quantification a forlorn hope. The impact of the Turks on Croatian culture is harder to assess. Grgin's opinion on this is forthright.

> The syndrome of society as a besieged fortress, created by constant clashes and wars from 1463 till 1791, spread to all social levels. It was aided by the concept of *antemurale christianitatis*, which revived the old ideology of the Crusades... One cannot underestimate the importance of these facts on the current [sc. contemporary] mentality of the Croatian population, as well as their relevance in the creation of modern national ideologies, myths, stereotypes, etc.[3]

Grgin's argument deserves to be debated, not just in the context of Croatian history but in that of all the Balkan countries and indeed the overarching European/Ottoman encounter. In this paper, I want to offer some thoughts based on research into the specifically crusading sources. I shall attempt first to position Croatia in terms of *antemurale* ideology. Then, I shall refer to some of the Croatian contributions to debate at the time. I shall conclude by looking at the career and outlook of Andrija Jamometić, a Croatian Dominican and diplomat who intervened in a remarkably explosive if short-lived manner in the crusading diplomacy of the later fifteenth century.[4]

Individuals and groups engaged in the arduous process of shaping a common crusading response to the Ottoman advance in the late Middle Ages created a discourse that was radically different from the one developed by their predecessors in the twelfth and thirteenth centuries. At its heart, lay a basic tension between the inherent universalism of crusade and the inescapable fact that most Catholics were not – at least

---

[1] *Hrvastski Latinisti: Croatici auctores qui latine scripserunt*, I (repr., Zagreb, 1969), 309.

[2] Borislav Grgin, 'The Ottoman Influences on Croatia in the Second Half of the Fifteenth Century, *Povijesni Prilozi*, 23 (2002), 87–104, including ample references to recent literature in Croatian. For the sixteenth century, see Catherine Wendy Bracewell, *The Uskoks of Senj: Piracy, Banditry and Holy War in the Sixteenth-Century Adriatic* (Ithaca and London, 1992), 20–5.

[3] Grgin, 'The Ottoman Influences', 102.

[4] The historiography is well covered by Patrick Hyder Patterson in 'The Futile Crescent? Judging the Legacies of Ottoman Rule in Croatian History', *Austrian History Yearbook*, 40 (2009), 125–40.

so far – physically threatened by the Turks. Their way of coping with this tension was in essence simple enough. A frontier community or state that was suffering Turkish attack was commonly described as a bulwark (*antemurale* or *propugnaculum*), or less frequently as a shield (*scutum* or *clipeus*). The *antemurale* metaphor served a number of purposes. It was colourful and dramatic, conjuring up a clear image of an embattled Christendom. Taken in conjunction with the *topos* of limitless Ottoman ambition forwarded by barbaric warriors whose origins lay in Asia's steppe lands, it made possible images of the sultan threatening to stable his horses in St Peter's or water them in the Rhine. And it could be coupled with another *topos*, that of a Christian faith that had not just been expelled from its ancestral homeland in the East but was now cornered in Europe (*angulum mundi*). To all intents and purposes, *Christianitas* was synonymous with *Europa*.[5] Hence, in 1501 the papal legate Raymond Perault asked the German diet at Nürnberg to consider where it would flee to if the Turks managed to breach the Hungarian *antemurale*. For the Turks would have no problem levelling the walls of this beautiful city with their cannon: perhaps the diet would reconvene at Lübeck and sail off to the Orkneys?[6]

Antemurale states shared a common image and function, but they varied widely in their configuration and *modus operandi*. The archetypal *antemurale* state was Hungary, where the rhetoric dated back to the Mongol incursions of the thirteenth century and had been subjected to considerable refinement since.[7] Here, the *antemurale* came close to being literal, because a veritable network of fortresses extended 375 miles, from Klis and Skradin on the Adriatic coast to Szörény on the Wallachian border. These fortresses formed part of the ambitious programme of defence that was devised by King Sigismund when the Ottomans first appeared on his southern border in the late fourteenth century. Hungary's perimeter of fortresses was symbolised by Belgrade, whose successful defence against Mehmed II in 1456 became a byword throughout Europe for heroic Christian resistance. To cite just one example from many, in February 1476 Pope Sixtus IV briefed his legate to Burgundy on the

5 Dieter Mertens, '"Europa, id est patria, domus propria, sedes nostra..." Zu Funktionen und Überlieferung lateinischer Türkenreden im 15. Jahrhundert', in *Europa und die osmanische Expansion im ausgehenden Mittelalter*, ed. Franz-Reiner Erkens (Berlin, 1997), 39–57.

6 Victor Felix von Kraus, *Das Nürnberger Reichsregiment, Gründung und Verfall, 1500–1502* (Innsbruck, 1883), 226–35, at 231. Useful commentary by Hermann Wiesflecker, *Kaiser Maximilian I. Das Reich, Österreich und Europa an der Wende zur Neuzeit* (5 vols., Munich and Vienna, 1971–86), III, 42–4.

7 Nora Berend, *At the Gate of Christendom: Jews, Muslims and 'Pagans' in Medieval Hungary, c. 1000–c. 1300* (Cambridge, 2001), 163–71 and *passim*. Most recently, see Attila Bárány, 'The Expansions of the Kingdom of Hungary in the Middle Ages (1000–1490)', in *The Expansion of Central Europe in the Middle Ages*, ed. Nora Berend (Farnham, 2012), 333–80, at 352–7 ('King Béla IV's new diplomatic doctrine').

repercussions of the Turkish capture of Caffa in the Crimea. Elated by victory, Mehmed II was preparing both his army and his fleet for further action. Charles of Burgundy was to be exhorted to help with men and money, on the grounds that 'if Hungary is conquered Germany will be next, and if Dalmatia and Illyria are overrun Italy will be invaded'.[8]

Venice consistently argued that its overseas territories, fleets and armies made up an *antemurale* that was different in kind from Hungary's but of equal importance for Christendom. The Venetians asserted that the fall of Negroponte in 1470 was just as disastrous a breach in the *antemurale* network as the capture of Belgrade fourteen years earlier would have been. 'It is our will and command', they instructed their envoys at Rome,

> that you immediately inform his Holiness the Pope that our eternal and relentless enemy the [Great] Turk has not just taken by storm a single city and island that were in Christian hands, important on account of their resources and population, but that he has overcome a bulwark that shielded Christians everywhere, opening up a path and clearing the way for the invasion, conquest and spoliation of Italy itself.[9]

The Knights of St John argued a similar case to that of Venice for their archipelago centred on Rhodes. Then, there is the intriguing case of Moldavia, an orthodox principality whose rulers nonetheless became adroit at weaving *antemurale* language into their negotiations for aid with the Catholic West. They argued that their lands sheltered Transylvania and Hungary, in effect forming an *antemurale* to an *antemurale*.[10]

Behind all this lively rhetoric, a hard core of moral argumentation was folded in with some gritty self-interest. Those rulers and peoples who were sustaining the bulwark had the right to enjoy support from their fellow-believers sheltering in its lee. States which denied help to current bulwarks would forfeit the right to put forward similar claims if circumstances later forced them to take on an equivalent defensive role. And if the rulers of the frontier states were not helped out, they would be justified – or at least harder to criticise – if they allowed Turkish raiders through, exchanging immunity for their own lands for guidance on how best to reach those of their Christian neighbours (with whom, of course, they were often at odds). Granted that a showdown with the Turks could not be avoided, surely it was better to stage it at a distance from one's own crops, vineyards, towns and markets? Croatian experience would certainly have backed up that argument.

---

[8] *Hungary as 'Propugnaculum' of Western Christianity: Documents from the Vatican Secret Archives (ca. 1214–1606)*, ed. Edgár Artner *et al.* (Budapest and Rome, 2004), no. 101, 112.

[9] *Magyar Diplomacziai Emlékek. Mátyás Király Korából 1458–1490*, ed. Iván Nagy and Albert Nyáry, Monumenta Hungariae Historica, acta extera, IV–VII (Budapest, 1875–8), II, no. 130, 184–5.

[10] Alexandru Simon, 'The Use of the "Gate of Christendom". Hungary's Mathias Corvinus and Moldavia's Stephen the Great, Politics in the late 1400s', *Quaderni della Casa Romena*, 3 (2004), 205–24.

These brief comments illustrate some of the versatility, not to say volatility, of the period's *antemurale* rhetoric.[11] The language of the bulwark was grist to the mill of Renaissance Europe's clever, classically educated humanists and diplomats. This can be misleading. All too often what they wrote has been construed as duplicity and pretence, fuelled by ambition, flattery and a dazzling way with words. But the impressive malleability of the dominant rhetoric should not lead us to dismiss it, any more than we should write off as stale and insincere the imposing corpus of anti-Ottoman oratory that the Renaissance generated.[12] Crusaders did not, for the most part, march or sail eastwards, as numerous enthusiasts for war ruefully commented, thereby paying homage to yet another *topos*, that of faith in decline. But what did occur was a pulsing traffic of individuals charged with the brief of discovering, informing, networking and persuading. And above all, this two-way traffic fertilised the exchange of ideas, data and modes of argument between Christendom's embattled frontier lands and its interior. Through reports, elaborate plans for action and desperate pleas for help, in speech and on paper, the frontier states instilled in the West a deep if tendentious consciousness of the Turkish threat and what it represented. From diets, assemblies and above all the papal court, responses were duly sent back. Arguably the greatest contribution that the Turks made to European life in this period was to make contemporaries think about who they were. Not only was a new vitality injected into the ancient debate about Christianity and Islam, but Europeans reflected on what it meant to be Catholic or Orthodox, not to say German, Hungarian or Croatian.

The Ottoman advance first impacted on Croatia in the mid-1460s, when neighbouring Bosnia fell, with astonishing rapidity, to Mehmed II's troops.[13] The collapse of medieval Bosnia in 1463 seems to have taken the sultan by surprise – he was heavily committed to operations in the Peloponnese, which held considerable attractions for him. Like his great opponent Pope Pius II, Mehmed faced difficult decisions about where to direct the bulk of his resources between the two competing areas of operation. Notwithstanding his youth and inexperience, and

---

[11] See Norman Housley, *Crusading and the Ottoman Threat, 1453–1505* (Oxford, 2012), ch. 2 *passim*, esp. 40–50. *Hungary as 'Propugnaculum'*, ed. Artner, is a useful collection of papal texts illustrating the general theme.

[12] See the ground-breaking study by James Hankins, 'Renaissance Crusaders: Humanist Crusade Literature in the Age of Mehmed II', *Dumbarton Oaks Papers*, 49 (1995), 111–207. Recently and specifically see Margaret Meserve, 'Nestor Denied: Francesco Filelfo's Advice to Princes on the Crusade against the Turks', *Osiris*, 25 (2010), 47–66.

[13] For a recent overview of the conquest, which is also insightful about Venetian management of the *antemurale* theme, see Emir O. Filipović, '*Ardet ante oculos opulentissimum regnum . . .* Venetian reports about the Ottoman Conquest of the Bosnian Kingdom, A.D. 1463', in *Italy and Europe's Eastern Border (1204–1669)*, ed. Iulian Mihai Damian *et al.* (Frankfurt am Main, 2012), 135–55.

the uncertain domestic situation that he confronted in the wake of dynastic change, Hungary's King Matthias stabilised what was left of the Christian position in Bosnia by retaking Jajce and setting up two frontier regions (*banovinas* or banates) centred on the recovered fortress and Srebrenica. Humiliated by his reversal at Belgrade in 1456, wary of taking on Matthias's impressive cordon sanitaire of fortresses, deflected by Iskanderbeg, and immersed in a gruelling sixteen-year war with Venice (1463–79), the sultan made little attempt to push further westwards during the remainder of his reign.[14]

The situation confronting Croatia in the six decades that separated the fall of Bosnia from the end of medieval Hungary in 1526 can conveniently be split into two phases, the hinge event being the disaster of Krbava Polje ('Krbava Field', near Udbina) in 1493. Up to 1493, Croatia suffered intermittent raiding; indeed, Grgin describes raids happening on an almost annual basis in the 1460s and 1470s.[15] The worst-hit area was the coastal region to the west of Bosnia, lying between Senj and Slunj. Turkish raiding parties frequently traversed this territory while making their way northwards towards Venetian Istria and Friuli, and Austrian Styria, Krain (Carniola) and Kärnten (Carinthia). As a satellite state of the Hungarian kingdom, Croatia was included, overtly or by implication, in the regular pleas for assistance that Matthias directed towards Rome. Dubrovnik was constantly alert to the menace facing it in the east and south, and was probably the most important feeder of information to the European powers. It is fair to say that it was in these decades that Croatia's political, ecclesiastical and cultural elite absorbed the language of *antemurale* discourse. They were well placed to do so. Despite such idiosyncrasies as the Glagolitic script,[16] Croatia was well integrated into the worlds of Italy and Hungary in the diplomatic, commercial and humanistic spheres, and we are increasingly aware of the importance of the Italian-Hungarian axis, in crusading terms as in so much else.[17] Studying the bulwark language that emanated from Buda and Venice could hardly have been surpassed as a means of learning the vocabulary and rhythms of the age's anti-Ottoman rhetoric.

---

[14] The best survey in English of Croatia in this period remains Stanko Guldescu, *History of Medieval Croatia* (The Hague, 1964). See most recently the various essays grouped as 'Croatia and Europe', in *Croatia in the Late Middle Ages and the Renaissance: A Cultural Survey*, ed. Ivan Supičič and Eduard Hercigonja (London and Zagreb, 2008), 5–84.

[15] Grgin, 'The Ottoman Influences', 92–4.

[16] See Eduard Hercigonja, 'Glagolism in the High Middle Ages', in *Croatia*, ed. Supičič and Hercigonja, 171–225.

[17] See most recently *Italy and Hungary: Humanism and Art in the Early Renaissance*, ed. Péter Farbaky and Louis Waldman (Florence, 2011); *Italy and Europe's Eastern Border*, ed. Damian et al.

From 1493 onwards, this became more relevant because Croatia suffered the calamity of Krbava Polje. In the report that was sent to Pope Alexander VI by his agent Antonio Fabregues in September 1493, and which was widely circulated, we gain a clear picture of how this latest disaster was interpreted. The rashness of the Croatian nobility in taking on the Turks as they marched through Croatia on their way back to Bosnia is accorded a charitable gloss: the Croatian army was attempting to free fellow-Christians who had been enslaved in Habsburg lands.[18] Christian losses had been terrible, only 300 soldiers escaping death or captivity out of 8,000 combatants. Fortresses, including Senj from where Fabregues wrote, had been stripped of their garrisons to field this army, so Croatia was ripe for conquest. Supplies were very limited and money from Italy was essential to pay troops to take on crucial defensive roles. Senj itself could be expected to fall in the immediate future, and with this port in their hands the Turks could easily invade northern Italy. This was the message that Alexander passed on to rulers including Giangaleazzo and Lodovico Sforza, summoning a meeting of envoys at Rome to take action.[19]

The planned meeting never took place, and Croatia's plight was soon little more than one tessera in the complex mosaic of European diplomatic interactions in the months leading up to the French descent into Italy. Following King Matthias's death in April 1490, the responsibility for defending Croatia had to all intents and purposes passed from Hungary to Austria. Maximilian could not ignore Croatia's military needs in terms of his imperial responsibility for the defence of Christendom. But a greater spur to involvement was the defence of his subjects in southern Austria. The potential was there for a more belligerent response to the Turks, one that would have served Croatia's long-term interests better than Matthias's compliance with – and arguably encouragement of – Turkish raids that used Croatian lands for convenient transit. But this was not to be. Renewed Ottoman pressure on the Danube began to exploit the chronic underfunding of Hungary's fortress perimeter, bringing about the series of conquests that culminated in the disaster at Mohács in 1526. Meanwhile, Maximilian's interventions in the region had proved to be at best intermittent, suffering like all of his policies from his prevaricating approach towards his many duties.

---

[18] Grgin, 'The Ottoman Influences', 90 (referencing work by Ivan Jurković at n. 11) points out that the slowness of Croatian mobilisation often lay behind such scenarios.

[19] For the response to Krbava Polje, see *Ausgewählte Regesten des Kaiserreiches unter Maximilian I., 1493–1519*, ed. Hermann Wiesflecker *et al.* (4 vols. in 7 pts so far, Vienna, 1990–), nos. 2764, 2777; Kenneth M. Setton, *The Papacy and the Levant (1204–1571)*, II: *The Fifteenth Century* (Philadelphia, 1978), 444–7.

After 1526, independent Croatian engagement in crusading discourse splintered into the various parts of the shipwrecked kingdom, the wistfully named 'remains of the remains of the once glorious kingdom of Croatia'. First, there were the various coastal cities that escaped occupation, ranging from Senj southwards to Dubrovnik. Thanks to Wendy Bracewell's monograph on Senj, we are well aware of the prominent role that holy war, of which *antemurale* rhetoric formed such a key part, played in the culture that was created by the uskoks.[20] There exists no comparable study for Dubrovnik, whose management of the shifting balance of power in the western Balkans would likely repay close analysis. The northern regions that passed into Austrian control naturally subscribed to the gradual absorption of holy war thinking into Habsburg imperial ideology. This had already begun under Maximilian I, and in due course it would result in the second genuine – as opposed to metaphorical – *antemurale* to which the region played host, the famed Austrian military frontier or *vojna krajina*. My subject, however, is ideas and their communication rather than structures, and from that viewpoint the political agencies that continued to represent Croatian interests are less significant than the range of individuals who continued to promote the cause of their occupied and divided country.

A good starting point for such an enquiry is Michael Petrovich's 1979 article on Croatian humanists who wrote about the Ottoman threat. Petrovich identified 'some two hundred' Croatian humanists, and provided useful résumés of the contributions that about a dozen of these men (mostly hailing from the Adriatic coastal towns) made to the literature frequently labelled as *Turcica*, early printed works about the Ottomans. It is regrettable but not surprising that so little of this bulky output has benefited from modern editions. Two points do, however, emerge from Petrovich's survey, when one compares these works with the overall spread of *Turcica*.[21] The first is the eclectic spectrum of genres to which they belonged. There was a literature (both poetry and prose) of lamentation, which described the destruction and sufferings of the Croats themselves without losing sight of the broader sequence of Christian setbacks and losses into which Croatia's plight fitted. Good examples of such texts are Šimun Kožičić Benja's poignantly titled *De Corvatiae desolatione* of 1516 and the letter appealing for a crusade that Marko Marulić wrote to Pope

[20] Bracewell, *Uskoks*, esp. 155–62.
[21] *Turcica: Die europaische Türkendrucke des XVI. Jahrhunderts, I. Bd, MDI–MDL*, ed. Carl Göllner (Bucharest, 1961); *idem, Turcica, III. Band, Die Türkenfrage in der öffentlichen Meinung Europas im 16. Jahrhundert* (Bucharest and Baden-Baden, 1978). Specifically on the humanists, see Nancy Bisaha, *Creating East and West: Renaissance Humanists and the Ottoman Turks* (Philadelphia, 2004); Margaret Meserve, *Empires of Islam in Renaissance Historical Thought* (Cambridge, MA, 2008).

Adrian VI six years later.[22] There was a literature of instruction, in which the enemy's strengths and weaknesses were described with a view to defeating him; though also, in a manner characteristic of the Renaissance *Feindbild*, of shaming fellow-Christians by reference to the military, moral and domestic virtues practised by the Turks.[23] There were texts that sprang from the personal experience of campaigning and captivity: these make for some of the most rewarding reading.[24] And naturally there were *pièces d'occasion*, texts intended to exhort and persuade envoys at assemblies and diets, with an eye on the particular situation faced by the Croatian *patria*.[25]

The other point to make is that *mutatis mutandis*, we find in these Croatian contributions a set of themes and *topoi* that are familiar from their Hungarian, Italian and German counterparts. Hence, the Turks are, by definition, the enemies not just of individual states but of Christianity. Croatia's sufferings are typical of the Christian countries that the Turks attack. Its young men are fighting for home and hearth – 'pro patria pugnans proque domibus suis'[26] – but they are also defending Christendom. For should they falter, which they will unless reinforced, others will pay a price. As Marko Marulić expressed it in 1522, 'in my judgement help must be despatched without delay to [Croatia], because if the enemy – God forbid – succeeds in conquering it, the road will be open to him to invade Germany and Italy, overcome all of Illyria, and subjugate the whole of the Christian world'.[27] In short, the vision is one of a stricken, meritorious and strategically vital *antemurale*.[28]

Thus, there was a strong commonality of both genre and theme between the output of Croatia's humanist elite and that produced by its various neighbours. But we should not infer that there was no difference between these outputs. For the same humanists who lamented what was happening to Croatia were at the same time composing its national history. They disseminated what they wrote not just through the press, but through their personal contacts; for they included bishops, legates and ambassadors, chancellors, men of letters, high-ranking city officials and a naval commander. So, at the very time that the nation faced catastrophe, talented and prominent members of its elite highlighted the glories of

---

[22] Michael B. Petrovich, 'The Croatian Humanists and the Ottoman Peril', *Balkan Studies*, 20 (1979), 257–73, at 266–7. For substantial extracts see *Hrvastski Latinisti*, 309–13, 509–13.

[23] Petrovich, 'The Croatian Humanists and the Ottoman Peril', 271–2.

[24] *Ibid.*, 258–61.

[25] *Ibid.*, 265–9.

[26] *Hrvatski Latinisti*, 141 (Šižgorić, 'Elegia').

[27] *Ibid.*, 311.

[28] Petrovich, 'The Croatian Humanists and the Ottoman Peril', *passim*.

Croatia's past and constructed its singularity.[29] Juraj Šižgorić (c. 1445–
1509), for example, wrote a text about the hinterland of his native town
of Šibenik and the ways of its people, as well as a poem describing the
destruction inflicted on its surroundings by Turkish raids. The celebratory
and the elegiac were bed fellows.[30]

It is worth glancing at the career at one of these lobbyists, Tomaso
Negri of Split (Spalato) to flesh out their *modus operandi*, motivation
and impact. Born probably between 1450 and 1460, Negri did not
have to leave his hometown to gain a sound education from a cluster
of gifted Italian teachers. Giuseppe Praga showed that Negri moved
within the overlapping orbits of three powers that for different reasons
were implicated in Croatia's defence against the Turks. The first was
Venice, of which Negri was legally a subject. Negri was talent-spotted by
Doge Loredan in 1503 when he gave an incisive report on Hungarian
affairs; thereafter, the Venetians listened attentively to Negri's views and
showed their gratitude by promoting his interests. In return, he viewed
the republic as one of Croatia's best hopes. It was at Venice, shortly
before his death, that he had his portrait painted by Lorenzo Lotto,
and commissioned his tombstone. Secondly, there was Rome, where on
several occasions Negri gave impressive orations about Croatia; his finest
speech, delivered at the Fifth Lateran Council in 1512, was immediately
printed. From this source too rewards followed, most importantly the
see of Trogir, where Negri ended his life in the 1530s. Then, there was
Croatia itself, or rather powerful individuals there. Negri served first the
archbishop of Split, the Venetian Bernardo Zane – in whose company
he came to Rome in 1512 – and following Zane's death Pietro Berislao of
Trogir, Croatia's ban. After Berislao in turn died (in battle) in 1520, Negri
appears to have functioned as a free agent, serving, as Praga put it, not a
person but a cause.[31]

We have learned not to expect purity of motivation from humanists,
who often had no means of support except their own talent.[32] Like his
peers, Negri was ambitious for fame, wealth and advancement, and
he managed to fashion a successful career, *inter alia*, from working for
Croatia's defence. But that is no reason to label him an opportunist. His

[29] E.g. *Hrvatski Latinisti*, 327–51 (Ludovik Crijević Tuberon, 'Commentaria de temporibus
suis'), 551–67 (Vinko Pribojević, 'De origine successibusque Slavorum').

[30] Michael B. Petrovich, 'Croatian Humanists and the Writing of History in the Fifteenth
and Sixteenth Centuries', *Slavic Review*, 37 (1978), 624–39. For Šižgorić, see the extracts in
Hrvastski Latinisti, 139–49.

[31] Giuseppe Praga, 'Tomaso Negri da Spalato, umanista e uomo politico del secolo XVI',
Archivio storico per la Dalmazia, 15 (1933), 159–201.

[32] Meserve, 'Nestor Denied'; *eadem*, 'Patronage and Propaganda at the First Paris Press:
Guillaume Fichet and the First Edition of Bessarion's Orations against the Turks', *Papers of
the Bibliographical Society of America*, 97 (2003), 521–88.

impact was varied. Praga showed that Negri is due much of the credit for bringing about the relief of Klis in 1524, thereby rendering a considerable service to his country.[33] Less susceptible to analysis is the effect of the speeches that he gave, but I would place most emphasis on the cross-pollination that took place as he and others like him moved between Croatia, Hungary, Venice, Rome and the other power centres of the day. There is a strong case for arguing that men like Negri, Šimun Kožićic Benja, Giovanni Stafileo and Antun Vrančić played the central role in both creating and disseminating Croatia's profile.

This choir of Croatian voices includes that of Andrija Jamometić. His views were unusually well articulated and distinctive; more to the point, for a few months in 1482, he triggered a full-blooded crisis in European diplomacy.[34] The early years of Jamometić are very obscure, thanks to the loss of so much documentation during the Ottoman conquest. We can surmise that he was born around 1420–30 into the aristocracy – indeed, his family origins have become relatively clear, though we still have no idea of either his birthplace or his education.[35] Jamometić entered the Dominican order and left his country for a career abroad. In joining the Croatian diaspora, he resembled many of Petrovich's humanists, though it is important to stress that Jamometić showed no sign of humanistic leanings: that is one reason why he is interesting. In 1476, he was appointed titular archbishop of Granea, now on the Montenegro–Albania border. He also entered the service of Frederick III, for whom he carried out several diplomatic missions to Rome between 1478 and 1481. One of the aspects of his brief was the promotion of a crusade against the Turks, and his imperial master placed particular emphasis on the need for Sixtus IV to adopt a more pacific policy in Italy – with specific reference to Medici Florence – as the essential preliminary to a substantial crusading venture. During his last Roman mission in 1481, Jamometić overstepped the mark in his criticism of the pope and suffered imprisonment in Castel Sant'Angelo. Forgiven by Sixtus, the errant envoy was released and made his way north of the Alps.

In the spring of 1482, the Croat enjoyed his brief moment of fame. At Basel on the Feast of the Annunciation, he dramatically proclaimed a general council of the church and issued a summons to the Pope to

[33] Praga, 'Tomaso Negri', 12–15.

[34] The seminal study of Jamometić remains Joseph Schlecht, *Andrea Zamometić und der Basler Konzilsversuch vom Jahre 1482* (2 vols., Paderborn, 1903), but Jürgen Petersohn, *Kaiserlicher Gesandter und Kurienbischof: Andreas Jamometić am Hof Papst Sixtus' IV. (1478–1481). Aufschlüsse aus neuen Quellen* (Hanover, 2004), is important for its new and corrected data, and its bibliographic updating.

[35] Jürgen Petersohn, 'Zum Personalakt eines Kirchenrebellen: Name, Herkunft and Amtssprengel des Basler Konzilsinitiators Andreas Jamometić', *Zeitschrift für historische Forschung*, 113 (1986), 1–14, at 2–8; *idem, Kaiserlicher Gesandter*, 11.

come to Basel to defend his behaviour. It was an astonishingly rash venture, one that he apparently embarked on without any preparation. Nonetheless, for a few weeks, the extraordinary proposal appeared to gain traction. Basel's patriciate was excited by the prospect of their city again becoming the seat of a general council, Frederick III did not immediately condemn his former diplomat, and Lorenzo de' Medici thought he saw the possibility of gaining a march on Sixtus IV, with whom he remained at odds in the wake of the Pazzi crisis. In theory at least, crusade and council alike appealed to the French. Meanwhile the pope was hemmed in at Rome by a Neapolitan army. Would this eccentric action by the titular archbishop of an obscure Balkan see bring about the fall of an anointed pope? The answer was no, because Sixtus recovered his position at Rome, Frederick intervened to stop Jamometić getting any further, and the man was arrested. In 1484 he died, most likely by his own hand, in his prison cell.

The significance for this paper of the Jamometić saga lies in the list of complaints that the Croat directed at the pope in 1482, the charges on which he proposed that Sixtus should stand trial. They were a mixture of items including simony, dynastic aggrandisement and the sponsorship of assassination (Sixtus's complicity in the Pazzi conspiracy was still fresh in people's memory). But there were also a number of charges specifically relating to the crusade. These did not all reference the Ottomans: Jamometić accused the pope of forming a covert alliance with the Mamluk sultan to forward his ambitions against the Medici and other Italian powers. But the Ottoman charges dominated. Jamometić accused the pope of neglecting the crusade by prioritising a series of unjust wars in Italy, 'lest an expedition be undertaken against the enemies of the Christian religion, who have shed innocent blood and thanks to you continue to do so'. Sixtus had compelled (*coegisti*) the Venetians to make peace with the Turks in 1479. He had stirred up Germans and Hungarians to attack Venice, 'as if the most illustrious lordship of Venice did not adhere to the Christian faith'. And he had permitted (*permisisti*) the Turks to invade southern Italy in 1480 in pursuit of his feud with Ferrante of Naples. In short, Sixtus was a friend of the Turks. 'Ecce opera Sixti.'[36]

The first thing that has to be said about these abrasively hostile comments is that they were more than just a cry of pain for a distressed *patria*. Jamometić did not single out his homeland for mention in his 1482 summons. As the archbishop of a see that had been occupied by the Turks, Jamometić had an *ex officio* duty to speak up on behalf of the Christians who had fallen under Ottoman rule, and as an imperial diplomat he had engaged closely with the minutiae of papal policy. The violence of his accusations could be ascribed to his insider knowledge of the duplicitous way in which Sixtus's court operated. It is possible to argue that Jamometić's Croatian origins played no role at all in his rebellion of 1482. But this seems unnecessarily cautious. During his imperial service at Rome, Jamometić had acted on several occasions on behalf of Croatian interests; in May 1480, for example, he lobbied alongside Dubrovnik's envoy for the supplying of the port in readiness for an Ottoman naval assault.[37] It is plausible that in the spring of 1482 Jamometić was not only expressing his own disappointment as a Croat, but the resentment of well-informed compatriots that behind Rome's constant assertions that it was working on their behalf, in practice the pope was pursuing aims that undermined the prospects of a crusade that would relieve their position.[38]

Even the restrained Šimun Kožičic Benja of Zadar, in appealing to Pope Leo X for help in 1516, was prepared openly to question the morality of building Roman palaces instead of ransoming fellow-Christians from Turkish bondage. Benja did not mince words. The prices that had recently been charged for captured Christian children showed that for a fraction of what the pope was spending on his construction projects, all the individuals rounded up by the Turks could be redeemed. If Leo did not rearrange his priorities, Benja went on to declare, the Croats would be driven by desperation and want to join forces with the enemies of the faith.[39]

So in the charges levelled against Sixtus IV by Jamometić in 1482, we witness a representative of the *antemurale* taking issue with the priorities and methods of Christendom's centre of authority. Such a challenge had both precedents in crusading history and echoes in Jamometić's own times. In the late thirteenth century, the defenders of the embattled crusader states had expressed their alarm that its needs were being placed second to the prosecution of the pope's goals in Italy. In the early fourteenth century, the enthusiastic lobbyist Marino Sanudo Torsello returned to the theme in the context of hopes to recover the Holy Land.[40] Just months after Jamometić launched his attempt to bring down Sixtus at Basel, the Venetian Girolamo Lando, who as titular patriarch of Constantinople bore a similar *ex officio* responsibility to the archbishop of Granea, confronted the pope in an analogous, though somewhat

---

[37] Petersohn, *Kaiserlicher Gesandter*, 91, citing a Milanese despatch. In practice, of course, the Turks attacked Otranto.

[38] Petersohn, *ibid.*, 111, adds a specifically Dominican grievance relating to Sixtus IV's unfair treatment of the claims of St Catherine of Siena. Additionally, Jamometić nursed a personal injury, having been turned down for promotion to cardinal, *ibid.*, 130–8.

[39] *Hrvatski Latinisti*, 509–13, quote at 511; Petrovich, 'The Croatian Humanists and the Ottoman Peril', 266–7.

[40] Norman Housley, *The Italian Crusades: The Papal–Angevin Alliance and the Crusades against Christian Lay Powers, 1254–1343* (Oxford, 1982), 75–97.

more restrained, way in conjunction with the republic of Venice.[41] And it is possible that similar charges originated with Jamometić's fellow-countryman Luca de Tolentis, bishop of Šibenik and crusade collector, whom Sixtus IV was trying to get his hands on in April 1484 because 'he won't stop making daily complaints about us'.[42]

What the complaints of Jamometić, Sanudo and Lando reveal is an ongoing and perhaps inevitable tension between warfare at home and crusade abroad, expressed as a confrontation between the agencies and spokesmen of centre and periphery (or *antemurale*). But the confrontation was never straightforward. King Matthias Corvinus, who faced similar criticisms of neglect and diversion to those that Jamometić directed at Sixtus, was the period's leading *antemurale* ruler. He had turned away from Bosnia following his early successes there, and the instigators of a rebellion that the king had to put down in 1471 included some prominent southern Hungarians and Croats. Jamometić was well aware of the equivocal character of the Hungarian king's *antemurale* stance. Jürgen Petersohn has surmised that Jamometić entered Habsburg service out of disappointment with Matthias's Turkish policy.[43] For his part, the emperor must have been tempted to make use of Jamometić's services by the man's first-hand acquaintance with conditions in Croatia. When Jamometić went to Rome on Frederick's behalf in 1478, he complained that Matthias was conducting an 'open door' policy with the Turks, allowing their raiders to ravage Austrian lands.[44] Additionally, the Croat's confrontation with Sixtus IV in 1482 went far beyond a demand that the pope adjust his priorities. Certainly, the Turks must be resisted, but Jamometić also called for a return to conciliar government, followed by root and branch reform of the church.[45] Indeed, writing to Frederick III in June 1482 defending his actions at Basel, he argued that unless the church was thoroughly reformed it was a waste of time trying to promote a crusade, as he had laboured so hard to do a few years previously at the emperor's behest.[46]

Jamometić's actions in 1482 and their background form a reminder of the complex hinterland to the period's *antemurale* rhetoric. In public discourse, it was beyond challenge, enjoying the sort of kudos that democratic values do today. But at the same time, it was constantly

---

[41] Dan Ioan Mureşan, 'Girolamo Lando, titulaire du patriarcat de Constantinople (1474–1497), et son rôle dans la politique orientale du Saint-Siège', *Annuario dell'Istituto romeno di cultura e ricerca umanistica di Venezia*, 8 (2006), 153–258, at 225–8.

[42] Alfred Stoecklin, 'Das Ende des Basler Konzilsversuchs von 1482', *Zeitschrift für Schweizerische Kirchengeschichte*, 79 (1985), 3–118, at 71–2 n. 280.

[43] Petersohn, *Kaiserlicher Gesandter*, 18.

[44] Schlecht, *Andrea Zamometić*, I, 28, II, 7.

[45] The association is overt in a citation of the pope that Jamometić issued on 14 May: *ibid.*, II, 66–8.

[46] *Ibid.*, II, 80–1.

subverted, most clearly by blunt political reality, but also by a potent counter-argument to the effect that a crusade against the Turks had to wait until peace had been secured within Christendom's interior. This peace entailed the subjugation of those – whether Medici Florence or Habsburg Austria – whose malevolence allegedly impeded the good work of the organising and contributing states.[47] In the past, recognition of the power interests that drove this counter-argument has often led to dismissal of the entire *antemurale* discourse as elaborate camouflage.[48] I think we have moved on from that polarised position. We can usefully learn from Cemal Kafadar's recent analysis of the way things worked on the Turkish side of the *antemurale*, albeit in a somewhat earlier period. Identities and values were no more absolute and clear-cut among the early Ottomans than they were among the Christian opponents of their successors. As Kafadar put it, 'All this commotion had a certain cosmic significance in the minds of the actors because it was, or one could occasionally and selectively remember it to be, played out in the name of a much larger struggle between two competing transcendental visions: Islam and Christianity.'[49] Both on the Muslim and on the Christian side of the frontier identities were fluid, values and beliefs interacted with circumstances and were affected by shifts of power and movements of people, and the conversions and religious commingling that they generated.[50] Croatian identity could cross over the religious divide, as evinced by the famous attempt by Bishop Antun Vrančić in 1559 to reach accommodation with an Ottoman official called Hasan-bey 'for the sake of our common Croatian origin'.[51] That instance, and others like it, does not negate the argument that the image of Croatia as an embattled and valiant *antemurale* played a significant role in sustaining Croatian national awareness during one of the most disastrous periods in the country's history. Given the political divisions of the time, it could not generate the military assistance that might have saved Croatia from collapse and division. But it did other things that are, regrettably, less susceptible of proof. Most clearly, it demonstrated Croatia's embrace of the humanist mode of debate that had become the fashionable means of communication across the entire Catholic community. More broadly,

---

[47] *Ibid.*, I, 33 (only Lorenzo de' Medici stands in the way of a crusade, 1478).

[48] For a thoroughgoing restatement of the ideal/reality paradigm, see Géraud Poumarède, *Pour en finir avec la croisade: mythes et réalités de la lutte contre les Turcs aux XVI et XVII siècles* (Paris, 2004).

[49] Cemal Kafadar, *Between Two Worlds: The Construction of the Ottoman State* (Berkeley, 1995), 141.

[50] The obscurity of Jamometić's origins enabled the legate Angelo Geraldini to make a maladroit attempt to use this situation against him in 1482, questioning 's'el sia christiano o Turcho': Petersohn, 'Zum Personalakt', 2.

[51] *Hrvatski Latinisti*, 637–9; Bracewell, *Uskoks*, 34; Petrovich, 'The Croatian Humanists and the Ottoman Peril', 265.

it affirmed Croatia's membership of that community, and it constituted a lasting reminder of an aspiration towards national unity.[52] Croatia was shown indubitably to belong to *Europa*, which in the reconfigured crusading discourse of the times was the Christian community threatened by the Ottomans. That the natural home for Croatia's freshly achieved national unity is seen as a European framework of political power is strikingly resonant of what was said and done in the fifteenth and sixteenth centuries and arguably owes much to it.[53]

[52] Cf. Petrovich, 'Croatian Humanists and the Writing of History', 638–9.
[53] This is not to deny that the 'European' debate remains highly politicised in Croatia: Patterson, 'The Futile Crescent?', 138–40.

Transactions of the RHS 24 (2014), pp. 165–81 © Royal Historical Society 2014
doi:10.1017/S0080440114000085

CROATS AND CROATIA IN THE WAKE OF THE GREAT WAR

By John Paul Newman

READ 27 MARCH 2013 AT THE UNIVERSITY OF LEICESTER

ABSTRACT. This article addresses the experiences of Croats and Croatia in the aftermath of the First World War, showing how the interwar Kingdom of Yugoslavia privileged the wartime sacrifice of Serbia and the Serbian army and how Croats were often depicted as the remnants of a defeated state, Austria-Hungary, and therefore less entitled to citizenship in the South Slav kingdom. It focuses on three large veteran associations: the Association of Reserve Officers and Warriors, the Union of Volunteers, and the Association of War Invalids.

Introduction

Croatia's 2013 entry into the European Union precedes a moment of reflection and remembrance for all Europeans, for 2014 is the centennial of the outbreak of the First World War, an anniversary – or rather the first year of a cycle of anniversaries – being marked throughout the continent and in a variety of ways. In many countries, the centennial is a tidal surge in what was already a fairly high water line: in Europe, popular and scholarly interest in the First World War has been continuously present, to a greater or lesser extent, since the war officially ended on 11 November 1918. The 'Great Seminal Catastrophe' of the twentieth century (George Kennan) has shaped the politics, society and culture of Europeans, and it has shaped the way Europeans think about their continent and its identity. And yet the vicissitudes of Europe's last hundred years have obscured the pan-European nature of the First World War. Thus, the Bolshevik Revolution of 1917 and the subsequent civil war drew a veil over Russia's First World War that has only recently begun to be lifted.[1] Europe's Cold War divisions of the second half of the twentieth century also generated alternate historical memories, realities, even; so whilst the First World War continued to feature prominently in French and British memory, it apparently left less of an impression in communist 'Eastern Europe', whose leaders preferred not to emphasise the importance of the

---

[1] The international project 'Russia's Great War and Revolution' looks set to address this research gap. See the project's website http://russiagreatwar.org/index.php (accessed 3 Jan. 2014).

'imperialist war' over their own revolutionary struggles, whose successes came later, usually in the wake of the Second World War. The end of communism and the gradual political integration of Europe – of which the eastward expansion of the European Union is an important part – has perhaps created the conditions, after a century, for a truly European understanding of the Great War and its impact, from Ypres to the Urals. Croatia's increasing institutional integration into Europe might, then, go hand-in-hand with greater integration into the mainstreams of European historical memory and identity.

The signs are, in fact, good. The centenary of the First World War in Croatia has generated official, academic and popular interest, just as it has throughout much of the rest of Europe: the Croatian government has appointed an official 'Centenary Committee' of historians and experts, presided over by the Minister of Culture; the Croatian Institute of History in Zagreb will hold a conference on Croats and the First World War in late 2014; a four-hour television documentary is forthcoming, too.[2] It is hoped that these initiatives will act as a corrective to decades of relative neglect, for until very recently the First World War and its impact on Croats and Croatia has been dealt with in a somewhat cursory fashion. Tito's socialist state had its own seminal conflict, the Partisan war, or the 'Anti-Fascist Struggle of 1941–5', in which, it was said, all Yugoslavs rose up in unison to rid their homeland of the fascist invader. The First World War was a footnote to the history of the discredited interwar kingdom, a state that was itself merely a preface to socialist Yugoslavia. According to the socialists' version of events, the First World War was a conflict waged by the imperialists; it led to the creation of the first South Slav state, in which political and economic power was monopolized by the Serbian bourgeoisie and wielded as an instrument of oppression against the state's other nationalities (and, of course, against the working class). Croats themselves were helplessly swept along in these historical currents, as a subaltern group in imperial institutions such as the Austro-Hungarian army, forced to fight not for their own interests (as they did during 1941–5) but as pawns for foreign capital.[3]

This, of course, is a very teleological perspective, and a response to the socialist regime's most pressing concern, that is, fitting the First World War into the inexorable historical process that led the South Slavs towards the formation of the socialist state in 1945. In keeping with the theme of Croatia's European integration, however, we could instead offer a new perspective on the First World War, one that emphasises the

[2] I am very grateful to Filip Hameršak for this information.
[3] A notable exception to this rule is Andrej Mitrović's excellent single-volume account of Serbia during the First World War, *Srbija u prvom svetskom ratu* (Belgrade, 2004), published (slightly abridged) in English as *Serbia's Great War 1914–1918* (2007).

European rather than exclusively the *Yugoslav* dimensions of the conflict and its consequences; one which places Croatia and the Croats in the context of the dramatic transformations in the political, social and cultural landscape wrought by the war throughout the continent. Some of the most consequential and enduring changes took place in the region to which Croatia belongs: the Great War completely altered the political borders of central and eastern Europe, laying to waste Austria-Hungary, the great continental empire (one of several great empires which became casualties of the conflict) of which the Croats had been subjects and for whom many had fought during the war, and replacing it with new 'successor-states', in theory if not in practice organised and governed on the principle of national self-determination. The most marked changes in borders and state structures, then, and with the possible exception of Russia, took place in central and eastern Europe, or 'New Europe'. After 1918, this region would become an unsuccessful experiment in liberal and democratic state-building; and experiment of which the Croats were a part.

National self-determination, of course, had been the vision of American President Woodrow Wilson, who had arrived in Europe belatedly and virtually unscathed, surveying the destruction and ushering in what he hoped would be a new, more enlightened and egalitarian epoch in the continent. It is now a truism of interwar history to note that Wilson's template for national determination was impossible to apply fully and uniformly throughout central and eastern Europe; in reality there was a significant shortfall between its universalist claims and the impossibility of these claims being applied universally. The eventual post-war settlement in Europe represented in part an attempt to draw borders which left the most number of Europeans inside territory governed by their own national group; but where this proved impossible, or undesirable, the peacemakers (and especially the French and the British) tended to favour those national groups identified as allies during the conflict at the expense of former enemies.[4] The states of 'New Europe' were compelled to sign up to minority treaties, the purpose of which was to guarantee the status of all peoples in 'New Europe', regardless of their nationality or country of residence. The problem of the minorities became one of the most acute of the interwar period. The Munich diktat of 1938, in which Great Britain and France colluded with Nazi Germany in the dismemberment of Czechoslovakia, demonstrates how the minorities question could be exploited with fatal consequences, in this case bringing about both the symbolic and actual end of the Allied-sponsored settlement of 1919.

[4] Zara Steiner, *The Lights that Failed: European International History 1919–1933* (Oxford, 2007), 80.

Quite rightly, then, the minorities question in interwar central and eastern Europe has attracted a great deal of scholarly attention. But I want to offer another category, one that might be a better fit for the Croat case. In addition to being ethnically heterogeneous, the new successor states cut across the fault-lines of the First World War, and countries such as Poland, Czechoslovakia, Romania and the South Slav state all housed subjects and citizens who had, until 1918, fought on different sides during the First World War. This division very often cut across ethnic and national lines, too. Take, for example, the veterans of the First World War: Frenchmen had fought in the French army, Britons in the British Expeditionary Force (the BEF); but Poles might have fought in the Russian army, with the Entente, or in the Austro-Hungarian or Prussian armies for the Central Powers;[5] subjects of Greater Romania had fought either in the Romanian army with the Allies, or as soldiers in the Austro-Hungarian army (recruited from Translyvania) with the Central Powers;[6] Serbs, Croats and Slovenes had fought either in the Serbian army, or in the Austro-Hungarian army. In the interwar period, reconciliation of former wartime enemies would become one of the great challenges facing Europe;[7] but in the successor states of eastern and central Europe, reconciliation was primarily a domestic matter.

The Croats found themselves on the wrong side of this division in the wake of the war. They were ostensibly one of the three constituent 'tribes' in the Kingdom of Serbs, Croats and Slovenes, but in reality they were politically subordinate to Serbia and its institutions, institutions that were transplanted from the pre-war Serbian state into the post-war South Slav state, often without significant alteration. So much is well known,[8] but the war and its outcome adds another dimension to our understanding of the development of Croatian national identity after the First World War and of the failures of the South Slav state in the interwar period. For the Kingdom of Serbs, Croats and Slovenes was strongly identified, both domestically and abroad, with Serbia's victory during the First World War and with the great sacrifices of the Serbian people and their army towards the creation of the state.[9] Serbia had been at the epicentre of the war's outbreak in 1914; its armies had fought successfully against overwhelming odds in the first year of the war; its people had made a harrowing winter

[5] Julia Eichenberg, *Kämpfen für Frieden und Fürsorge. Polnische Veteranen des Ersten Weltkriegs und ihre internationalen Kontakte, 1918–1939* (Munich, 2011).

[6] Irina Marin, 'World War One and Internal Repression: The Case of Major General Nikolaus Cena', *Austrian History Yearbook*, 44 (Apr. 2013).

[7] See *The Great War and Veterans' Internationalism*, ed. Julia Eichenberg and John Paul Newman (2013).

[8] See Ivo Banac, *The National Question in Yugoslavia: Origins, History, Politics* (Ithaca, 1984).

[9] John Paul Newman, 'Allied Yugoslavia: Serbian Great War Veterans and their Internationalist Ties', in *The Great* War, ed. Eichenberg and Newman.

retreat through Albania in the winter of 1915; and in the face of defeat and even destruction, Serbia had 'resurrected' itself with the victory of 1918. The great cost of the war to 'gallant little Serbia' was recognised and lauded throughout the countries of the Entente. A kind of Serbian 'culture of victory'[10] reigned supreme in the interwar kingdom, one that tended to emphasise Croatia's past as part of a 'defeated state' – Austria-Hungary. It was a culture that justified consigning Croats to the status of second-class citizens in a country that supposedly recognised them as one of three constituent 'tribes'. It therefore undermined the Croats' sense of citizenship in the new state, contributing to their alienation and inhibiting the formation of a properly integrated Yugoslav culture.

Veterans' associations: micro and national

I want to examine this problem further by focusing on South Slav veterans of the First World War and the associations of which they were members in the interwar period, an area that remains relatively under-researched.[11] Many such associations sprang up throughout the country (although mainly in the Serbian lands) in the years immediately after the First World War. The majority of them were what we might term 'micro-societies', that is, ephemeral groups comprising rarely more than twenty members, established solely for the purpose of raising funds for a war monument or memorial at local level. Such associations could apply for subventions to the Royal Court in Belgrade in order to raise enough money to build their monuments, and it is in these records that we start to see the imbalance caused by the war throughout the South Slav state: the boxes of requests received by the Royal Court were overwhelmingly sent from Serbian associations, that is, associations formed by war veterans of the Serbian army, and they were most frequently raising monuments which celebrated Serbia's victory or commemorated its war dead. Far fewer came from associations formed by Croat or Slovene veterans of the Austro-Hungarian army, and those that did were treated with suspicion (although their requests were not always turned down).

The micro-societies rarely needed to broach the question of post-war reconciliation between the men who had fought in the Serbian army and those who had not, because they operated only at a local level and almost never crossed the boundaries between the two contingents of the wartime generation. They asked only that the local dead, the men

[10] This term, an inversion of Wolfgang Schivelbusch's notion of a 'culture of defeat', is explored by John Horne in his essay 'Beyond Cultures of Victory and Defeat? Interwar Veterans' Internationalism', in *The Great* War, ed. Eichenberg and Newman.

[11] There is an important study of the interwar 'Chetnik' associations in Bosnia – many of whose members were veterans of the Great War – by Nusret Šehić, *Četništvo u Bosni i Hercegovini (1918–1941): politička uloga i oblici djelatnosti četničkih udruženja* (Sarajevo, 1971).

who hailed from their village and who had lost their lives fighting in the Great War, were honoured with a plaque or monument. Once this demand had been fulfilled, the associations tended to disappear from the record. But matters were quite different for the handful of national associations that formed in the years after the war and that were active throughout the country. The ambitions of such associations were grander: they aspired to memberships that crossed tribal boundaries, and their corporate identities were more fixed. Thus, it was with three of the largest and most important national associations in the interwar kingdom: the 'Association of Reserve Officers and Warriors' (*Udruženje reservnih oficira i ratnika*), a patriotic association whose members were largely although not exclusively veterans of the First World War (of all nationalities); the 'Union of Volunteers' (*Savez dobrovoljaca*), an association formed by men who had volunteered to fight for the Serbian army during the Balkan wars and the First World War; and the 'Association of War Invalids' (*Udruženje ratnih invalida*), a national association which promoted and protected the welfare of disabled veterans of the wars (again, of all nationalities). Croats were represented at every level in the membership of each of these associations. Their experiences in them, however, show the way in which the legacy of the war continued to divide the country and to marginalise Croats.

The Association of Reserve Officers and Warriors

The Association of Reserve Officers and Warriors, in most respects, defined the commemoration of the First World War in the interwar kingdom to a greater extent than any other.[12] This association represented on a macro level what the tiny, local associations mentioned above represented on a micro level: its members were concerned with the commemoration of the war in the interwar kingdom, as well as the welfare and well-being of its members and their families. The society had started small: its first meeting, in Belgrade, was attended by just a few hundred people, but it claimed to have as many as 20,000 members in 1930,[13] making it one of the largest patriotic or veteran associations in the country at the time. The reserve officers had close ties with the army and with the Royal Court of King Alexander Karadjordjević; delegates of both often attended commemorative and festive ceremonies organised by the association, as did the king himself. They were responsible for raising some of the most striking monuments of the First World War, including the first monument to the unknown Serbian soldier at Avala, in 1922 (which would later become a monument to the 'Unknown Yugoslav Hero'); a

[12] For a good overview of the association's activities, see Danilo Šarenac, 'Udruženje rezervnih oficira i ratnika 1919–1941', *Istorija XX. veka*, 1 (2011), 27–38.
[13] *Ratnički glasnik*, May–June 1930.

monument to Chetnik Vojvoda Jovan Stojković 'Babunski' in Veles; and a monument to Rudolf Archibald Reiss, the Swiss criminologist who had published reports of Austro-Hungarian wartime atrocities against Serbs, and who had made Yugoslavia his home after 1918. In 1931, the reserve officers unveiled a huge monument and ossuary to the 'Defenders of Belgrade' – the men who fought against the Austro-Hungarian invasion of 1914 – in the Serbian capital's New Cemetery. Needless to say, it was the achievements of the Serbian army that the Association of Reserve Officers wanted to pass on to future generations. The monuments and commemorative activities of the reserve officers, initially, at least, were largely silent about the tens of thousands of men who had fought in the Austro-Hungarian army during the First World War.

It should be noted, however, that beyond these initiatives for monuments to Serbia's war, the reserve officers did make efforts to build relations between Serbian and Austro-Hungarian veterans, and especially with Croat veterans. As well as their domestic activities, the association was part of the inter-Allied veterans' movement, through their membership (from 1921) in the international war veterans' association, the *Fédération Interalliée des Anciens Combattants* (FIDAC). Throughout the 1920s, FIDAC agonised about the correct relations between war veterans of the Entente and veterans of the Central Powers.[14] The Association of Reserve Officers and Warriors were aware of a corresponding gap in Yugoslavia between veterans of the Serbian army on the one hand, the 'victors', and those who had fought for Austria-Hungary on the other, the 'vanquished'. The Italian section of FIDAC repeatedly underlined (at FIDAC conferences during the 1920s) that South Slavs – and especially Croats – had fought against Allied interests during the war.[15]

These relations were subject to the winds of international diplomacy and reconciliation, for just as the Locarno Treaty of 1925 advanced cultural demobilisation throughout Europe,[16] in the latter half of the 1920s the reserve officers internalised a kind of 'Locarno Spirit'. Thus, in summer 1926, a few months after the treaty was signed, the Association of Reserve Officers and Warriors held a Gala in Zagreb in an attempt to reach out to the Austro-Hungarian contingent of South Slav veterans into its ranks. The association claimed that about 2,500 of its 12,000 members were Croats and Slovenes, many of whom, presumably, were

---

[14] See their report on the FIDAC congress in London, Sept. 1924, at which the discussion of relations with 'former enemies' was discussed, mentioned in *ibid.*, Oct. 1924.

[15] See *ibid.*, Nov. 1925. See also Martina Salvante 'The Italian Associazione Nazionale Mutilati e Invaldi di Guerra and its International Liaisons in the Post-war Era', in *The Great War*, ed. Eichenberg and Newman.

[16] See John Horne, 'Démobilisation culturelle de l'après-guerre', in *Sortir de la Grande Guerre, le monde et l'après-1918*, ed. Stéphane Audoin-Rouzeau and Christophe Prochasson (Paris, 2008), and Steiner, *The Lights that Failed*, 387–452.

also veterans of the Austro-Hungarian army.[17] The glittering ceremonies in the Croatian capital were attended by, *inter alia*, the Yugoslav Minister of the Interior and the Minister of the Army and Navy, and by Colonel Fred Abbot, chairman of FIDAC's 'Propaganda Committee'. The secretary of the Zagreb branch of the Association of Reserve Officers and Warriors welcomed his comrades and spoke of how 'All eyes, and especially those of our neighbours [i.e., Italy], are fixed on us at this solemn moment.' To this, a delegate from Belgrade replied 'We are today united and will always remain so.'[18] An ostentatious display of unity with a double purpose, the organisers intended to show FIDAC and the world that Yugoslavia belonged wholly to the inter-Allied camp, and to show that South Slav veterans were all comrades together, without regard for their wartime past. The ceremonies in Zagreb exemplified the contradictory interests of the reserve officers and, more broadly, the contradictions inherent in celebrating Serbia's war victory above all else in the South Slav state. On the one hand, the reserve officers wanted to place the culture of Serbian and inter-Allied victory at the core of Yugoslavia's national culture; on the other hand, they wanted to find a way to reconcile Allied veterans with those of the Austro-Hungarian army, including, of course, Croats.

How successful was the Association of Reserve Officers and Warriors in integrating Croats who had fought in the Austro-Hungarian army into their ranks and into their narrative of war victory and sacrifice? In terms of the commemorative projects that the association initiated and sponsored, as indicated above, non-Serbs were entirely absent: their monuments featured exclusively motifs and themes from Serbia's war. The only partial exception was the monument to the Unknown Soldier at Avala, which went from honouring an 'Unknown Serbian Soldier' to honouring an 'Unknown Yugoslav Hero'. This change, which was a long time coming (the monument to the Unknown Yugoslav Hero was not unveiled until 1938), was an attempt to create a more inclusive, Yugoslav commemoration of the war to replace the solely Serbian memory which had predominated throughout much of the interwar period. But the commemorative culture of the Association of Reserve Officers and Warriors, like that of the network of micro-societies beneath it, and like the state itself, remained first and foremost a Serbian affair.

The Union of Volunteers

Perhaps more promising for Croats, then, was the Union of Volunteers an association formed by South Slavs of all nationality that had served

---

[17] *Ratnički glasnik*, May 1926.
[18] *Ibid.*, June–July 1926.

or fought in the Serbian army's volunteer divisions during the wars.[19] The volunteer legions were the wartime initiative of a small group of pro-Entente South Slav émigrés, mainly from Dalmatia. They had fled the monarchy at the beginning of the war and had formed the 'Yugoslav Committee' (*Jugoslovenski odbor*, or JO) through which they worked assiduously to promote the cause of South Slav union outside of the Austro-Hungarian monarchy. To this end, the JO had recruited a South Slav volunteer force, from the diaspora throughout the world and from prisoners of war in Entente countries (mainly pre-revolutionary Russia). Arguably, the propaganda value of these divisions outweighed their military value: the JO needed a counterweight to the many thousands of South Slavs whose presence in the ranks of the Austro-Hungarian army undermined their case for the pro-Entente sympathies of the Habsburg South Slavs.

The volunteers were first and foremost a symbol of Yugoslav unity, then, and they continued to serve as such a symbol once the war was over. In the South Slav state, the volunteers would assume a prominence that belied their wartime contribution,[20] for to celebrate the volunteer sacrifice was to celebrate a more inclusive culture of victory, one that encompassed not just Serbians but all South Slavs. It was a means of breaching the Serbian/Austro-Hungarian gulf that divided veterans in Yugoslavia. The most prominent figures in the volunteer movement in the interwar period were great examples of 'Yugoslav warriors', Serbs, Croats and Slovenes whose sacrifice showed how the legacy of the war could transcend tribal distinctions and contentious wartime histories. The volunteers also had their own association, similar in size and scope to the Association of Reserve Officers and Warriors, and based in Sarajevo.

The outstanding figure of the Union of Volunteers was a Croat, Captain Lujo Lovrić, who was also, arguably, the outstanding figure of the interwar veteran movement in Yugoslavia. And he was truly remarkable, a kind of composite figure who embodied all the fissures and fault-lines of the South Slav wartime generation. Hailing from Bakar, as a student Lovrić had been influenced by Frano Supilo (who became a leading figure in the JO) and the pro-Yugoslav newspaper *Novi list*; he started the war as a reluctant reserve officer of the Austro-Hungarian army but ended up in the uniform of a Serbian infantry captain.[21] Lovrić had deserted the empire in Galicia and thereafter volunteered for the Serbian army,

[19] For a history of the Union of Volunteers, see Novica Pešić, *Udruženje ratnih dobrovoljaca 1912–1918, njihovih potomaka i poštovalaca: nekad i danas* (Belgrade, 2005).

[20] Andrew Baruch Wachtel, *Making a Nation, Breaking a Nation: Literature and Cultural Politics in Yugoslavia* (Stanford, 1998), 99–100.

[21] For Lovrić's biography, see Boris Grbin, *Portret Luja Lovrića* (Zagreb, 1985); and Arhiv Jugoslavije (Archives of Yugoslavia, hereafter AJ) 74–234–200.

distinguishing himself fighting with the First Serbian Volunteer Division. Indeed, there were few Serbians who had sacrificed as much and fought with such distinction as this Croat, who held some of the highest honours the Serbian army bestowed upon its soldiers. A bullet to the temple from enemy fire permanently blinded Lovrić, but did not stop him becoming a prolific writer (he learnt Braille during the war, at Saint Dunstan's School for the Blind in England) and a prominent veteran activist after 1918. He attended official ceremonies both at home and abroad in full uniform, adorned in medals and wearing his signature dark glasses.

From 1928 onwards, Lovrić served as president of the Union of Volunteers, beginning a spell of great activity and prominence for the association, both at home and abroad. It was Lovrić who linked the Union of Volunteers to the international veterans' movement, joining FIDAC soon after his presidency began. The affiliation of the Union of Volunteers with FIDAC further 'proved' the pro-Allied sympathies of all South Slavs (including the Croats), since the Union of Volunteers was apparently a fully fledged 'Yugoslav' association whose membership bridged the Serbian/Austro-Hungarian divide, was composed of Serbs, Croats and Slovenes and was presided over by a Croat. He produced two volumes about his wartime experiences, *Tears of Autumn* (1922) and *Through Snow and Fog* (1923), but abandoned a third volume, putatively titled *Return in Spring*, which would have dealt with the hardships faced by veterans in Yugoslavia after 1918. Lovrić claimed (plausibly) that this highly critical account of the state's politics would not have made it past the censors.[22] Because of all this activity, Lovrić became a kind of veteran 'celebrity' in interwar Yugoslavia; he met several times with King Alexander, and even, in Berlin in 1937, with Adolf Hitler. A sincere believer in South Slav unity, Lovrić was used by the likes of Alexander and Hitler for their own ends.

Like the Association of Reserve Officers and Warriors, the volunteers had their monuments and their days of celebration and mourning. Of their monuments, most notable was the pyramid ossuary marking the 'Battle of Dobruja', the volunteer 'epic' of 1916. The Battle of Dobruja had taken place in the second half of 1916, when the First Serbian Volunteer Division fought on the flanks of the Romanian army against Bulgaria. The battle itself was not a success: Romanian and South Slav troops failed to capture their objective despite numerous and, in terms of casualties, costly assaults. The defeat had had an adverse effect on discipline and morale within the volunteer movement, as did the revolutionary changes taking place in Russia at the time. The corps' Serbian officers, responsible for maintaining the fighting efficiency of the units, resorted to force to restore order amongst the volunteers. On 23 October 1916, three units revolted

---

[22] *Ibid.*, 80.

against 'Serbian terror'; in quelling the mutiny, Serbian soldiers shot dead thirteen Croat volunteers. Josip Horvat, a Croat publicist who served in the Austro-Hungarian army and spent much of the war in Russian captivity, would later write of how the volunteer movement revealed in embryonic form many of the problems that would plague the first Yugoslavia, claiming that 'the mistakes and the fallacies began in Russia'.[23] Such omens were ignored in the interwar period: the disappointments on the battlefield and the unedifying aftermath of Dobruja were virtually erased from the record after 1918.

The Battle of Dobruja, like the volunteer movement, lent itself to mythologisation: it became the most important symbol of the volunteer sacrifice in the interwar period. From 1926 onwards, the Union of Volunteers organised an annual pilgrimage to Dobruja to commemorate the anniversary of the battle.[24] Dobruja was said to be the place 'where all three brothers, Serb, Croat, and Slovene, fought for the first time shoulder-to-shoulder for liberation and unification'.[25] In the 1930s, Alexander would frequently court the Union of Volunteers and attend their celebrations: Lujo Lovrić and the Battle of Dobruja were precisely the kind of symbols useful to the king in shoring up his Yugoslavising dictatorship.

The mythologisation of the wartime volunteer movement was, then, an alternative strategy for breaching the gulf caused by the legacy of the war in Yugoslavia; one that differed from that of the Association of Reserve Officers and Warriors. The volunteers offered a set of symbols, including Lovrić himself, that offered a more inclusive memory of the First World War, one that could integrate the Croats rather than alienate them. And yet on closer inspection the volunteer 'myth' barely papered over the fault-lines within the association itself; the facts were that non-Serbs were seriously under-represented among the volunteers, that the movement itself, both now and during the war, was wracked by controversies and conflicts. Even within the volunteer movement itself, veterans such as Lovrić were unusual, part of an articulate and literate minority (mainly reserve officers educated in Austria-Hungary's gymnasia and universities) that defined the volunteer legacy in the interwar period by promoting their own experiences at the expense of others, just as the British war poets had projected their own experiences of combat onto popular perceptions of the Great War in Britain. The South Slav volunteer movement, like the South Slav veteran movement itself, was in reality deeply divided.

[23] Josip Horvat, *Živjeti u Zagrebu 1900–1941. Zapisci iz nepovrata* (Zagreb, 1984), 85.
[24] See AJ 69–159–248.
[25] AJ 74–349–72.

Disabled veterans

If the Association of Reserve Officers and Warriors, and the Union of Volunteers, show the difficulties of creating a set of binding symbols and narratives about the war that would include the Croats, the problems faced by Croat disabled veterans show in the starkest terms the institutional prejudices that operated against Croat war veterans in the interwar state. In the associations formed by disabled veterans in the 1920s, it was welfare provision rather than commemoration of the war that was of paramount importance.

Croat veterans of the Austro-Hungarian army formed an association in Zagreb, in June 1919. Its records show that from the outset its members were painfully reminded of their wartime pasts. At one meeting, in June 1920, an attendee told of how he had been to see an official at the Ministry of Social Policy and had been asked 'were you at the front at Salonika? [t]hen go to [deposed Habsburg emperor] Karl, maybe he will give you something'.[26] Another speaker, a former officer of the Austro-Hungarian army, agreed that such accusations were common at the ministry, and were unfair since 'We fought because we had to . . . you did not want to fight, but you had to, if you did not, you would be shot.'[27] Apparently, the Habsburg stigma was enough to discount the Croat veterans' claims on the social conscience of the new state: attendees of these early meetings had the impression that only those who fought in the Serbian army were entitled to welfare. This was ironic, since many far worse offenders were able to shed their wartime pasts with ease: 'Those same gentleman, those same devils, who were the greatest black-and-yellow clamourers, that Frankist rabble who didn't even know how best to express their dog-like loyalty towards the Austrian eagle, are now the greatest Yugoslavs and Serbophiles.'[28] The Zagreb veterans, then, were victims of an institutionalised hostility against Croats who had fought or served in the Austro-Hungarian army.

The disabled veterans were deeply divided between Austro-Hungarian and Serbian wartime contingents: it was necessary for them to find a shared sense of wartime sacrifice, but the war could not bind veterans of the Serbian army to those of the Austro-Hungarian army. Disabled veterans had fought on different fronts, and even against one another. The disabled veterans, without a shared sense of victory, needed to find a common language of entitlement with which to confront the state's welfare institutions. This was not always easy, when disabled veterans themselves were divided over the legacy and meaning of the war, and

[26] Hrvatska državni arhiv (Croatian State Archives, Zagreb, hereafter HDA), Pravila društva 4684.
[27] *Ibid.*
[28] *Ratni invalid* (Zagreb), 1 July 1920.

many bureaucrats and officials harboured prejudices against disabled veterans who had fought in the Austro-Hungarian army.

In such circumstances, the disabled veteran movement made halting progress towards unification, forming a national association at the end of 1922, following an international congress on disabled veterans held in Yugoslavia that summer. The central council of this 'Association of War Invalids of the Kingdom of Serbs, Croats, and Slovenes' (*Udruženje ratnih invalida Kraljevine Srba, Hrvata, i Slovenaca*) was based in Belgrade, and it drew the majority of its membership from veterans of the Serbian army. By 1925, the unified association claimed to have a membership of about 38,000 with branches throughout the country, making the society of comparable size and scope as the Association of Reserve Officers and Warriors.[29] Tensions did not disappear entirely, however, and the unified association would continue to experience internal divisions and disagreements along the Austro-Hungarian/Serbian fault-line throughout the 1920s.[30]

For its part, the state pondered the extent of its responsibility to disabled veterans, attempting to weigh this against economic scarcity (especially in the 1930s) and the possibility that the duty of care for these men could be shifted to the private sphere of the family. There was a shortfall between the amount of welfare that could be realistically delivered and the amount that disabled veterans had been promised in the years immediately after the war. Moreover, disabled veterans were seriously disappointed by the legislative and political paralysis that marked the national affairs of Yugoslavia during the 1920s. This failure was felt keenly by disabled veterans since the inability of the state's political parties to pass new laws left them in a kind of legislative limbo, their status as recipients of welfare and social care undefined, or defined through pre-war or temporary arrangements. But whilst the state assumed responsibility for the retraining and reintegration of disabled veterans, it also assumed responsibility for providing disabled veterans with adequate facilities. On this matter, a complex of facilities at the Holy Spirit in Zagreb, and the sanatoria at Brestovac (on Mount Medvedica, outside of Zagreb) and Moslavina (also in Croatia) offer insights into the experiences of disabled veterans. The records of these institutions reveal a litany of complaints on the part of disabled veterans about living and working conditions due to inadequate funding and bad relations between staff and pupils/patients.

---

[29] John Paul Newman, 'Forging a United Kingdom of Serbs, Croats, and Slovenes', in *New Perspectives on Yugoslavia: Key Issues and Controversies*, ed. Dejan Djokić and James Ker-Lindsay (2010), 52.

[30] Although the association was better organised and more united in the following decade. This, according to the Royal Court, was due to the administrative skill of its new president, Božidar Nedić brother of Milan Nedić, the head of the Axis-affiliated Serbian quisling state during the Second World War. See AJ 74–233–366.

Problems arose within just a year of the Holy Spirit opening. In summer 1922, disabled veterans complained that despite grand talk of reintegrating them into society, the school was still woefully underfunded, and disabled veterans were finding it to hard to gain employment on leaving.[31] At the end of 1922, 140 pupils at the school downed tools in protest at the poor conditions. The pupils presented a note of protest to officials in Zagreb and called (unsuccessfully) for the dismissal of the school's director.[32] Disabled veterans made similar complaints about Brestovac, a former barracks located at Sljeme at the top of Mount Medvedica that now served as a sanatorium for soldiers suffering from tuberculosis, which had space for 120 patients and forty-two members of staff. Disabled veterans made complaints about the standard of treatment in these facilities from a very early stage. In September 1921, the Society for War Invalids in Croatia (*Udruženje ratnih invalida u Hrvatskoj*, see below) printed a list of complaints about conditions at Brestovac. Disabled veterans, they claimed, were given sub-standard food and drink whilst staff kept the better food for themselves. They complained further that horse-drawn coaches, the most comfortable way of getting to and from Sljeme, were used exclusively by the staff, whilst disabled veterans were made to travel in freight cars. One disabled veteran, they noted, died two days after being sent down the mountain to another hospital in such a car. Finally, they drew attention to the dilapidated state of the barracks due to lack of funds, and how this was of critical importance during the winter months.[33]

Disabled veterans at Brestovac made national headlines when they started a hunger strike in protest at poor conditions in the sanatorium,[34] prompting a commission from the Ministry of Social Policy that arrived from Belgrade to address their demands.[35] Complaints persisted, however, and in November 1926 patients went on strike once again, demanding warm clothes for the approaching winter.[36] Indeed, complaints from disabled veterans persisted throughout the 1920s. Similar problems arose at Moslavina, whose history in the 1920s is marked by bad relations between staff and disabled veterans. So serious were the problems here that Moslavina became the subject of two investigations by the Ministry of Social Policy (1925 and 1930) after disabled veterans lodged official complaints against staff there. The first occasion for complaint came in September 1920, when disabled veterans at Moslavina expressed

---

[31] *Ratni invalid* (Zagreb), 8 July 1922.
[32] *Ratni invalid* (Belgrade), 21 Dec. 1922.
[33] *Ratni invalid* (Zagreb), 10 Jan. 1921.
[34] *Obzor*, 17 Oct. 1924.
[35] *Ibid.*, and 20 Oct. 1924.
[36] HDA 137–468.

dissatisfaction about the treatment they received from the institute's director.[37] At the end of 1924, disabled veterans, as well as a number of blind students who were receiving training at Moslavina, submitted a further list of complaints against staff at the school to the Ministry of Social Policy. One in particular stood out: three disabled veterans who tried to raise complaints with the institute's director, they were dismissed with the response, 'I am in charge here, and if you don't like it, you can go to Franz Joseph.'[38] It was neither the first nor the last time that Austro-Hungarian veterans claimed to have been insulted in this way, that is, on the basis of their having served or fought in the Austro-Hungarian army.

Just as at Brestovac, however, complaints persisted, and Moslavina was investigated again in 1930, following further complaints about conditions and staff at the institute. Again, the commission heard of how disabled veterans complained that staff had made insulting and derogatory remarks about their war records. In this investigation, a disabled veteran complained of how the school's Serbian director had called him a 'kraut whore' (*švapska kurva*) after getting drunk, and threatened to 'turn his brains into schnitzel'.[39] The complaint was upheld and the director, who conceded both to being drunk on duty and to the possibility that he had made such a remark, lost his job. The report found that this comment was not only characteristic of his attitude to work, but that it reflected more generally the bad state of relations between staff and patients at Moslavina over the years.[40] The director was a Serbian, and almost all of the residents at Moslavina had served in the Austro-Hungarian army during the war, hence the insult 'kraut whore' (and the references to Franz Joseph before that). Such prejudices match the kind of attitudes found in the records of the Ministry for Religious Affairs and the Royal Court when dealing with requests for money from Austro-Hungarian veterans' associations. Indeed it is difficult to refute evidence of prejudice against Austro-Hungarian veterans when it is supported by an independent investigator.

One of the most successful 'invalid authors' of the interwar period was Josip Pavičić, a Croat disabled veteran who wrote about his experiences as a disabled veteran in Yugoslavia in the interwar period. Pavičić had been called up by the Austro-Hungarian army in 1915 at the age of twenty and lost a leg fighting in Galicia, in 1917. Pavičić had visited many of the mainstays of disabled veteran life in the 1920s, staying at Ciglana, Brestovac and the Holy Spirit, where he worked briefly as a support teacher. In 1928, he graduated from the law faculty in Zagreb

[37] *Ratni invalid* (Zagreb), 15 Sept. 1920.
[38] HDA 1363–16.
[39] AJ 39–7.
[40] *Ibid.*

and went on to work as a civil servant until his retirement in 1939.[41]
Yet, Pavičić never escaped from his status as a disabled veteran, and his
experiences in what he called the 'invalid catacombs' of Yugoslavia made
an indelible mark on him. Pavičić wrote about his debilitating sense of an
'invalid identity' in short stories, which he started to publish in 1931. In
these stories, the end of the war was depicted ironically, as the beginning
of a new phase of agony: 'And so began the roaming down tortuous
paths of the invalid catacombs, from hospitals to the invalid barracks at
Ciglana . . . , from the barracks to the invalid home at the Holy Spirit,
ending at last in the sanatorium for invalids with tuberculosis on Sljeme.'[42]
Pavičić did not equate this common sense of suffering with any kind of
post-war camaraderie, however: there was no 'trenchocracy' that could
bind disabled veterans together. Instead, the 'invalid' experience was one
of isolation and ultimately death, often by suicide. It was a process that
Pavičić referred to as 'silent liquidation'. The bitter irony of the invalid
question stemmed from the fact that whilst in the immediate post-war
period these men were encouraged to hope for so much, by the end of the
1920s they were 'silently liquidated', empty-handed and long-forgotten
by the very people who had sworn to help them. Pavičić was very explicit
about this when he wrote a new preface to his short stories in 1946.
Speaking of his experiences in the interwar period, he remarked:

> Those were difficult days . . . Whilst the system concealed the tragedy with endless
> solutions to the 'invalid question', the problem was resolving itself – with alcohol, with
> the tuberculosis bacillus, with a bullet, a knife, with poison . . . And ten years later, whilst
> the 'invalid question' was still filling up sheets of paper, it had in reality resolved itself
> long ago.[43]

Pavičić wrote these words immediately after a new war had produced a
new generation of veterans, disabled and otherwise, in Yugoslavia. Pavičić
had reworked his stories, adding four new tales about the Partisans and
the anti-fascist struggle and renaming the collection *In Red Letters*. It was
to be the final chapter in what had proven to be a long and difficult
publication history. The ten stories of invalid life in interwar Yugoslavia
had originally been published under the title *Memento* in 1937, only to
be withdrawn and pulped after two weeks, banned by the royal regime
of Prince Paul. In 1946, Pavičić, now with the socialists, wrote of how
'Those [invalid] masses were for the capitalist order too much of an
encumbrance, ballast which needed to be cast away so as not to hamper
the rise of their balloon. And so the ballast was cast away.'[44]

[41] Biographical details from Vladimir Popović, *Izabrana djela: Josip Pavičić, Antun Boglić, Mato Lovrak* (Zagreb, 1971), 7–16.
[42] Josip Pavičić, preface to *Crvenim slovima* (Zagreb, 1946).
[43] *Ibid.*, 5.
[44] *Ibid.*, 6.

Conclusion

The years 1914–18 are of critical importance for understanding the development of Croat national identity in the twentieth century and of the Croatian experience in Yugoslavia. Still in the process of national integration at the war's outset, Croats were, like many other Europeans, cast into the maelstrom of the world war; they fought on many of the conflict's fronts (in the east, in the Balkans, in Italy), and by war's end they had lurched from an imperial state and into a (South Slav) nation-state. National identity would hereafter have to be mediated in a country dominated by its Serbian contingent and a state (Serbia) whose experience of the world war was in most cases very different from the Croats. The prominence of Serbia's culture of war victory in the interwar state further alienated many Croats, especially those who had fought in the Austro-Hungarian army during the war, since their sacrifice and therefore also their sense of citizenship was rendered of secondary importance, even, in some cases, as being in opposition to the interests of the state itself. Attempts to bridge the divide were unsuccessful. The Association of Reserve Officers and Warriors did much to construct a monumental and commemorative culture of the war that emphasised Serbia's sacrifice and victory, but largely excluded non-Serbians; their attempts to draw Croats into their ranks were not wholly successful. The Union of Volunteers placed Croats very prominently in its leadership and offered an complementary narrative of the First World War that was more Yugoslav than Serbian, but like unitary Yugoslavism itself, it failed to take deep roots in the interwar state. And the experiences of disabled veterans show how deeply ingrained prejudices based on the war years were in the institutional culture of the interwar kingdom.

Perhaps all this goes to show how precarious a state's national culture is when it rests so heavily on a myth of the war years that excludes so many of the state's citizenship. If so, it was nevertheless a mistake repeated by the socialists after 1945, who built their country on the foundations of the Partisan struggle against the fascist invader, ostensibly a pan-Yugoslav myth, but one that concealed the messier and more complex experiences of the South Slavs during the war years, in the same way as the privileging of Serbia's war did in the interwar kingdom. Perhaps now that the Yugoslav story has reached its conclusion, Croats and Croatia will be able to explore the history of the years 1914–18 more fully.

Transactions of the RHS 24 (2014), pp. 183–203 © Royal Historical Society 2014
doi:10.1017/S0080440114000097

DISSIMILATION, ASSIMILATION AND THE UNMIXING OF PEOPLES: GERMAN AND CROATIAN SCHOLARS WORKING TOWARDS A NEW ETHNO-POLITICAL ORDER, 1919–1945*

By Alexander Korb

READ 27 MARCH 2013 AT THE UNIVERSITY OF LEICESTER

ABSTRACT. This paper deals with a transnational network of scholars and their demographic concepts of ethnic homogenisation of Europe. Focusing on the ethnographer Karl Christian von Loesch and the sociologist Max Hildebert Boehm, it sheds light on German supremacist scholarship and its international entanglements in the interwar years. Loesch and Boehm headed the Institute for Borderland and Foreign Studies in Berlin, where they developed concepts of a new European demographic order based on ethnic segregation, border shifts, assimilation and population transfers. They closely cooperated with non-German nationalists. Indeed, Loesch and Boehm had a big impact on non-Germans scholars, who studied at their institute and who would later try to apply similar concepts of ethnic homogenisation to their countries. By discussing the work of three of their students, Franz Ronneberger, Mladen Lorković and Fritz Valjavec, the paper presents a case of transnational cooperation between German and south-eastern European scholars. Using Croatia as an example, the paper demonstrates how these scholars worked towards nation-states freed of ethnic minorities. The Second World War would bring them into a position to try to implement their projects. Yet, the brutal dynamics of the war quickly altered the reality scholars had planned to design. The grand demographic schemes paved the way for ethnic cleansing, but had not much to do with the way they were carried out.

Introduction

'This war will bring about a Europe more united; though uncertain in terms of international law, it's a fact that it will be.'[1] When the later famous journalist Otto Schulmeister concluded a book on the European economy in 1942, he expressed a position that was by no means marginal. For him and many other intellectuals, the Second World War

---

* I would like to express my gratitude to Sarah Ehlers, Dr Michael Goebel, Dr Ian Innerhofer, Dr Katherine Lebow, Dr John Paul Newman, Prof. Kiran Patel, Dr Ulrich Prehn and Prof. Sven Reichardt, and my anonymous reviewer for their comments on earlier versions of this paper.

[1] O. Schulmeister, *Werdende Großraumwirtschaft. Phasen ihrer Entwicklung in Südosteuropa* (Berlin, 1942).

did not only bring about death and destruction. They associated the war with hope for something new, with constructive feelings for a new European order, or even with ideas of a European unification. Indeed, the overcoming of the post-First World War order and the destruction of the 'system of Versailles' triggered a multitude of ideas how a future European order should look like. The political borders of central and south-eastern Europe shifted as result of the Munich Agreement of 1938 and the Vienna Awards of 1939/40. Germany had become the leading power on the continent, and the Nazis pursued the reshaping of Europe with astonishing speed. For German scholars who had worked against 'Versailles' for decades, these events must have seemed like a dream come true. They had constantly called for such border shifts and justified the destruction of the post-Versailles order with historic, cultural and demographic arguments. Ethnic cleansing before and during the Second World War was grounded in an academic discourse on population transfers, and academics advocating ethnic engineering paved the way for violent expulsions. Those German researchers who focused on German minorities in eastern Europe and were skilful in Europeanising the issue of minority rights stand at the centre of this paper.

The involvement of experts in population transfers and their cooperation with the SS in the cases of ethnic cleansing and genocide in Poland and Yugoslavia are well known.[2] The passionate debate on the character and the aims of the German *Ostforschung* not only demonstrated that scholars paved the way for genocidal crimes intellectually, but it also showed that one did not need to be a Nazi to support imperial and genocidal takes on eastern Europe. Scholarly involvement was by no means limited to the years between 1933 and 1945, or to Nazi ideologues only. Apolitical, conservative and even some liberal scholars shared visions of a redesigned order in eastern Europe mastered by Greater Germany. Recent scholarship also unveiled the paths of continuities of such ideas from the German Empire to the Federal Republic.[3] The debate was so passionate because a generation of German scholars discussed the genocidal involvement of their own teachers and forefathers.[4] It largely focused on eastern Europe, where the Nazi genocidal project unfolded with unrestrained force. The issue of scholarly involvement needs to

[2] Götz Aly and Susanne Heim, *Architects of Annihilation: Auschwitz and the Logic of Destruction* (Princeton, 2002); M. Burleigh, *Germany Turns Eastwards. A Study of Ostforschung in the Third Reich* (Cambridge, 1988), 13ff.

[3] See for instance *Paths of Continuity. Central European Historiography from the 1930s to the 1950s*, ed. H. Lehmann *et al.* (Cambridge, 1994).

[4] See *Deutsche Historiker im Nationalsozialismus*, ed. Winfried Schulze *et al.* (Frankfurt am Main, 1999).

be debated regarding south-eastern Europe.[5] Research on scholarly involvement on the Nazi genocidal project in this part of Europe, however, faces two blind spots: cooperation and Europe.

The main feature is that national entities in central eastern Europe, namely Poland, were to be destroyed and to be subjected to direct German rule, whereas the south-eastern European nation-states were to be included into the New Order with a certain degree of autonomy. That does not only explain why local perpetrators had carried out the bulk of wartime-mass crimes in south-eastern Europe (and Germans to a lesser extent). But the dominant focus on German supremacist ideology and genocidal violence in eastern Europe involved an underestimation of certain aspects of collaboration. Whilst collaboration on the ground has recently received the attention it deserves, the cooperation between German and (south)-east European intellectuals is a relatively under-studied field.[6] This leads to the second blind spot: most German historians and Slavists who studied Polish, Bohemian, Baltic or Russian history and culture had a relatively hostile stance towards the region they studied, their inhabitants and, most importantly, their gentile scholars. In a nutshell, they claimed German racial superiority over the Slavic peoples of eastern Europe.[7] In contrast to that, German scholars who dealt with south-eastern Europe were far more cooperative, and their supremacist prejudices were less widespread. German and south-eastern European scholars had intensive and persistent contacts. The scholarly cooperation between Germans and their colleagues in Hungary, Romania, Yugoslavia and other countries before and during the war allowed them to have a transnational debate regarding the question what a New European Order should look like. They might not have agreed on the details, but they did agree that Europe needed to have a modern, anti-liberal order based on ethnically homogeneous nation-states. By taking such ideas seriously, this paper hopes to contribute to the debate on German *Ostforschung* and its European implications, and to measure the tension between German supremacist scholarship on the one hand, and European cooperation on the other.

Historical research has pointed out that ideas of Europe had been popular well before 1945, and that anti-liberal and right-wing movements

[5] A first pioneer study was published in 1968, see Dietrich Orlow *The Nazis in the Balkans: A Case Study of Totalitarian Politics* (Pittsburgh, 1968); an edited volume published in 2004 marks the current state of research, see *Südostforschung im Schatten des Dritten Reiches. Institutionen – Inhalte – Personen*, ed. Mathias Beer *et al.* (Munich, 2004); *Deutsche Historiker im Nationalsozialismus*, ed. Winfried Schulze *et al.* (Frankfurt am Main, 1999).

[6] C. Unger, *Ostforschung in Westdeutschland. Die Erforschung des europäischen Ostens und die Deutsche Forschungsgemeinschaft, 1945–1975* (Stuttgart, 2007); *Paths of Continuity. Central European Historiography from the 1930s to the 1950s*, ed. H. Lehmann *et al.* (Cambridge, 1994).

[7] Unger, *Ostforschung in Westdeutschland*, 60.

could well have a European horizon, whether it was the cooperation between fascist movements, or between Germans and their local partners in western and eastern Europe during the Second World War, or right-wing intellectual exchange.[8] Transnational right-wing and fascist concepts of race, space and culture are part of the shared intellectual history of Europe and it is time to attend to such ideas. Believing that only German domination would make the continent heal and prosper, German intellectuals were ardent supporters of both the right-wing and Nazi movements. However, being German supremacists did not prevent them from having a European horizon. In his seminal book on Nazi rule in Europe, Mark Mazower analysed how the Nazis tried to build a European empire founded on the idea of the dominance of the German race. As the Nazi leaders thought in large-scale categories of race instead of nation, Mazower concludes, they were neither interested in meeting the demands of other nations nor in seeking cooperation between European nation-states. In such a perspective, they could only exploit the pro-European sentiments of the peoples Germany dominated. 'One of the reasons why Germans failed to think deeply about Europe was because for much of the war they did not need to: Europeans fell into line and contributed what they demanded anyway.'[9] Mazower's statement might be true for the higher echelons of the Nazi party, but it fails to acknowledge that many scholars and intellectuals in Nazi Germany did, in fact, think deeply about Europe.

This paper thus highlights such European agendas and argues that many Völkisch scholars believed in the necessity of genuine cooperation among the nations of Europe. To this end, I will focus on scholarly cooperation between German and Croat scholars and their focus on the ethnic and demographic history of south-eastern and eastern Europe. The paper centres on a group of Völkisch scholars who serve as a good example of cooperation across national boundaries. The ethnographer Karl Christian von Loesch (1880–1951) and the sociologist Max Hildebert Boehm (1891–1968), who were key figures of the Völkisch movement in Germany, devoted their careers to fighting the Paris peace system by incorporating non-German scholars and activists into a transnational alliance. Thus, they stood for scholarly cooperation on a European level with the goal of designing a new territorial and ethnic order in the eastern

---

[8] See for example M. Mazower, *Dark Continent: Europe's Twentieth Century* (New York, 2008); for conceptional overviews, see or R. Gerwarth and S. Malinowski, 'Europeanization through Violence? Experiences of War and Destruction in the Making of Modern Europe', in *Europeanization in the Twentieth Century. Historical Approaches*, ed. M. Conway and K. Patel (Oxford, 2010), or D. Gosewinkel, 'Antiliberales Europa – eine andere Integrationsgeschichte', *Studies in Contemporary History*, 9, 3 (2012), 189–210.

[9] M. Mazower, *Hitler's Empire. Nazi Rule in Occupied Europe Hitler's Empire: Nazi Rule in Occupied Europe* (London, 2008), 6.

and south-eastern parts of Europe. Over the decades, they spun a large network of colleagues and former students who – during the Second World War – would try to put their ideas of a new ethnic order into practice. That applies in particular to three of their disciples: the German social scientist Franz Ronneberger (1913–99), who during the war formed a Nazi think-tank that became a hub for information regarding the Balkan states; the German-Hungarian historian Fritz Valjavec (1909–60), who was perhaps the most dynamic figure within German *Südostforschung* in the twentieth century; and the Croat lawyer Mladen Lorković (1909–45), who was a key figure of the separatist Croatian Ustaša movement and who became Croatian foreign minister in 1941 once Croatia was awarded independence by Hitler and Mussolini. These three men were young intellectuals who hoped to change the world they lived in and perceived demographic changes as the key to an altered future. Ronneberger stated how he, already as a student, was tempted by the idea 'to plough the unworked field of south-eastern Europe'.[10] They were students when the Nazis came to power, and their professional careers started well after 1933. But during the war, their careers skyrocketed. They would come into a position to put the ideology their teachers planted into genocidal practice, at least in part.

In the first part of this paper, I will discuss how unfulfilled Wilsonian promises led to a certain degree of frustration amongst ethnocentric nationalists throughout Europe after the Paris Peace Treaties. I then introduce Loesch and Boehm and their proposals for a new European demographic order based on the principles of border shifts, assimilation and dissimilation or population transfer and the impact these ideas had on younger scholars such as Ronneberger, Valjavec and Lorković. I conclude with a discussion of the attempted violent implementation of demographic plans during the Second World War in the Independent State of Croatia and elsewhere, the role scholars had in campaigns of ethnic cleansing, and the ultimate failure of schemes of grand planning.

The impact of the Paris Treaties on the Völkisch movements

The Wilsonian policy of fostering nation-states in Europe based on ethnicity paved the way for the breakthrough of the ethnic paradigm. President Wilson had promised in 1917 that 'national aspirations *must* be respected; people may now be dominated and governed only by their own consent. Self-determination is not a mere phrase; it is an imperative principle of action'.[11] The problem was that the hopes for sovereignty

---

[10] F. Ronneberger, 'Zwischenbilanz der Südosteuropa-Forschung', *Südosteuropa-Mitteilungen*, 20, 1 (1980), 3–17.

[11] *Woodrow Wilson: His Life and Work*, ed. W. D. Eaton *et al.* (Whitefish, 2005), 415.

and statehood Wilson had nourished could never be satisfied. In the eyes of many central, eastern and south-eastern European nationalists, this promise had not been applied to their nations; those who belonged to the losers of the Great War especially felt betrayed by the signatory powers. Frustrated, political activists now aimed at putting the Wilsonian paradigm into reality in the way they had understood it: only if Europe consisted of sovereign ethnically homogenised nation-states, they argued, could a just territorial and political order in Europe be reached.[12] The historian Eric Weitz has pointed at the links between the interwar debates surrounding minority rights protection, on the one hand, and campaigns for ethnic homogeneity, on the other.[13] Indeed, German diplomats learned to turn the tool of internationally monitored minority rights against their initiators, and skilfully used the League of Nations framework not only for the protection of German minorities in the neighbouring states, but as a weapon in its fight against the Paris peace order as such. And Germany served as a role model for eastern European governments on this front: looking at Romania and Hungary, the historian Holly Case demonstrates that local leaders 'had come to associate minority rights not only with . . . international agreements . . . and the League of Nations, but also – perhaps primarily – with Germany's resistance to the League'.[14] And they felt encouraged that the international community would accept 'demographic solutions' as they demanded it for their countries. Had not the League of Nations acknowledged the paradigm of ethnic homogeneity by agreeing on population exchanges, or by sanctioning them *ex post facto* at the treaty of Lausanne?[15] In this respect, the protagonists of this article managed to be both fervent activists in the field of minority rights in the 1920s and 1930s and promoters of ethnic homogeneity at the

[12] See H. Case, *Between States: The Transylvanian Question and the European Idea during World War II* (Palo Alto, 2009), 39; for contemporary perceptions of the Paris Treaties see F. Ronneberger, 'Parlamentarismus – ein Mittel der Großmachtpolitik', in *Volk und Führung in Südosteuropa. Aufsätze aus dem Grenzboten, Jg. 72*, ed. F. Ronneberger (Preßburg, 1942).

[13] E. D. Weitz, 'From the Vienna to the Paris System: International Politics and the Entangled Histories of Human Rights, Forced Deportations, and Civilizing Missions', *American Historical Review*, 113, 5 (2008), 1313–43; for a case-study that demonstrates this context, see Case, *Between States*.

[14] Case, *Between States*, 39 and 59; for joined lobbyism of Germany and east European partners see p. 243. It would be wrong, however, to claim that all south-eastern European scholars promoted concepts of ethnic disentanglement. For example, Hungarian representatives of a Völkisch historiography (*Volksgeschichte*) advocated a multi-ethnic Hungarian empire with Magyars being the dominant, but not the only group; see Á. v. Klimó: 'Volksgeschichte in Ungarn (1939–1945). Chancen, Schwierigkeiten und Folgen eines "deutschen" Projektes', in *Historische West- und Ostforschung in Zentraleuropa zwischen dem Ersten und dem Zweiten Weltkrieg: Verflechtung und Vergleich*, ed. M. Middell, U. Sommer (Leipzig, 2004), 151–78.

[15] For an overview, see P. Ther, *Die dunkle Seite der Nationalstaaten. 'Ethnische Säuberungen' im modernen Europa* (Göttingen, 2011).

same time. This is the context in which scholars from Germany, eastern Europe and south-eastern Europe cooperated, and tried to provide their governments with demographic ammunition against the Paris peace order. Most plans for restructuring the demography of Europe were thus inextricably intertwined with the idea of German dominance over eastern and south-eastern Europe.[16]

Two Völkisch eminences: Boehm and Loesch

The ethnographer Karl Christian von Loesch and the sociologist Max Hildebert Boehm were luminaries in the field of ethnicity and minority studies, anti-Versailles activists and counsellors to German governments before and after 1933. They stood for a stream of nationalist activism that was in opposition to Nazi racial scholarship, in particular to its neo-pagan and blood-mystifying tendencies; but their scholarly opposition quickly faded away after 1933, and they tried to find accommodation with the Nazi party. Boehm's and Loesch's interest in eastern and south-eastern Europe stemmed from their biographical backgrounds: Loesch was born in Silesia, Boehm in Livonia. During the Great War, both held positions within the German occupation regime in eastern Europe and had the opportunity to travel in and study eastern Europe.[17] After the war, they were leading figures in what they called *Volkstumskampf*: an integral strategy that consisted of political, academic and educational elements with the aim of justifying the historically German character of lost territories, preserving the alleged or real Germanness of the population in the eastern borderlands, and fostering German culture and 'Germanic' historical awareness in East and south-eastern territories. Both Loesch and Boehm developed a focus on German minorities in eastern Europe and were skilful in Europeanising the issue of minority rights, thus feeding the question of German minorities into a larger context. Boehm headed an inter-party committee for minority rights. Loesch, as a leading figure of the 'German League for the Protection of Germans in the Borderlands and Abroad', an umbrella organisation addressing itself to concerns of the German borderlands, at times advocated a pan-European solution for all ethnographic and minority questions and sympathised with a union of

---

[16] For Western geopolitical concepts, see C. B. Hagan, 'Geopolitics', *Journal of Politics*, 4 (1942), 478–90; for Germany see Burleigh, *Germans Turn Eastwards*; J. Elvert, *Mitteleuropa! Deutsche Pläne zur europäischen Neuordnung (1918–1945)* (Stuttgart, 1999); *German Scholars and Ethnic Cleansing, 1919–1945*, ed. I. Haar et al. (New York, 2005); S. Salzborn, *Ethnisierung der Politik. Theorie und Geschichte des Volksgruppenrechts in Europa* (Frankfurt am Main, 2005).

[17] For Boehm, see U. Prehn, *Max Hildebert Boehm (1891–1968). Radikales Ordnungsdenken vom Ersten Weltkrieg bis in die Bundesrepublik* (Göttingen, 2013); for Loesch, see H.-W. Retterath, 'Karl Christian von Loesch', in *Handbuch der völkischen Wissenschaften. Personen*, ed. I. Haar et al. (Munich, 2008), 386–9; see also German Federal Archives, BA/BDC, REM, Personal File K.C. v. Loesch, 9 Nov. 1939, p. 4.

the European peoples. That was, however, to be achieved under German leadership. It is therefore not surprising that Loesch fervently fought against cooperative visions of Europe like Coudenhove-Kalergi's 'pan-Europe'. Instead, he highlighted ideas of Europe with Germany being the dominating power. Therefore, it is no coincidence that he intensified his European propaganda after 1938.[18]

In 1926, Boehm and Loesch founded the Institute for Borderland and Foreign Studies (IGA) in Berlin-Steglitz, with Boehm as director and Loesch as his deputy.[19] Another important body was the Institute for Southeastern Studies (SOI), founded in 1930 in Munich. After 1936, similar institutes mushroomed in Leipzig, Vienna and Graz, which all, to a certain extent, advocated applied sciences and provided the Nazi authorities with their demographic expertise. The Nazi takeover in 1933 did not mark any relevant caesura regarding German Balkan studies or German policies towards south-eastern Europe.[20]

Boehm and Loesch continued their scholarly careers. Boehm was appointed professor of ethno-national sociology (*Volkstumssoziologie*) at the University of Jena in 1933. Loesch was running the institute and was appointed professor for 'Germandom abroad' at the Faculty of Foreign Studies at the Friedrich-Wilhelms University Berlin in 1940. Their successes after 1933 notwithstanding, their relationship to Nazism was ambiguous. For one thing, their offer to become Nazi party members was rejected rather coolly by Reichsleiter Rudolf Heß, given their request that their membership not be made public, lest it disrupt their international academic activities.[21] In addition, Boehm was under constant attacks from the League of National-Socialist Lecturers, because his definition of *Volk* was not entirely based on biological grounds.[22]

Nonetheless, Boehm and Loesch inspired a generation of scholars with their focus on social and demographic issues and their combination of national and European approaches, and they dominated the discourse in the 1930s and the early 1940s. They also trained a number of students from south-eastern Europe and had a considerable impact on their political and demographic theories. Loesch later looked back full of praise at the early

[18] M. H. Boehm, *Europa Irredenta. Eine Einführung in das Nationalitätenproblem der Gegenwart* (Berlin, 1923); for Loesch's activities, see Deutscher Schutzbund, *Bücher des Deutschtums*, ed. K. C. von Loesch and E. H. Ziegfeld (Breslau, 1925); Loesch also edited a volume on the ideas of a European league of peoples (*Völkerunion*), see *Staat und Volkstum* (Berlin, 1926).

[19] For the IGA, see C. Klingemann, 'Angewandte Soziologie im Nationalsozialismus', in *1999. Zeitschrift für Sozialgeschichte des 20. und 21. Jahrhunderts*, 4, 1 (1989), 10–34, at 15.

[20] For continuities before and after 1933, see H.-J. Schröder, 'Deutsche Südosteuropapolitik 1929–1936. Zur Kontinuität deutscher Außenpolitik in der Weltwirtschaftskrise', in *Geschichte und Gesellschaft*, 2 (1976), 5–32.

[21] C. Freytag, *Deutschlands 'Drang nach Südosten': Der Mitteleuropäische Wirtschaftstag und der 'Ergänzungsraum Südosteuropa' 1931–1945* (Göttingen, 2013), 170.

[22] See Prehn, *Boehm*, 317ff.

years of his *Volkstumsarbeit*, and highlighted the interdisciplinary character of the work of geographers, historians, linguists, economists, racial scientists, human biologists, ethno-psychologists, social psychologists and pedagogues researching German and non-German minorities in the ethnic shatter-zones of eastern Europe.[23]

With their foci on eastern-central Europe (Boehm) and south-eastern Europe (Loesch) both scholars entered a fascinating field of study that offered the opportunity to build up international networks of nationalistic scholars, who fought for independence and ethnic purity against great powers or powerful neighbours. In their view, both regions were underdeveloped and paralysed by their multi-ethnic demographic design. This view sat well with the goal of many (South)-Eastern European nationalists finally to 'arrive' in Europe by transforming their homelands into proper nation-states and by rebuilding the demographic and social structure of their states.[24] German scholars interested in ethnic homogenisation agreed that population policies needed to be pursued and systematically coordinated by Germany as an intermediary power. But non-German nationalists also welcomed the war, as they saw it as an opportunity not only to revise the Paris order, but to achieve their own national demographic goals. There was a match of interests, because such a new order would finally bring peace, security and a reconstruction of economic and cultural life, and thus, as Loesch put it, safeguard the supremacy of European civilisation.[25]

Concepts of dissimilation and assimilation

According to Loesch, south-eastern Europe consisted of seven state-building peoples: Hungarians, Romanians, Bulgarians, Serbs, Croats, Greeks and Albanians, each with a size of between one and a half and fourteen million people. The Turks were seen as a non-European people (and the emigration of Turks as a non-European people from the Balkans as desirable). Loesch sought to reestablish the primordial order and pre-modern ethnic cores of these nations.[26] He called for the demographic separation of the south-eastern European nations from

---

[23] K. C. von Loesch, 'Volkstumskunde und Volksgruppenfragen', in *Jahrbuch für Politik und Auslandskunde*, ed. Franz Alfred Six (Berlin, 1941), 93.

[24] For ideas of national purity (and their transfers), see *Definitonsmacht, Utopie, Vergeltung. 'Ethnische Säuberungen' im östlichen Europa des 20. Jahrhunderts*, ed. U. Brunnbauer et al. (Berlin, 2006). The notion that south-eastern Europe is 'underdeveloped' is of course not reserved to Germany; see J. Evans, *Great Britain and the Creation of Yugoslavia: Negotiating Balkan Nationality and Identity* (2008).

[25] K. C. von Loesch, 'Die Umsiedlungsbewegung in Europa', in *Jahrbuch für Politik und Auslandskunde*, ed. Franz Alfred Six (Berlin, 1942), 47–8.

[26] That, of course, is not different from the classical theories of nation building; see E. Gellner, *Nationalism* (1997).

each other and the reerection of what he saw as the natural boundaries between them by 'harmonising' political and ethnic borders. According to Loesch, 15 per cent of the population of south-eastern Europe belonged to ethnic minorities: this included Jews, Gypsies and ethnic pockets within the mainland. What he was more concerned with, however, were the ethnically mixed borderlands, which he perceived as a source of instability between the remaining ethnic cores. Everything that blurred these boundaries and weakened the ethnic cores – be it individual migration; pan-Slavism; shifts in religion, identity or language; or assimilation – was seen as a danger to the natural order.[27] But Loesch's horizon as an ethnic engineer was much broader: the remedy he prescribed to Europe was to turn back time and undo early modern and modern migration as a whole. Loesch, the international lawyers Werner Hasselblatt (1890–1958) and Viktor Bruns (1884–1943), as well as Boehm, thought that the time had come for a new legal status for minorities in Europe (*Volksgruppenrecht*), and they initiated a think-tank called *Arbeitsgemeinschaft für Völkerpolitik* with the aim of developing a continental master plan for a new system of inter-ethnic and inter-state relations in Europe.[28] The goal was to initiate a continental dialogue between Germany and smaller nations regarding the ethnic, demographic and geographic future of Europe and its nationalities. Censuses based on ethnicity and large-scale assessments of the ethnic *character* of the population of the multi-ethnic borderlands (*volkstumsbiologische Prüfungen*) were to be organised by a trust.[29] An arbitration board would collect the concerns and ideas of smaller nations and feed them into the general framework. At the end of the process, a new phase of orderly migration and settlement would bring about a New European system based on the principle of ethnicity.[30]

How was this new system to be achieved? According to Loesch, only a combined application of two methods could lead to success: assimilation and dissimilation. Both terms he borrowed from the biosciences.[31] Those ethnic minorities that would stay within a nation-state's borders, because migration was not an option, should be assimilated or absorbed by the majority ethnic group. As Loesch put it, they needed to undergo a

[27] K. C. von Loesch, W. E. Mühlmann, and G. A. Küppers-Sonnenberg, *Die Völker und Rassen Südosteuropas* (Berlin, 1943), 8–9.

[28] W. Hasselblatt, *Begründung einer 'Arbeitsgemeinschaft für Völkerpolitik'*, Berlin, Nov. 1941, Hoover Institution Archives, Collection Loesch/8. For the Academy for German Law (Akademie für Deutsches Recht), see Schlomoh Gysin, '(Zu) viele offene Fragen nach Interpellationsbeantwortung', in *Israelitisches Wochenblatt*, No 23, Zurich, 11 June 1999.

[29] K. C. von Loesch, 'Die Lebensgemeinschaft der europäischen Völker', in *Jahrbuch für Politik und Auslandskunde*, ed. Franz Alfred Six (Berlin, 1944), 90–1.

[30] Six, 'Gedanken zu Reich und Europa', in *Jahrbuch*, ed. Six (1941), 27.

[31] See A. Pinwinkler, '"Assimilation" und "Dissimilation" in der "Bevölkerungs-geschichte", ca. 1918 bis 1960', in *Bevölkerungsforschung und Politik in Deutschland im 20. Jahrhundert*, ed. R. Mackensen (Wiesbaden, 2006), 3–48.

'liquidation of their ethnic character' including language, religion and culture.

'Dissimilation' was the second wing of Loesch's demographic master plan. Those ethnic minorities in between the ethnic cores that populated contested borderlands were to be dissimilated, in other words physically segregated by means of forced migration. Loesch and like-minded colleagues took great interest in population exchanges between Greece, Turkey, Romania and Bulgaria in the decades between 1910 and 1930, which Loesch saw as 'adjustment of ethnic territories (*völkische Siedelböden*) and state borders'.[32] Many scholars were thrilled to be able to contribute to that process, and eager to avoid the mistakes that had been made during earlier population transfers, for example between Greece and Turkey after the Treaty of Lausanne of 1923. Loesch fervently criticised the population transfers that followed the treaty, because religion and not ethnicity was made the decisive criterion for resettlement, calling it an example of harmful dissimilation.[33] Analogously, he saw the migration of Muslims from Yugoslavia to Turkey as a 'loss of Caucasian blood', as they were not Turks but Croats who had been converted to Islam under the Ottomans.[34] In contrast, Loesch illustrated cases of necessary and useful dissimilation using the example of the Jews. Holding Jews to be an obstacle on the path to a new European order, he suggested an 'all-European dissimilation of Jews' (*alleuropäische Judendissimilation*). Loesch imagined the resettlement of the Jews on a continental scale, even though he did not say where the European Jews should be concentrated. In his earlier writings, Loesch sympathised with a Palestinian solution of what he perceived to be the Jewish question. After 1939 however, he made increasing use of terminology inspired by Nazi racial anti-Semitism: since intercontinental resettlements were no longer an option, Loesch suggested regional 'spatial solutions of the Jewish question', which indicated concentration and segregation of Jews in Europe or elsewhere.[35]

A key flaw of Loesch's ethnographic theories, however, remained unresolved. Although he asserted that neither religion nor language, in the case of Jews and Muslims, should be taken as a proxy for ethnicity, he was unable to offer a clear method by which ethnicity (*Volkstum*) was to be proven. Loesch acknowledged that his project of 'dissimilation' of the Jews was extraordinarily difficult, especially due to the high degree of intermarriages and Jewish assimilation in the Balkans. Loesch, in his

---

[32] Loesch, 'Umsiedlungsbewegung', 47–8.

[33] K. C. von Loesch and Hans Harmsen, *Die deutsche Bevölkerungsfrage im europäischen Raum. Beiheft der Zeitschrift für Geopolitik*, V (Berlin, 1929).

[34] Loesch relied on the findings of one of his disciples, see Mladen Lorković, *Narod i zemlja Hrvata* (Zagreb, 1939), 219.

[35] Loesch, Mülmann and Küppers-Sonnenberg, *Völker*.

post-1945 writings, never reflected on the possibility that his suggestions could be seen as a blueprint for the Holocaust as a giant murderous 'dissimilation'. In this regard, he is typical of his generation of Völkisch scholars.

Croats in Berlin

As an example of the impact of German Völkisch scholarship on non-German scholars, I will highlight the career of Croatian intellectual Mladen Lorković, who was the youngest member of the leadership of the Ustaša movement, a terrorist organisation supported by Italy with the aim to dissociate Croatia from Yugoslavia by force. Once that goal was achieved in 1941, Lorković became Minister of Foreign Affairs of the Independent State of Croatia.[36]

Non-German nationalists started populating German universities once more from the mid-1920s. In 1925, for instance, the Humboldt Foundation was reestablished and offered scholarships for foreign students. Here, the funding bodies made a distinction between eastern and south-eastern Europe. They tried to make sure that students from eastern Europe had an ethnic German background in order to strengthen their German identity and to segregate them from elites critical of Germany. In contrast, students from south-eastern Europe were seen as future partners and possible multipliers of the Völkisch ideology. This went hand in hand with the efforts of the German industry to intensify its presence in south-eastern Europe. German managers organised the Council of the Central European Economy and started promoting a united European economy. German industry became increasingly interested in peacefully penetrating south-eastern Europe. One element in the strategy was to bring young elites from the Balkan states to Germany to train them. The rationale was that they would form Germany-friendly opinion leaders upon returning to their homelands. The number of stipends for Yugoslav students skyrocketed as a consequence of Hermann Göring's visit to Yugoslavia in 1934. Ironically, and in contrast to Göring's Yugoslavia-friendly stance, the beneficiaries of these stipends were to a large extent Croatian separatists. In the 1930s, 40 per cent of all foreign students at German universities came from south-eastern European states, and their share was still growing.[37] Semi-official bodies such as the German

[36] For Lorković, see N. Kisić-Kolanović, *Mladen Lorković. Ministar urotnik* (Zagreb, 1998), and T. Debelić, 'Mladen Lorković, 1909–1945. Biographische Studien zur kroatischen Zeitgeschichte' (unpublished manuscript, Freiburg i.B., 2001). I thank Thomas Debelić for having generously shared his research results with me.

[37] H. Impekoven, *Die Alexander von Humboldt-Stiftung und das Ausländerstudium in Deutschland 1925–1945. Von der 'geräuschlosen Propaganda' zur Ausbildung der 'geistigen Wehr' des 'Neuen Europa'* (Göttingen, 2012), 314.

Academy for Politics announced that foreigners were welcome to study in Germany and to get a feeling of the new spirit of the German *Volksgemeinschaft*.[38]

Many Humboldt-fellows saw Berlin as a particularly fitting locale for their studies and their activism directed against the Paris peace order. The presence of a number of lobbyists, pressure groups, and scientific and political organisations and the new air of Nazism provided an attractive mix.[39] Important discussions regarding the demographic reshaping of Germany, the Balkans and Europe also took place at the IGA, where Boehm and Loesch mentored young German and (south)-east European scholars and activists; Loesch's and Boehm's institute received students from Croatia, Slovakia and the Ukraine after its founding in the late 1920s, and partly sponsored their fees. In the 1930s, a good part of the later leadership of the Croatian state (founded in 1941), studied or resided in Germany. South-eastern European intellectuals received an excellent education at German universities, broadening their intellectual horizons and sharpening their analytical toolkits.

In September 1930, Lorković arrived in Berlin as a nineteen-year-old student. As a teenage political activist, he had been forced to leave Yugoslavia and pursue his academic studies in Innsbruck, where he became acquainted with Fritz Valjavec. He moved on to Berlin, where he conducted research at Boehm's Institute for Borderland Studies. With a study on the violation of minority rights by the Yugoslav government in Macedonia, he skilfully positioned himself as an expert on all demographic questions regarding minority rights in south-eastern Europe.[40] Shortly after, he was awarded a doctorate at Berlin's Friedrich-Wilhelms University with a study arguing that the existence of the Yugoslav state was actually a violation of international law, because the Croats had not given their consent to the creation of the state.[41]

Croatian nationalist intellectuals portrayed the demographic situation of their homeland as a doomsday scenario. Yet, the problem could be fixed, as Croatia still had a 'healthy, safe and sound ethnic value'.[42]

---

[38] Paul Meier-Benneckenstein, interview, *Deutsche Kurzwellensender*, 15 Apr. 1937, Geheimes Staatsarchiv Preußischer Kulturbesitz, I.HA Rep. 303 neu Nr. 81.

[39] This becomes evident in memoirs and letters of former Ustaša activists, see J. Jareb, *Političke uspomene i rad dra. Branimira Jelića* (Cleveland, 1982), 65; for a letter from Lorković to his mother, Innsbruck, 1 Sept. 1930, see Croatian State Archives, SBUO, 3021/1931, Box 203.

[40] M. Lorković, *Das Recht der Makedonier auf Minderheitenschutz. Dokumente: Die Verhandlungen d. 'Komitees f. neue Staaten' u. des Obersten Rates über d. makedonische Frage Mai–Nov. 1919* (Berlin, 1934); the book was reviewed by Boehm's assistant H. Raschhofer, in *Zeitschrift für ausländisches öffentliches Recht und Völkerrecht*, 5 (1935), 496.

[41] E. Bauer, *Život je kratak san. Uspomene 1910–1985* (Barcelona, 1986), 60.

[42] K. C. von Loesch, *Croatia Restituta* (Berlin, 1941), 9–16.

Large-scale resettlement of minorities would bring peace and social stability to the Balkans. Out of six million inhabitants of the Croatian state, two million were seen as non-Croats. Some hundred thousand were to be resettled to Serbia, or – in the case of Jews – to other countries, whilst the remaining majority of Serbs was to be merged with the Croatian population, as they were said to be actual Croats by blood.[43] These measures were presented as a historic task: reestablishing the supposedly natural ethnic order in a part of the world troubled by ethnic diversity, Loesch argued, would add value to Europe as a whole.

Ethnic cleansing during the Second World War

Hitler's decision to split up the Yugoslav state along ethnic lines was a break with Nazi foreign policy prior to 1941, but it went along with Nazi ideology and set in motion what Völkisch scholars had advocated for a long time. Thus, they could offer their expertise for one of the most extensive projects of wartime ethnic cleansing. Hitler set the scene at his first meeting with Ustaša leader Ante Pavelić – who had been appointed head of the Croatian state in April – at the Obersalzberg in June 1941: only clear spatial segregation between ethnic groups would enable peaceful and stable relations between ethnicities. Deportations and resettlements would be temporarily painful for those affected, but in the long run, their effect would be healing and beneficial.[44] Hitler preached to the converted, as Pavelić was already obsessed with the idea of an ethnically homogenised Croatian state. Pavelić must have understood Hitler's sermon as a licence to set in motion what would become one of the largest resettlement programmes during the Second World War.

It is remarkable, however, that – with the exception of the Vienna Awards, where their institute served in an advisory capacity – Boehm and Loesch were relatively uninvolved when it came to border shifts and large-scale resettlements, and their aspirations to practise applied sciences remained unfulfilled. Boehm continued to teach throughout the war, maintained contact with most of his non-German colleagues and gave a series of talks in south-eastern European states; Loesch also maintained his theoretical work, and was appointed professor for 'Germandom abroad' at the Faculty for Foreign Studies at the University of Berlin in 1940. In 1941, his former students, who had all high posts within the new Croatian government, invited him to visit the Independent

---

[43] See A. Korb, *Im Schatten des Weltkriegs. Massengewalt der Ustaša gegen Serben, Juden und Roma, 1941–1945* (Hamburg, 2013), 195ff, and M. Biondich, 'Religion and Nation in Wartime Croatia: Reflections on the Ustaša Policy of Forced Religious Conversions, 1941–1942', *Slavonic and East European Review*, 83, 1 (2005), 71–116.

[44] Minutes of the meeting, 9 June 1941, in *Akten zur deutschen auswärtigen Politik XII 2, 6. April bis 22. Juni 1941* (Göttingen, 1969), 813ff.

State of Croatia, and he toured the country together with his family.[45] Even though both scholars still had a number of opportunities to get involved in hands-on projects, their impact on the war-time population transfers was minimal. It was rather the younger generation of scholars who had aligned themselves smoothly to the new realities after 1933, seeing Nazism in power as an opportunity for the launching of their careers, which advanced remarkably thereafter, enabling them to attain positions in which they could apply their science in practice during the war. Lorković, Valjavec and Ronneberger can serve as examples of a generation of young scholars who offered their expertise to the SS or branches of the Nazi government, thus getting involved in Nazi mass crimes during the war. They found it easier to bring their Völkisch ideals and Nazi ideology in line as their teachers, who had started their careers in the 1920s or even before the First World War. Ronneberger was a frequent visitor to several south-eastern European countries during the war and worked as an intermediary between various German and south-eastern European politicians. He became a member of the SS in 1939 and advisor for the Security Service of the Nazi Party (SD) in south-eastern European matters. In Vienna, he founded a public-relations office that edited weekly digests and provided the Foreign Office as well as the SD with both intelligence and public information on south-eastern Europe. Through his expertise, he was a valuable asset for a number of governmental institutions.[46] Valjavec, already a shooting star in the field of *Südostforschung* and managing director of the SOI, offered his expertise to the SS as well. In the wake of the attack on the Soviet Union, he gave up his Hungarian in favour of German citizenship; he was awarded German citizenship and was part of the 'Task Force 10b' of the *Einsatzgruppe*, which was dispatched to the northern Bukovina.[47]

Valjavec found himself in a region whose multi-ethnicity had always been one of his key research interests. And he was there at a time when Romania tried to engineer the region ethnically by oppressing Ukrainians and by deporting Gypsies, and killing Jews in collaboration with the *Einsatzgruppe*. Valjavec was having meetings with Ukrainian officials and tried to play off their separatism against the Romanian authorities. Ultimately, the Romanian governor asked for Valjavec's removal from the

[45] Heinrich von Loesch, interview, Reichertshausen, 13 Dec. 2013, in possession of author.

[46] See P. Heinelt, 'Portrait eines Schreibtischtäters. Franz Ronneberger (1913–1999)', in *Die Spirale des Schweigens. Zum Umgang mit der nationalsozialistischen Zeitungswissenschaft*, ed. W. Duchkowitsch *et al.* (Münster, 2004), 197–8.

[47] G. Grimm, 'Georg Stadtmüller und Fritz Valjavec. Zwischen Anpassung und Selbstbehauptung', in *Südostforschung*, ed. Beer, 237–55; I. Haar, 'Friedrich Valjavec: Ein Historikerleben zwischen den Wiener Schiedssprüchen und der Dokumentation der Vertreibung', in *Theologie und Vergangenheitsbewältigung. Eine kritische Bestandsaufnahme im interdisziplinären Vergleich*, ed. L. Scherzberg (Paderborn, 2005), 103–19.

region.[48] In 1943, he was appointed professor at the Faculty of Foreign Studies, thus becoming Loesch's colleague.

As for Croatia, a wave of articles and monographs introduced the new state to a broader German public, in which the authors called for ethnic engineering in the former Yugoslav state and for the physical segregation of Serbs and Croats.[49] The upcoming ethnic engineering was also prepared by an extensive output of ethnic maps produced in the first half of 1941 by research institutes such as the Southeast German Research Council (SOFG, or *Südostdeutsche Forschungsgemeinschaft*).[50] They comprised detailed information on the ethno-religious composition of eastern and south-eastern Europe down to the village level, building on Mladen Lorković's research. Indeed, his book was quickly translated in 1941 by the SOFG 'for official use only'.[51] At the same time, German ethnographers, cartographers and geographers entered a bizarre contest regarding the question of who had been the first to map the ethnic boundary between Serbs and Croats (most of the pre-1940 maps did not distinguish between the nationalities). One of the protagonists was Johann Wüscht (1897–1976), an ethnic German geographer from Yugoslavia, who was praised for the quality of his maps, on which he distinguished between ethnic groups, and on which he also visualised post-1919 migration such as the arrival of 'colonist settlers' (war veterans who were awarded with formerly imperial lands). Ronneberger and Valjavec were highly interested in safeguarding his services for their purposes. Such maps were sharp tools in the hands of experts especially after the German occupation of the countries concerned. Ronneberger and Valjavec were keen to offer such services to the authorities. Hence, they tried to keep Wüscht away from other German *Südostforscher*, which they saw as competitors.[52]

Of all the scholars discussed here, Mladen Lorković had the most significant impact. In 1941, he was appointed Croatia's Minister of Foreign Affairs, and in 1943, Minister of Interior Affairs, thus bearing

---

[48] A. Angrick, *Besatzungspolitik und Massenmord. Die Einsatzgruppe D in der südlichen Sowjetunion 1941–1943* (Hamburg, 2003), 158.

[49] See for instance H. Raschhofer, 'Der kroatische Staat', *Monatshefte für auswärtige Politik*, 6, 8 (1941), 613–24; *idem*, 'Entwicklung und Funktion des neuen Volksgruppenrechts, 1941/42', *Zeitschrift für ausländisches öffentliches Recht und Völkerrecht* (1942); Loesch, *Croatia*; *Kroatien marschiert. Erste Jahreslese in Wort und Bild aus der Wochenschrift 'Neue Ordnung'*, ed. L. Scherzberg (Zagreb, 1942).

[50] See M. Straka, *Die volkliche Gliederung Südslawiens* (Graz, 1940); W. Sattler, *Die deutsche Volksgruppe im Unabhängigen Staat Kroatien* (Graz, 1943); W. Schneefuß, *Politische Geografie Kroatiens* (Graz, 1944).

[51] M. Lorković, *Das Volk und das Land der Kroaten* (Vienna, 1941).

[52] C. Klingemann, *Soziologie und Politik. Sozialwissenschaftliches Expertenwissen im Dritten Reich und in der frühen westdeutschen Nachkriegszeit* (Wiesbaden, 2009), 247; see also J. Wüscht, *Volkszählungsergebnisse der Donaubanschaft (Wojwodina) in Südslawien 1931. Nur f. d. Dienstgebrauch* (Vienna, 1940).

responsibility for a number of mass crimes committed by the Croatian government including the deportations of Jews. Very quickly after the Croatian state was proclaimed, Germany and Croatia agreed on a resettlement programme that resembled the master plan Lorković had published in 1939. On 4 June 1941, the German ambassador to Croatia, Siegfried Kasche, led a meeting of German and Croatian officials who agreed on a resettlement scheme that would ultimately affect half a million persons in four countries. Lorković, by then Croatian Minister of Foreign Affairs, attended the meeting as well as two historians from the South-East German Institute in Graz (Helmut Carstanjen and Heinz Hummitzsch). Up to 260,000 Slovenes from German-annexed Lower Styria and Upper Carniola were to be deported partly to Croatia, partly to Serbia. In exchange, the Croatian state was granted permission to deport an even higher number of Serbs from Croatia to Serbia.[53]

It is not the aim of this paper to analyse how the resettlement programmes were performed. It is, however important to note that the plans discussed in this paper largely failed. The euphoria of Croat nationalists in the summer of 1941, and the figures they were juggling with, belied the utopian character of their demographic endeavour: the Independent State of Croatia was a multi-ethnic and multi-religious state with a highly heterogeneous population. It was simply impossible to resettle or to assimilate a third of the population. Therefore, the ambiguous consequences of the Ustaša´s demographic plan were foreseeable. On the one hand, the Ustaše unleashed a brutal programme of ethnic cleansing, thus coming closer to the ethnically homogenised Croatian nation-state they desired. On the other hand, the brutal expulsions involved massacres and triggered Serb resistance on a massive scale. Thus, the consequences were a civil war within Croatia that considerably weakened the Ustaša regime. Due to the sheer size of the Serb community, as well as its readiness to resist, Serbs were partly successful in rebuffing the Ustaša militias and Croatian state organs in their attempt at ethnic cleansing. Being resettled was a desperate experience for those affected, which often ended in a deadly catastrophe. The same applies for the overblown plans to bring home the Croat communities from abroad. None of this was ever realised, with the exception of the 'return' of a few hundred Croatian settlers from Macedonia and the Kosovo in late 1941.[54]

The fact that the German-Croatian cooperation regarding the resettlement of Serbs brought the Ustaša movement closer than ever

---

[53] Minutes of the resettlement conference, 4 June 1941, in T. Ferenc, *Quellen zur Nationalsozialistischen Entnationalisierungspolitik in Slowenien 1941–1945* (Maribor, 1980), doc. no. 58.

[54] See J. B. Schechtmann, *European Population Transfers, 1939–1945* (New York, 1971).

to the ethnically homogenised nation-state they had always desired also radicalised their policy toward other minorities, namely Jews and Gypsies. In the summer of 1941, the Croatian government started to discuss 'spatial projects' as goals of Jewish 'resettlement': remote islands, 'reservations', ghettoes, as well as deportations of Jews to Serbia (which the Germans declined).[55] The intention of Loesch´s idea of 'Jewish dissimilation' might not have been genocidal, but its consequences, as practised in Croatia and elsewhere, were: Lorković in his capacity as Foreign Minister tried to get permission from the Germans to deport Jews from Croatia to other countries as early as the summer of 1941.[56] But none of these 'spatial solutions of the Jewish question' was feasible. Assimilation had turned into dissimilation, and dissimilation into annihilation: from the summer of 1941, Croatian Jews were deported to the Ustaša camps, where the vast majority perished, or, from 1942 onwards, to Auschwitz, where they were killed upon arrival. As for the resettlement of Serbs, the Germans had to realise that their utopian scenario of population transfers was not feasible, and that the Ustaša constantly violated their mutual agreements. Ultimately, frustrated German partners withdrew their support for any further resettlements. The consequence was that the Ustaša militias acted even more ruthlessly. More massacres and more expulsions without German consent were the consequence.

Conclusion

Most Völkisch scholars were not directly involved in executing population transfers on the ground. Inside as well as outside the sphere of German influence, police forces, armies and militias were responsible for ethnic cleansing and genocide; more often than not, it was local personnel that pushed for action motivated by local goals, rather than great schemes of ethnic engineering. The grand demographic schemes paved the way for ethnic cleansing, but had little to do with the way they were carried out. Yet, all wartime efforts at ethnic cleansing can be said to have arisen from the academic debates on population transfer in the decades succeeding the Great War. Scholars such as Boehm, Loesch, Ronneberger, Valjavec and Lorković contributed to demographic debates in Germany and in the countries they studied, and they ignited national aspirations by internationalising them and integrating them into their all-European framework of ethnic homogenisation.[57]

During the Second World War, the way ethnic cleansing was performed mostly led to the opposite of what social engineers had initially envisaged.

---

[55] See Korb, *Im Schatten*, 204–5.

[56] See C. Browning, *The Final Solution and the German Foreign Office. A Study of Referat D III of Abteilung Deutschland 1940–1943* (New York, 1978), 93.

[57] Loesch, 'Volkstumskunde', 94.

The widespread destruction of existing social structures that resulted from ethnic violence went against all theories of ethnic reorganisation: where villages had been looted and destroyed, and where the population had been expelled or massacred, measures of social engineering could not possibly be implemented. The dynamics of mass violence prevented most attempts of resettlement. But even where ethnic cleansing did not turn into mass murder, the ambitious project of large-scale social engineering mostly failed.[58] When it came to plans to alter the social composition of villages and regions, to improve the demographic distribution of occupational groups or the agrarian structure of the rural economy, almost nothing could be implemented. In Croatia as everywhere else, the state was too weak and its staff too inexperienced, and greed and the readiness to loot prevented all attempts at the redistribution of property.

Moreover, Völkisch scholars were frustrated when the principle of ethnic homogenisation was violated. In Yugoslavia, for instance, the German–Italian annexation of Slovenia and the subsequent deportation of Slovenes to Croatia and Serbia were opposed to Völkisch principles. Such resettlement projects were undertaken in the spirit of Nazi imperialism, and they sometimes led to conflicts between scholars and activists on the one hand, and the official or party line on the other. But when it came to actual resettlement projects in eastern and south-eastern Europe, Völkisch advocates of ethnic homogenisation rather disregarded their own reservations for the sake of the 'greater good'. They were, however, disillusioned by the way their concepts were put into reality. By highlighting Nazi criticism of their work after the war, they presented themselves as opponents of the Nazi movement. In terms of content, however, they followed the old tracks after 1945.

After the war, the younger generation of scholars found it much easier to adjust themselves to the new realities and to start new careers. This is somewhat ironic as Valjavec and Ronneberger were far less ambivalent towards the Nazi movement than their teachers' generation, represented by Loesch and Boehm. The former died in 1951 without having the opportunity to start a new career, not least because he was too old and exhausted at the end of the war.[59] The latter had a somewhat bumpy restart of his career; after his flight from Jena in 1945, German universities did not appoint him again. But he was able to found another institute in Lüneburg in 1951, which he called the 'Ost-Akademie'. Boehm did not even try to reform his old Völkisch viewpoints, as he based his theory on the same assumptions as prior to 1945.[60] The younger scholars who made

---

[58] For the failures of social engineering see J. C. Scott, *Seeing Like a State. How Certain Schemes to Improve the Human Condition Have Failed* (New Haven, 1998).

[59] Heinrich von Loesch, interview, Reichertshausen, 13 Dec. 2013.

[60] Prehn, *Boehm*, 407.

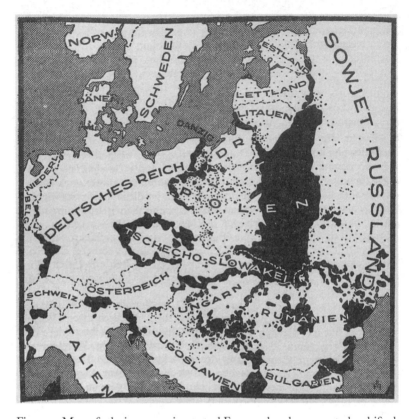

Figure 1 Map of ethnic groups in central Europe: borders were to be shifted; minorities were to be assimilated or dissimilated.
Source: Zehn Jahre Versailles. Die grenz- und volkspolitischen Folgen des Friedensschlusses, III, ed. M. H. Boehm and K. C. Loesch (Berlin, 1930), 445.

a fresh start after 1945 did not have to reinvent themselves. Ronneberger's and Valjavec's experiences in the Balkans during the war, based on tasks they had fulfilled for the Foreign Office, the Security Service or the SS, allowed them to position themselves as apolitical experts after the war. They could promote the same picture of Europe they had before the war. The narrative that the nations of Europe had to defend themselves against eastern threats remained largely unchanged. The focus on ethnic homogenisation was slightly revised into a narrative of minority rights, thus coming back to where they had started in the years after the Paris treaties. Their enthusiasm for south-eastern Europe prevailed. In 1952, they became founding fathers of the *Südosteuropa-Gesellschaft* in Munich, a lobbyist association that aimed to improve relations between the Federal Republic of Germany and the south-eastern European states.[61] The fate of Mladen Lorković is the one exception. For him, the fields of scholarship and political activism had always been muddled. But when he was appointed minister in 1941, he crossed a line. Ironically, he did not to have face justice, as his own men executed him in April 1945 because of his participation in a conspiracy to join the Allies towards the end of the war. His goal had always been to safeguard an independent, ethnically homogenised Croatian state, so it is not surprising that it was secondary whether this state would be part of the Axis or of an Allied world.

---

[61] See Haar, 'Friedrich Valjavec'; for Ronneberger, see P. Heinelt, *PR-Päpste. Die kontinuierlichen Karrieren von Carl Hundhausen, Albert Oeckl und Franz Ronneberger* (Berlin, 2003).